Femina Perfecta

Femina Perfecta

The Genesis of
Florida State University

by Robin Jeanne Sellers

The FSCW/FSU Class of 1947

Cataloging information

Sellers, Robin Jeanne.
Femina Perfecta: the Genesis of Florida State University.

  Bibliography.
  Includes index.
  1. Florida State College for Women (1905–1947). 2. Florida State University—History. 3. Women's colleges—History. I. Title.

LD1771.F92S45 1995a   376.8
ISBN 0-9648374-1-2

Library of Congress Catalog Card Number 95-78724

Orders for books should be addressed to
FSU Foundation, Inc., Class of 1947
Hecht House, 634 West Call Street
Tallahassee, Florida 32306.

For the
Mason women—
they know of whom
I speak

Table of Contents

Part III

Message From the President

From early childhood I viewed Florida State College for Women with respect and affection because so many of my female relatives, including my mother, attended the institution. During summer visits with my maternal grandparents, who lived just blocks from the present FSU School of Law here in Tallahassee, I came to associate both a love of learning and a love of tradition with the red-brick towers and arches at the end of College Avenue.

It was gratifying to discover shortly after I assumed the presidency of Florida State University that the first comprehensive history of FSCW was being written as a doctoral dissertation by Robin Sellers. I was further pleased when the FSCW/FSU Class of 1947 chose to publish this history, and I was happy to serve as a witness to the contract between author and publisher.

The history of FSCW is a story of motivated students, gifted faculty, and dedicated leaders who built one of the best colleges for women in the country. The strong foundation we inherited explains how FSU became one of the great teaching and research universities of the nation in less than half a century.

It is fitting that we who enjoy the prestige of that rapid development have knowledge of the women's college that made it possible. This book provides that insight.

Talbot D'Alemberte, President
Florida State University

Publisher's Foreword

When Florida State College for Women became Florida State University just three weeks before June graduation, diplomas for the Class of 1947 had already been printed. As there was too little time to do it again, the FSCW diplomas were overprinted "issued by Florida State University," giving our class the unique distinction of having both institutions' names on our diplomas. While researching projects for our class's 50th anniversary celebration as the Omega of FSCW and the Alpha of FSU, we discovered that Robin Sellers was writing the history of FSCW for her doctoral dissertation. What better way to commemorate our anniversary than to publish this history? With the author's blessing, our gift committee quickly voted to publish *Femina Perfecta*, a title using the motto from FSCW's seal.

Robin's choice of this title seemed especially appropriate and delighted us. Though as students we often took the "perfecta" with a bit of humor, we were more often touched by its deeper meanings. In Latin the "perfecta" implied not so much the "perfect" woman as the "completed" woman—all the hopes, aspirations, and potential of womanhood. Despite its strict rules, FSCW was a place to grow toward that ideal. Relieved of playing assigned feminine roles in the world outside the gates, FSCW students were free to expand their talents, abilities, and imaginations along with their knowledge. Within the safety of the campus community, where students seldom saw an unfamiliar face, even the timid were inspired to dare. This nurturing environment broadened the ambitions of many girls into fields beyond FSCW's liberal arts orientation.

Therefore, in the 1940s, coeducation with its expanded university curriculum became a preference for many serious FSCW students. Certainly, some students opted for coeducation just to have men around. Yet a significant minority of students would have preferred to perpetuate FSCW as it was—a prestigious liberal arts women's college steeped in tradition.

Looking back to the spring of 1947 (now a longer span of time than FSCW's whole existence) invites retrospection. Coeducation did, indeed, broaden educational choices for Florida's young women at what is now a major university. As for having men around, they now constitute almost half the student population, and FSU possesses that most masculine of distinctions, a national football championship. As for the prestigious liberal arts women's college steeped in tradition, it is preserved forever in the records, in our memories, and now in this book.

—FSCW/FSU CLASS OF 1947

Sarah Lewis Marxsen,
Permanent President

Mary Lou Norwood,
Gift Committee Chair

(Full Gift Committee membership listed in Appendix C.)

Publisher's Acknowledgements

The Class of 1947 embarked on the project of publishing *Femina Perfecta* with a great deal more enthusiasm than experience or know-how. Without the aid and whole-hearted support of many individuals on campus and in the community, we would have been overwhelmed.

Our very greatest appreciation goes to Robin for having written the history of FSCW and for telling our story with wit and grace. Her efforts on our behalf have gone far beyond that of authorship. She has been de facto typesetter, proof reader, photographic consultant, indexer, collector of archival and anecdotal material, and a genial, tireless collaborator. A special word of thanks to Robin's mother, Joy Mason, for her help with the book cover artwork.

We were fortunate to have Jeanne Ruppert, former Director of the Florida State University Press, to guide us through the perils of publishing. Her knowledge and professional editorial expertise, plus her enthusiasm for the project, made it possible for us to get the book-making job done.

Special thanks are due Jim Melton, President of the Alumni Association, and all the staff at the FSU Alumni Office, for standing in the wings, cheering us on, and supporting all our efforts. We are especially indebted to Linda Henning, Alumni Services Coordinator, for recognizing the potential value of the book at its inception and for hanging in with us through it all. In particular, we are grateful to her for providing access to her collection of photographs, scrapbooks, and other memorabilia accumulated during more than 20 years of planning reunions for FSCW classes. Special thanks, also, to the Alumni Office for generously lending us the time and talent of Graphic Arts Specialist, Gayle Norris. We are grateful beyond measure for her patience and skill in designing and formatting the book, scanning the dozens of photographs, and correcting and correcting again copy and proofs.

Without the wise financial and legal counsel given by the FSU Foundation, through Paula Fortunas, Vice President for Planned Giving, we could never have attempted so ambitious a project. We are truly grateful for her strong support and encouragement, and for the time and energy she and her secretary Clara Penny devoted to the book.

The two photographic sections of the book have been made possible through the kind assistance of staffs at the FSU Special Collections of Strozier Library, the FSU Photo Lab, and the Florida State Archives. We are particularly indebted to David Poindexter for his computer enhancement of twelve stained, torn, and faded early photographs.

To the editors and staffs of the *Flastacowo* we pay special tribute. In the days before the university had its own media department to record history in the making, camera-toting student photographers for the *Flastacowo* were the main providers of our visual record.

We are, of course, grateful for the many faculty, alumnae, and friends of FSCW who have contributed the scrapbooks, interviews, histories, memorabilia, interest, and encouragement that have made this history possible.

Lastly, we are deeply grateful for President Talbot D'Alemberte's interest and support, from his joining us in signing the author's contract to his signing of commemorative editions.

Author's Foreword

Florida State College for Women existed from 1905 to 1947, during which time it offered the women of Florida a superior liberal arts education for minimal cost while it achieved national prominence. By concentrating primarily on liberal arts rather than teacher-training or industrial and technical training, FSCW differed from other Southern state-supported institutions of higher learning. Its solid academic program created a substantial foundation upon which its successor, Florida State University, has been able to establish its own reputation.

During the period of rapid growth and development that began in May 1947, with the creation of Florida State University, newcomers to the faculty and administration showed an understandable tendency to take the past for granted and look to the future. Consequently, many of the accomplishments of the women's college, while recognized, went unheralded. With the fiftieth anniversary of Florida State University on the horizon, it is time to acknowledge the contributions of Florida State College for Women and its graduates.

I am indebted to a vast number of persons and organizations whose cooperation, advice, and encouragement played an important part in the completion of this book. Among them are Florida State University faculty members Edward Keuchel, for his outstanding (and understanding) direction of my Ph.D. dissertation, and William W. Rogers, for sharing his personal research materials and expansive knowledge of Tallahassee history. Retired FSCW/FSU faculty members Lynette

Thompson, Grace Fox, and Elizabeth Thomson generously shared recollections and information. James P. Jones made his personal collection of FSCW memorabilia available for my use.

Staff in the Alumni Association offices, Dean of Faculties office, and Special Collections at Strozier Library extended valuable assistance and good-natured camaraderie while I searched for elusive and long-forgotten documents. Edward Conradi's family graciously allowed me to use any and all of his papers relating to FSCW.

I owe a very special thank you to Mary Lou Norwood and Sarah Lewis Marxsen, FSCW Class of 1947 graduates, who tirelessly read and critiqued the manuscript and offered many valuable suggestions.

Many other persons contributed information and memorabilia, and generally encouraged my research by responding to questionnaires, answering specific inquiries by letter or telephone, and providing diaries, scrapbooks, annuals, and newspaper clippings. All of this help was invaluable.

—RJS
Tallahassee, Florida
August 1995

 # Part One

Chapter I

In the Beginning: 1851–1905

lorida created its first and only state-supported college for women on June 5, 1905, when Governor
Napoleon Bonaparte Broward signed House Bill
Number 361. This new law, known as the Buckman Bill, eliminated all existing state educational institutions and established
in their stead four new ones: the Florida Normal and Industrial College for Negroes; the Institute for the Blind, Deaf, and
Dumb; the University of the State of Florida; and the Florida
Female College. The governor's action was drastic but not
uncalled for. Duplication of services, acrimonious rivalries,
and expensive competition had characterized the state's educational system for some time. The Buckman Bill seemed to
solve those problems.

BEFORE 1857

Florida became a possession of the United States in 1821.
At that time, Congress followed a tradition dating from the
Northwest Ordinance of 1787, which mandated that land be
set aside for the support of public education. Accordingly,
the national government dedicated two townships (a township is six square miles and encompasses 23,040 acres), one
to the east of the Suwannee River and one to the west, to be
used for the establishment of institutions of higher learning.
The townships were not meant to be the sites of the schools,
but rather their lands were to be used in a way that provided

income to support such institutions. At the time, Escambia County, west of the river, had a population of approximately 5,800 and St. Johns County, east of the river, about 7,400; just 317 persons lived in the undelineated southern part of the territory. Because the sparse population meant a consequent lack of common or lower-level schools capable of preparing students for higher education, the territorial government moved slowly in its selection of those township lands, setting aside only a few parcels over the next twenty years.

Florida grew rapidly during those decades and, by 1840, had an estimated population of 55,000, almost half of which lived between the Apalachicola and Suwannee rivers.[1] When Florida finally attained statehood in 1845, a Congressional act increased the earlier educational endowment to four townships of land, two each for a seminary or university on either side of the Suwannee River. A survey to determine the need for such institutions of higher learning showed that, based on an estimated population of 85,000, and excluding Santa Rosa and Dade counties, which failed to respond, only 9,966 white children between the ages of five and eighteen years lived in the state.[2] Only one-fifth of them could read, and over one-half of them could neither read nor write. Despite this discouraging report, in 1851 the General Assembly of Florida passed "An Act to provide for the establishment of two Seminaries of Learning, one upon the east, the other upon the west side of the Suwannee River."

In the decades just prior to the Civil War most of Florida's inhabitants, forty percent of whom were slaves, lived in the northern and central sections of the state. Florida's mostly agricultural economy relied on the plantation system or yeoman farmers who grew cotton, tobacco, rice, and sugar cane. The state during the early 1850s seemed less than ready for one, let alone two, universities. A majority of legislators recognized that the state's frontier conditions were suited to graduates of practical rather than liberal studies. Accordingly, they decided to meet the requirements of the act by establishing two normal schools as soon as funds realized from the sale of lands produced sufficient interest to support the institutions. These schools would prepare trained teachers for the community schools that would follow statewide settlement, and those lower schools would in turn furnish students for the teaching academies. Such a reciprocal arrangement would enhance both the number of teachers and the competence of the fledgling state school system. With this in mind, the state government prescribed for each university a teacher-training course and additional "instruction in the mechanic arts, in husbandry and agricultural chemistry, in the fundamental laws, and in what regards the rights and duties of citizens."[3]

The act that established the two seminaries located them only generally to the east and west of the Suwannee River. Subsequently, a joint resolution created a legislative committee to consider inducements, defined as land, buildings, or money offered by various counties, and to recommend sites at the next biennial session. As a result, in January 1853 a bill located the Seminary East of the Suwannee at Ocala, that city having offered

> sixteen town lots in a square, valued at two hundred dollars each, also a building standing thereon, built in the form of an L . . . together with two other buildings erected on the said lot . . . the three valued at three thousand eight hundred dollars, also one thousand and six hundred dollars in money, and the whole amount of the donation being eight thousand six hundred dollars.[4]

The location of the Seminary West of the Suwannee remained undetermined. Tallahassee, which had been named the state capital in 1824, seemed a logical site. Residents of the city had seriously considered bidding for the seminary since passage of the act in 1851, but they had no building to offer as an inducement until 1854. That year the City Council committed more than $6,000, secured from the Fire Fund and through the sale of bonds and public subscriptions, to finance a new school building on land owned by the city. They sweet-ened their offer with $10,000, consisting of the value of the property plus cash to make up any difference in appraisal, payable immediately to the seminary, and $1,500 per year every year that the seminary remained in the city.[5] The site, Gallows Hill (so called since 1830, when a woman who had killed her baby was hanged there), drew considerable criti-cism because of its location on the western outskirts of town in an undeveloped area, but supporters prevailed.[6] Once the construction work began, the city superintendent approached the legislature and presented his case. State officials failed to render a decision during the remainder of that session, so the school opened on April 30, 1855, as the independent Florida Institute. It offered both a college program with a junior, middle, and senior class, and preparatory departments, but did not include a normal school or a teacher-training program.[7]

The next year the city reiterated its bid for the seminary, and this time the legislature granted the request. On January 1, 1857, the governor signed the bill designating Tallahassee as the site of the Seminary West of the Suwannee. Rather than restrict its curriculum to that of a normal school as the legis-lature had prescribed, the new seminary maintained the lib-eral arts program as set forth by the Florida Institute.[8] Its regu-lating board promptly added four adjacent lots to the existing land, enlarging the campus to 13.5 acres.

In general Floridians and residents of Tallahassee were pleased with the seminary, though some local citizens no-ticed that it had not opened its doors to young ladies. After all, schools like Troy Seminary, founded in 1821, and Mount Holyoke Seminary, established in 1837, both made classics and sciences available to young ladies. Oberlin College in Ohio had accepted women students in a "female department" in 1837, becoming the first coeducational college in the coun-try. Tallahassee had offered an opportunity for education to its female residents since 1843, when the "Misses Bates School" had opened.[9] That had become the Leon Female Academy.

After much discussion, the academy's trustees consigned the school's frame building and two lots to the seminary board.[10] In the fall of 1858, the West Florida Seminary admitted girls, though they attended classes on the erstwhile academy campus across town. The Female Academy ceased to exist except as a branch of the seminary.

Too soon Florida's secession from the Union and affiliation with the Confederate cause interrupted the progress of the school. During the Civil War, the state diverted funds normally used for the seminaries to the war effort. That, coupled with the difficulty in securing qualified male faculty members while the fighting continued, caused unanticipated hardships for both seminaries. The Female Department of West Florida Seminary, not dependent on male teachers, operated continuously throughout those years except for a few weeks in the fall of 1864.[11] The Male Department had prudently and prophetically added military instruction to its curriculum in 1859, but a severe shortage of suitable male teachers finally forced it to close in the spring of 1862 and remain closed until the fall term. Once reopened, it contended with further faculty and funding shortages. But the seminary struggled along, and on March 6, 1865, its young men put their military training to the test when Federal troops attempted to capture the state capital. A company of cadets from the school joined the battle south of the city at Natural Bridge and helped halt the Yankee advance from the coast,[12] allowing Tallahassee to remain the only Confederate capital east of the Mississippi not captured by Union forces. Of course, the respite was short-lived. On May 10, 1865, just two months after they were repulsed at Natural Bridge and one month after Robert E. Lee surrendered to Ulysses S. Grant at Appomattox, Federal troops entered Tallahassee. That summer 300 Northern soldiers lodged in the West Florida Seminary building.[13]

The residents of Tallahassee had invested too much time and money in securing their seminary to have thoughtless Yankees destroy it. Once the troops vacated the school building, citizens pitched in to repair the damage inflicted on the structure and ready it for reopening. Generous and patriotic community members guaranteed sufficient funding for adequate faculty for both the male and female departments, and the school accepted students for the Fall 1866 term.[14]

East Florida Seminary had not fared as well. It had ceased to function as a state institution after the first two years of the conflict, but carried on as a private academy. It reopened under state auspices just as the war ended. In January 1866, the legislature, hoping that affiliation with the private Gainesville Academy established during the war would raise the seminary's standards, moved the school from Ocala to Gainesville. In contrast to Tallahassee's enthusiasm for its seminary, this relocation occasioned slight interest on the part of Gainesville's citizens. Perhaps because of a lack of encouragement from the residents, the transfer proved fruitless, and the East Florida Seminary remained little more than a local elementary school.[15]

Federal Reconstruction in Florida accomplished little for either seminary. Adequate financing continued to be a problem. The State Constitution of 1868 had abolished tuition; uncertain salary payments meant undependable faculties, and the need for building maintenance was largely ignored. Both schools operated more on elementary or secondary levels than as institutes of higher education whose primary purpose was teacher training. By the time Reconstruction ended in 1877, some citizens and legislators questioned the seminaries' value to the state. The schools seemed to catch the drift of legislative winds, for East Florida Seminary established a normal department in 1881, and West Florida Seminary followed suit in 1882.[16] Their actions paid off. Tourism picked up considerably throughout the 1880s, and many visitors decided to settle in Florida. These temporary and permanent newcomers vastly improved the state's economy. The legislature spread the resulting prosperity to public higher education by allocating annual funds for operation of the newly established seminaries' normal departments.[17]

As the state's population rapidly increased over the next twenty years (from 269,500 in 1880 to 752,619 in 1900), Florida's educational institutions grew in number, relocated, and changed names. The Florida Agricultural College, of little consequence when originally established in Eau Gallie during Reconstruction, moved to Lake City in 1884. During the next few years the school prospered, though its annual enrollment never topped fifty. It offered traditional classical and military programs in addition to agricultural training.[18]

Under a renewed commitment to teacher training, the legislators who met in 1887 established the Florida State Normal School for white teachers at DeFuniak Springs and the Florida Normal and Industrial School for black teachers at Tallahassee, both funded through state appropriations. In deference to the new teacher-training schools, the seminaries suspended their normal-school programs. Still in an expansive mood in 1895, the legislature created the South Florida Military and Educational Institute (later called the South Florida Military College) at Bartow. In 1901, the legislature appropriated funds for the St. Petersburg Normal and Industrial School, though it did not assume total financial responsibility for the institution. It also approved West Florida Seminary's name change to Florida State College (FSC). In 1903, the state established the Florida Agricultural Institute, located in Kissimmee, and permitted Florida Agricultural College in Lake City to adopt the name University of Florida.[19]

By 1905, state appropriations financed all or part of the activities of eight educational institutions. Six were state-owned and, of those, two had a respectable number of collegiate-level students: the University of Florida at Lake City (with an enrollment of 225 male students, 87 of whom were considered college-level) and the coeducational Florida State College at Tallahassee (with 308 students, of whom 152 were enrolled in college-level work).[20] Students at the remaining four of the six—the East Florida Seminary at Gainesville, the

South Florida Military College at Bartow, the Florida State Normal School at DeFuniak Springs, and the Florida Normal and Industrial School for Negroes at Tallahassee—maintained a high quality of work but below college level.

In their desire to make higher education available to all, the past several legislatures had unwittingly created a monster. As each of these schools stridently pressed its monetary demands, dissatisfaction with their petty rivalries and competitions mounted. The institutions made a fatal error in the spring of 1905 when they submitted a combined budget request, undoubtedly padded, in the amount of $700,000 for the 1904–1906 biennium, a figure nearly three times as large as that for the preceding two years. They realized their action had backfired when members of the state House of Representatives requested an investigation into the feasibility of dispensing with some of the institutions. The schools quickly reduced their collective request to a realistic $174,000,[21] but it was too late. An educational reorganization act proposed by H. H. Buckman had abolished them outright.

THE BUCKMAN BILL

H. H. Buckman represented Duval County in the state House of Representatives. In his opinion, Florida needed a designated state university, a girls' school, and a state normal school. All others, to his mind, should be run at the high school level. Other legislators expressed the opinion that a clean break with the past was needed to solve the higher education problems of the state. Buckman picked up on their thinking and introduced House Bill No. 361, which abolished all existing institutions and replaced them with four state-supported facilities. Two of these, the Florida Normal and Industrial College for Negroes at Tallahassee and the Institute for the Blind, Deaf, and Dumb at St. Augustine, remained essentially the same as prior to the reorganization. A third, the University of the State of Florida, so called in order to avoid confusion between it and the old pre-Buckman University of Florida at Lake City, permitted enrollment of only white males and offered agricultural, mechanical, and classical programs. The fourth, Florida Female College (FFC), proposed to offer both a classical and practical higher education to the white females of the state.[22]

Limitation of enrollment to one gender in an educational institution was something new to Florida law, and reasons for its inclusion by Buckman are not clear. Since none of the educational system's problems had stemmed from coeducation, it's possible that the University of Florida's administration perceived an advantage for their school, and deliberately fostered such a plan. Whatever their motives, the Buckman Bill's supporters expected inherent differences in curricula in the university and college to reduce competition and duplication of programs between the two,[23] ultimately accomplishing the intended financial savings for the taxpayers without the legislature's reprising the role of Solomon or accepting any responsibility for difficult decisions.

The bill also created a supervisory Board of Control, whose members met immediately in joint session with the State Board of Education to determine the locations and elect the presidents of the new institutions. Attention focused first on a site for the university. In a less than cost-conscious move the board chose the city of Gainesville, which offered appropriate political and financial considerations, though it lacked a physical plant for immediate use by the school. Students of the new university attended classes in Lake City for a year while the state financed construction of usable buildings at the central Florida site. In the fall of 1906, the University of the State of Florida opened its doors to students in Gainesville.

THE WOMEN'S COLLEGE

Florida was the last state in the Deep South to make separate provisions for the higher education of women. During the late nineteenth century other Southern states had barred females from both land grant and private institutions of higher learning. Often at the insistence of local agricultural interests such as the Grange or Farmers' Alliance, these states established publicly supported schools for women.

Mississippi State College for Women opened in October 1885 with a regular enrollment of 312. Georgia State College for Women held its first session in fall 1891, enrollment 220. North Carolina State Normal and Industrial College also began in 1891 with 449 students. Winthrop College of South Carolina opened at Rock Hill in the fall of 1894 with 353 students. Alabama College embarked on its program at Montevallo in October 1896 as a technical high school for women with an attendance of 226, and offered its first college-level work in 1910. Texas State College for Women offered two years of high school and two years of college beginning in September 1903, with 186 women attending that year. Until well into the twentieth century, all of these state-supported women's schools stressed industrial, technical, and/or teacher training. Florida Female College differed considerably in both content and intent. Unlike other Southern state women's colleges, Florida Female College considered liberal studies its primary focus, with teacher training and industrial education as secondary functions.[24]

The newly created Board of Control had turned its immediate attention to a site for the university, and ostensibly there had been some question concerning the location of that school. However, the original version of the Buckman Bill that went to committee had specified that the school for women be located in Tallahassee.[25] The final bill stopped short of designating the capital city, but the board seemed to think that site had been predetermined. Though relatively modern, Tallahassee reflected a gentility reminiscent of an earlier time in the South. With a population of less than 5,000, the community offered social opportunities and refinements deemed desirable for the education of young ladies without subjecting them to the tawdry elements of a larger municipality.

Another consideration in Tallahassee's favor was that relocation of the university from Lake City to Gainesville entailed expensive construction, whereas the successful Florida State College provided an acceptable physical plant that included 13.5 acres of land and three buildings. The college grounds were located well to the west of downtown Tallahassee at the end of Clinton Street, where "a broad avenue, lined with majestic oaks, formed the approach from the center of the city to the main entrance to the campus." The campus area was bounded by Jefferson Street on the south, Park Avenue on the north, and Copeland Street on the east. The more nebulous western boundary consisted of an imaginary line extending from Jefferson Street northward through a neglected cornfield, a small pond, an area of wild shrubbery, and on to Park Avenue (little more than a driveway into the campus at that time).[26]

The board offered the presidency of Florida Female College to Albert Alexander Murphree, who until the advent of the Buckman Bill had been head of Florida State College. After some hesitation, he accepted the position. He had come to the West Florida Seminary in 1895 as a mathematics teacher and had become its head two years later, at the age of 27. That same year he had married Jennie Henderson, who was a member of an old and highly respected Tallahassee family.[27] His new father-in-law, Colonel John Henderson, had once been a trustee of the old seminary. Murphree and his family were extremely popular in Tallahassee. They lived in the Henderson home on Adams Street across from the Capitol. One Florida State College professor's son remembered that

> Dr. Murphree would come driving up the hill every morning behind his big roan horse. Occasionally he would walk the mile from his home to the College, but most of the time he drove the roan hitched to his one-seated top buggy.[28]

Under Murphree's far-sighted leadership the seminary had by 1901 metamorphosed into the highly successful Florida State College. With his school thriving, he had opposed wholeheartedly any changes in the state's educational system.[29] When the Buckman Bill passed despite his objections, he had expected to be appointed head of the new university since he believed its proposed program closely resembled the one he had created at Florida State College. He deluded himself on that point, for the curriculum of the Florida State College for the 1904–1905 session consisted of six divisions: the Liberal Arts College, the School for Teachers, the School of Music, the School of Oratory and Physical Culture, the Commercial Department, and the College Academy (the high school department). The curriculum mandated for the university included a School of Language and Literature comparable to his Liberal Arts College and a Normal School, but there the similarities ended. The Florida Female College curriculum embraced Schools of English, Modern Languages, Ancient Languages, Mathematics, Natural Sciences, Philosophy, Elocution, Physical Culture, Music, Art, Domestic Science, History and Political Science[30]—a perfect meld with the curriculum of Florida State College.

Murphree's dissatisfaction with his appointment as president of the women's college proved extremely fortunate for the young ladies of Florida, for it ensured the scholastic preeminence of Florida Female College among Southern institutions. While he never publicly voiced his ambivalence over the assignment, he privately acknowledged to many friends and supporters his disappointment in not being made head of the university. In July he wrote:

> It was a disappointment, of course, and the friends of education predict absolute failure at Lake City, and they tell me that I will go with the University to Gainesville next year. Hence, I am reconciled to undertake the Female College position and make the very best thing out of it possible.[31]

To J. A. Forsythe, Jr., the Florida State College football coach for the 1904–1905 season, he penned, "I am grievously disappointed but my friends tell me that next year will set matters right."

Even though he believed his tenure in Tallahassee would be short-lived, he was determined to make the Female College "the greatest state college in Florida" as well as "the biggest college for women in all the South." He intended the "girls' school" to outshine the new university at every opportunity, and spent much of his time assuring that. His future and that of the college depended upon whether the population of Florida accepted and supported the new school. To that end he spent the summer of 1905 in determined preparation for the successful opening of Florida Female College that coming September.[32]

Summer 1905

As much as Murphree wanted the college to surpass the university in enrollment, he recognized the necessity for high moral as well as educational standards. The admission policy followed the guidelines of the Association of Colleges and Preparatory Schools of the Southern States. Florida Female College accepted only those students who met specific scholastic requirements, *and* provided "satisfactory evidence of good moral character," *and* promised to obey the authorities and rules of the campus. Prospective dormitory residents even signed a pledge to honor all rules made "with reference to...student's conduct outside of the regular school hours."[33] As far as the administration was concerned, a student's off-campus deportment directly affected, positively or negatively, the reputation of her college.

The Board of Control prescribed the curriculum for the Florida Female College.[34] Within that agenda, the college offered six programs of study: Liberal Arts, leading to either a Bachelor of Arts or a Bachelor of Science degree; Industrial Arts, consisting of studies in home economics combined with specified liberal arts courses; the School of Music, culminating in a music certificate; the School of Art, and the School of Expression, both offering appropriate certificates; and the State School for Teachers, familiarly called the Normal School, granting a Licentiate of Instruction.[35]

Applicants for admission to the Liberal Arts program had to be at least 16 years old and to have satisfactorily completed the 11th grade. The college accepted a certificate from an accredited high school or credits from a college or university as proof of that accomplishment. In the absence of those documents, the school administered examinations in various fields. A Committee on Admissions judged each applicant individually; a Committee on Curriculum and Terms of Admission determined the course work most suitable for that student.[36]

According to the catalogue, the Normal School was not established as an addendum to the Florida Female College, but as a separate and distinct institution for the training of teachers. It included a model school and kindergarten. Despite their distinction from liberal arts participants, Normal students were able to take advantage of courses offered in other departments. Applicants for admission to the School for Teachers had to be at least 14 years of age and to have completed eighth grade, but all applicants holding a teacher's certificate were admitted regardless of age or level of schooling. Anyone interested in the Kindergarten Course, which prepared a student specifically for teaching pre-school children, had to be at least 18 years old. Moral requirements for the State School for Teachers matched those of the regular college.[37]

Because a scarcity of accredited high schools still existed in Florida, the college also established a class composed of girls who had completed the tenth grade. This 'sub-freshman' class prepared students for a regular college curriculum. Actual freshmen were those who satisfied the 11th grade minimum admission requirements. Young ladies with diplomas or certificates from the 12th grade usually entered the sophomore class, but the Committee on Admissions allowed graduates of accredited Duval High School in Jacksonville to enter at the junior level. Though the admissions policy seemed extremely lenient, the public education system in the state was such that the Committee still referred many applicants to Stetson College in Deland or to Rollins College in Winter Park, private coeducational institutions in Florida that offered courses at a preparatory level.[38]

The faculty expected students in the college to possess a respectable knowledge of English, Latin, mathematics, history, and science. Candidates for a Bachelor of Arts or Bachelor of Science degree studied a second language—Greek, French, or German. Those seeking the Bachelor of Science added botany and zoology to their course work.[39] Murphree considered a bachelor of arts or science degree from Florida Female College sufficient for admission to Vassar, Smith, or Wellesley at the graduate level.[40]

Individual expenses were nominal. State residents paid no tuition; out-of-state students paid $20 per year. Each girl incurred an annual registration fee that consisted of a $5 incidental fee and a $2 library fee. The state expected the boarding department of the college to be self-sustaining. To assure that, unless a student lived with an immediate family member in town, she was required to board in one of the college dormitories, East Hall or West Hall. A boarding fee of $100 per year entitled a student to meals, a furnished room, fuel, and lights. Miscellaneous expenses for books, stationery, gym suits, laundry, and sundries were estimated at $20–35 per year.[41]

Students in the College of Industrial Arts paid a $3 annual fee to use the domestic science laboratory. A student of expression paid $18 annual tuition for her program. The Art Department charged $24 per year for advanced instruction and supplies. The School of Music depended entirely on student fees to pay its faculty. That department charged piano students $64 per year for two weekly lessons; 45 minutes of practice daily cost another $10 per year, and each additional weekly practice period raised that by $2. Two voice culture lessons per week cost a student $48 per session. Courses in music history, theory, and harmony were included free of

charge when taken with piano or voice. Similar course offer-
ings at Rollins or Stetson cost about $10 more per year.[42]

Even though the school charged no tuition, some parents
felt the boarding costs were too high, and other parents were
simply unable to pay even the smallest assessment. Murphree
realized that the greater the enrollment, the more successful
the college would appear to the citizens of Florida and to the
Board of Control; nevertheless, he refused to compromise
high moral and academic standards. Instead, whenever possible, he tried to make suitable financial arrangements in the
students' favor. At one point during the preparatory summer
he confidentially offered a scholarship for one-half the boarding costs to "Miss Nellie" in return for approximately two
hours work per day grading handwritten English theses. When
a mother complained about expenses, he offered her daughter one year free board if the mother could show him a comparable institution in the South that charged less than Florida
Female College. In the same letter, he mentioned the possibility of offering board plus a salary of $3 or $4 a month to
approximately 15 students in exchange for their waiting tables
in the dining room; however, nothing came of the idea for
some time.[43]

Florida Female College was scheduled to open on the last
Wednesday in September 1905. As the date drew near, an
epidemic of yellow fever in northern Florida caused the State
Health Officer in Pensacola to quarantine that city and the
surrounding area. Though the disease never reached Tallahassee, Murphree spent long hours reassuring concerned
parents that their daughters would face no health threat at
the college. Determined not to lose students already registered, he advised those who lived in areas of restricted travel
to review their Latin and pursue readings on their own. He
suggested resources for their studies that included Caroline
Brevard's *History of Florida* and Tarr's *New First Physical Geography*. He was extremely relieved when faculty members in
the North reached the college in time for the beginning of

classes by using state-issued health certificates stamped at various locations in Alabama and Georgia.[44]

❧

Murphree worried needlessly about opening day. By anyone's standards, Florida Female College debuted to favorable notices. Governor Broward, State Superintendent of Public Schools W. M. Holloway, and most of the citizens of Tallahassee joined the students for ceremonies in the College Hall chapel and later that day attended a formal reception held on the campus. With nearly one hundred students registered for classes and more expected by the end of the week, the new school was on its way.

lbert Alexander Murphree accepted more than the
presidency of Florida Female College in June 1905—
he accepted a tremendous challenge. Thanks to the
"foresight" of the Board of Control, the college possessed a
reasonably adequate physical plant of three buildings on 13.5
acres of land. However, the new institution lacked faculties
and students. Though his heart was with the men's university
in Gainesville, between June and September Murphree recruited
an outstanding cadre of teachers and a respectable number of
bright, well-qualified students for the women's college.

THIRTEEN AND ONE-HALF ACRES

College Hall, the main building on the small campus, sat
upon the crest of a hill at the western end of Clinton Street.
Erected in 1855 to lure the seminary to Tallahassee and
remodeled in 1891, it was an impressive two-story brick edifice with a wooden shingle roof and copper gutters and down-
spouts. The college held most of its liberal arts classes in the
building's thirteen lecture rooms, four study halls, and four
scientific laboratories. College Hall also contained a chapel
and a library, which were actually small lecture rooms converted for those purposes.[1]

The other two buildings on the campus, East Hall and
West Hall, were wooden dormitories built in 1901 for use by
the coeducational college.[2] East Hall afforded living space for

80 students in 40 small sleeping rooms, each one crowded with a double bed, wash stand, basin, and clothes cupboard.[3] The college held most of its social functions in the building's parlor, the reception room, or the dining room which seated 200 persons. Separate kitchens were connected to the northwest wing. West Hall not only housed students in 30 dormitory rooms but also doubled as a classroom building for the Domestic Science, Domestic Arts, and Fine Arts departments. Residents found both buildings comfortably equipped with modern plumbing facilities and steam heat. All students not living with family in Tallahassee resided in East or West Hall.

Shortly before the start of its first session, the college purchased adjoining land and buildings from the Lincoln Academy, once a small school and church serving Tallahassee's Negro community. This property lay immediately north of the campus. The college remodeled part of the school/church building to make space for the Model School and Kindergarten Departments of the State School for Teachers. A gymnasium and an indoor swimming pool filled the rest of the interior.[4]

Since there was no popular demand for a state women's school in Florida, it fell to Murphree to "drum up business." Aware that his future as an educator in the state depended on his success in Tallahassee, he initiated a statewide campaign to elicit support for the school and encourage girls of college caliber to attend. "We must get people to realize this is not a secondary school," he often declared.[5]

The roundup of prospective students succeeded, and attendance quickly surpassed expectations. With both residence halls filled to capacity by Christmas, Murphree arranged for students expected to arrive in January to room in a house two blocks from the campus.[6] Classrooms were overcrowded; too many music students and too few pianos in College Hall meant that girls often practiced their lessons at night. Murphree fretted about the dark grounds and lack of paved pathways between buildings, but he knew of no way to improve conditions. Street lighting in the area consisted of a single arc light adjacent to the campus on Clinton Street. Until the state created the Female College, the city's electric power plant had little incentive to extend its resources westward from the downtown area. Fenton Davis, a day student who lived on West Jefferson Street, remembered when electric street lights went up around the campus about 1907. Hoards of large beetles swarmed around the light globes. When the bugs fell to the ground Davis scooped them up and put them in the bedrooms of college music instructor Margaret Buchholz and Normal School teacher Hallie Lewis, both of whom boarded with her family.[7]

A near disaster on the campus directed legislative attention to the serious nature of the overcrowding. At dawn on the Sunday before Christmas 1906, clanging fire bells awakened the city. West Hall was ablaze. Tallahassee's volunteer fire department hurried to the scene but arrived too late to save the building. Thankfully, most of the students had left the campus for the holidays, and those who remained had moved temporarily into East Hall for dining convenience. Bedroom furnishings, private property, seven pianos, most of the sheet music, the art studio and its supplies, the domestic science labs and equipment—all were lost.[8]

The next day Murphree leased five cottages near the campus as temporary housing for the 40 or so girls who had resided in the dormitory portion of West Hall. College Hall somehow managed to absorb the Art Department. In the gymnasium, athletic activities now shared space with cooking and sewing classes. Music studios ended up in both College Hall and East Hall, with replacement pianos placed in private rooms, halls, corridors, and anywhere else they would fit.[9] The campus became a cacophony of music lessons, voice and piano practice, and classroom lectures.

If not for the fire and the resulting immediate demand for more dormitory space, it is doubtful that the legislature would have funded any new buildings for the campus for some time. But the local newspaper editorialized that the situation compelled the upcoming legislature to provide for campus improvements.[10] During the 1907 legislative session, Murphree subtly drew attention to the overcrowded situation by inviting lawmakers to a musical program and reception on the campus. The Tallahassee *Morning Sun* estimated that at least 500 people, excluding students, attended the events, and reported:

> The word campus is used advisedly, for there is no one room or even one building of the inadequate plant of the college that would accommodate the large crowd attracted there to take part in and enjoy the concert and reception given by President Murphree and his faculty. About ten times as many people as the little chapel could hold . . . crowded into the halls and listened from windows and other points.[11]

The legislature quickly provided funds for a brick dormitory to be located behind College Hall.[12] The Board of Control had already employed the South Carolina architectural firm of Edwards and Walter on a contract basis for work at Gainesville and Tallahassee. The architects designed buildings in the popular Collegiate Gothic style for both campuses. For the new Female College dormitory, they revised their plans twice before anticipated construction costs and the legislative allocation coincided. The construction contract finally went to the W. T. Hadlow Company of Jacksonville, which had already erected buildings on the Gainesville campus.[13] The contractors started work during the 1907 Christmas holidays, almost exactly one year after the fire. Digging, hammering, and concrete work continued on this project throughout the spring and summer of 1908.

Meanwhile, Gilmore and Davis, original contractors for the two wooden dormitories, renovated East Hall and enlarged its dining room and kitchen facilities. By fall a driveway composed of sand and clay mixed with refuse coal from furnace fires skirted the central area of campus; flower-lined walkways connected College Hall, the new dormitory, and "old" East Hall.[14] As a safety measure, the Tallahassee Fire Department installed another fire plug in the immediate vicinity of the campus.

The college named its new dormitory in honor of the late U.S. Senator William James Bryan of Jacksonville. The very popular Bryan had died of typhoid fever just three months after he assumed the senatorial seat left vacant by the death of Stephen Mallory, Jr., in December 1907. Statewide, Bryan's constituents applauded the idea of bestowing his name on Florida Female College's new building. Of course, the college realized that the late Senator Bryan had also been the brother of Nathan P. Bryan, Chairman of the Board of Control.

When Bryan Hall opened in September 1908, 40 two-bedroom suites connected by studies became homes for 160 girls. J. G. Kellum, business manager for the college, furnished the parlors and reception rooms with furniture in the currently popular Mission style. An infirmary was initially located in a suite on the first floor and was later moved to the southeast corner of the third floor. A nurse had to carry meals to her patients from the East Hall dining room.[15]

Just days after Bryan Hall opened, President Murphree's eight-year-old daughter, Mary, died of diphtheria in the new hospital rooms. The school suspended activities and called in state health officials to consult with college physician F. Clifton Moor. Moor acted quickly to quarantine the Murphree family as soon as he recognized the disease, and gave antitoxin injections to anybody who might have come into contact with Mary while she was contagious. The diphtheria outbreak was statewide, but Tallahassee fared much better than other areas of the state; still, students and their families were understandably concerned. The college was fortunate that no other cases of the disease materialized.

Bryan Hall quickly replaced East Hall as the social center of the campus. Students held such refined and proper affairs as Japanese teas and masquerade balls in the parlor, the sun room, and the entry/reception area later known as the Atrium. Faculty members served tea in the new dormitory during weekly "at homes." These events provided an opportunity for Tallahassee residents to visit the college and exchange ideas with the faculty and students. When girls stayed on campus over Christmas and New Year's, they celebrated the holidays around a tall Christmas tree in the parlor.[16] The wide marble entry steps and porch served as an outdoor stage, and the sunken garden in front of the dormitory provided a grassy spot for ceremonies or seating for spectators. In 1909, the seniors held Class Day exercises there and started a tradition that lasted for many years.

NO CRANKY OLD MAIDS

Even as Murphree worked through the summer of 1905 securing the physical plant for the new school, he was also pulling together a qualified faculty for the students that he fervently hoped were coming to Florida Female College. Based on the proposed curriculum, he retained several well-qualified scholars who had been members of the Florida State College faculty. These included John C. Calhoun, Arthur Williams, Samuel M. Tucker, Elmer R. Smith, Jerome McNeill, and Mary Apthorp. All but Apthorp were mature married men who had either master's degrees or doctorates. Apthorp had just received her bachelor of arts degree from Florida State College and remained to manage the existing library. New to the liberal arts college was B. C. Bondurant, who had recently received his Ph.D. from the University of Chicago. Murphree chose him over several other applicants, although at first he feared Bondurant's relative youth and bachelor status would prejudice the Board of Control against him.[17] Bondurant had the distinction of being the only unmarried male on the faculty.

Murphree shied away from any connotation of a traditional "female seminary" for the new college. He intended to be president not of a "women's college" but of a modern institution of higher learning whose students happened to be females. He stressed this concept repeatedly as he contacted colleagues in the South, East, and Midwest for faculty recommendations. Over and over he admonished, "For these positions we desire ladies of some experience, of good disposition and agreeable manners. We do not want cranky old maids."[18] Unfortunately, women who possessed this complement of characteristics seemed hard to find. With the exception of Inez Abernethy, Director of Art, few of those he eventually hired stayed longer than one or two years. Though each contributed in some way to the development of her respective department, it was not until after Murphree left Florida Female College that traditional "women's" programs solidified. Consequently, during the college's first four years, its Music Department, Industrial Arts Department (cooking, sewing, housekeeping, horticulture, and industrial drawing), and School of Expression seldom had the same faculty members two years in a row.

In contrast to the industrial instructors, the liberal arts faculty changed seldom or not at all. Arthur "Pi" Williams, an eccentric Welshman, remained at the college until 1937. He had acquired his nickname from his daughter, Edna, whose first attempts to say "Papa" sounded like "Pi." Young men under his charge at Florida State College quickly picked up the name and added "mister." So "Mr. Pi" and later plain "Pi" it was. His sister-in-law, Rowena Longmire, accepted a position with the State School for Teachers in 1906 and stayed until her death in 1938. In 1912, she received the first honorary master of arts degree bestowed by the college.[19]

Classics professor Bondurant stayed only a short while but made a lasting impression on the young women who attended his classes. Students of Latin waited in vain each year for Christmas presents from the bachelor professor. In 1908, a Leap Year, flirtatious students often left bunches of wild violets on his desk. Unfortunately, this popular teacher contracted tuberculosis, or "consumption" as it was called then. When failing health forced him to take a leave of absence during the Spring 1909 semester, several competent graduate students took over his teaching schedule. Fenton Davis taught his sophomore and junior Greek classes, while Ruth Reynolds and Irita Bradford taught those in Latin. The young women were paid for their teaching, and Davis gave her pay to Bondurant to help out with his medical bills.[20]

The Buckman Bill had abolished the several state-funded normal schools charged with training teachers and had established new ones at both the college and the university. The first catalogue stated "the State School for Teachers is established not as an addendum to the Florida Female College, but as a separate and distinct institution for the training of teachers."[21] Because its requirements both for admission and in course work were not as stringent as those of the college, students enrolled in the Normal School were indeed separate for many years. Ludwig W. Buchholz, with a recent master of arts degree from Florida State College, served as principal for the school. Hallie C. Lewis and Anna Chaires, teachers from the old normal school at De Funiak Springs, assisted Buchholz. Lewis was Director of the Observation and Practice School (which taught classes in the first through third grades), and Chaires was Director of the Kindergarten School component. In addition to these three instructors, all members of the liberal arts faculty taught in the State School for Teachers.

Buchholz resigned the principalship in 1908. Murphree offered the position to Dr. Edward Conradi, head of the Normal and Industrial School in St. Petersburg, Florida, but Conradi had already committed himself to the St. Petersburg position for another year. The following year Murphree again offered the Normal School directorship to Conradi, and this time Conradi accepted.[22]

COLLEGE LIFE

Florida Female College existed to provide an education for the approximately 225 girls who graced the campus each year during Murphree's four-year tenure.[23] Because many of them were as young as 14, 15, and 16 years old; because it was early in the twentieth century; and because this school was in the South, the college closely regulated and supervised not only classes but all activities. The school required students "to submit to such regulations as will insure faithful study and exemplary conduct."[24]

As the first Lady Principal of the dormitories, Mrs. W. H. Reynolds, widow of the State Comptroller, endeavored to replicate home life for the girls. During the first two years, with no infirmary on campus, she ministered to the students in a motherly manner when they suffered minor injuries or mild indispositions. If necessary, she called in a local physician, usually Dr. Henry Palmer, at the patient's expense. She also instructed students in table manners and social graces.[25] She held regular "at homes" on Monday evenings, attended by all on campus, where she provided both refreshments and light but meaningful instructional programs.

Although the college was nonsectarian, its mission and activities reflected a decidedly Southern Protestant orientation. Students attended chapel every weekday morning as part of their daily schedule. These services brought the entire student body together as a captive audience, making it relatively easy for the administration to offer first a morality lesson through a Bible reading, singing, and prayer, then supervisory announcements and/or pronouncements. On Sundays, all dormitory residents attended church; the only dispensation was for documented illness.

Given the assumptions of the times, most girls accepted the religious emphasis without question. Forty-two students created a campus chapter of the Young Women's Christian Association in the fall of 1905. The new group offered a Bible-study class every Sunday afternoon and religious services on Sunday evenings.[26] The college encouraged membership in the YWCA and allowed students to substitute attendance at the Sunday evening services for morning church.

Florida parents expected their daughters to be safe and well cared for while away at school. The college complied with its own interpretation of *in loco parentis*. Designated chaperones, at this time usually a female faculty member or a male faculty member and his wife, accompanied students every time they left the campus. A system of bells regulated the girls' lives, from waking at 6:30 A.M. for 7:15 breakfast through enforced study period after supper and light flash at 9:45 P.M.[27]

Until 1907, the administration mandated student membership in either the Minerva Club or the Thalian Literary Society. These scholastic organizations, more like debating societies than social clubs, held weekly meetings and annual commencement debates. Together, the societies published a literary and current-events magazine, *The Talisman*. Beginning in April 1906, the issues appeared bimonthly until the advent of the student newspaper, the *Florida Flambeau*, in January 1915. *The Talisman* contained stories and plays written by students, editorials, news of campus organizations, and social accounts of interest to the young ladies. A third literary society, The Anvil Society, appeared briefly in the mid-teens but failed to flourish.

ATHLETICS

Athletics immediately became an important part of college life.[28] Barely three weeks into the Fall 1905 semester, students formed a college-wide Athletic Association to which all belonged. The next year the association organized two basketball teams, Cockleburs and Prickly Pears, from among the liberal arts students. The victor in two out of three matches became the "college team."

At the time, a small but active intercollegiate sports network existed among the older, private institutions in the state. Soon women's basketball teams from Stetson and Rollins colleges challenged the new school. In March 1907, the Female College team traveled to Deland, where they lost a hard-fought game to Stetson. The team went on to Winter Park where it was beaten by Rollins. Dejectedly, the FFC girls returned to the capital city where, to their surprise and delight, a contin-

gent of students greeted them at the railway depot with cheers
and banners. That night the college feted its team members
with a dinner party in the dining room.[29]

As enthusiasm for intercollegiate basketball spread through
the campus, the faculty intervened. With a mind to the importance of scholarship and decorum (admittedly, the athletic
"costume" of cotton stockings, bloomers that ended just below
the knee, and middie blouses lacked dignity), the administration decided that when the current season ended they would
allow no further public games. "Public" denoted the presence of any young men except members of the faculty. Under this cloud Florida Female College played its last game of
the season against Stetson College. A crowd of both students
and townspeople attended and cheered the FFC girls on to
victory. Unfortunately, bickering between the umpire (a Stetson
student) and the referee (a Female College student who had
recently transferred to the Tallahassee institution from Stetson)
added fuel to faculty fires, and the season ended on a tenu-
ous note.[30]

In the fall of 1907, an accumulation of circumstances pre-
vented the girls from playing their favorite sport. First, exceptionally dry weather meant not enough rain to pack the clay
courts. Second, on a campus that had been littered with piles
of lumber all summer as construction on Bryan Hall progressed,
there was a curious shortage of wood with which to build
backboards.[31] Third, the faculty recalled the rowdy disputes
with Stetson the previous year and refused to condone intercollegiate competition. The girls nevertheless anticipated playing against local "faculty approved" teams in the spring.

Much to the students' dismay, when time for basketball
finally arrived, the administration reminded the girls of its
earlier edict regarding spectators at athletic events: all men
except relatives of students or members of the faculty were
excluded from the audience at basketball games. That ruling
eliminated the possibility of local competition, for none of
the other teams were willing to bar male relatives and friends

from the games. Prohibited from participating in intercollegiate contests and frustrated in attempts to play local teams, students created two new campus teams, Stars and Crescents, and inaugurated a formal intra-college rivalry between the two.[32]

TRADITIONS

Life at Florida Female College seemed to lack zeal after the administration vanquished intercollegiate sports contests. During the Murphree years, Florida Female College had neither a past nor traditions, elements that bring cohesiveness to an institution. The new college did have school colors of garnet and gold, but when those colors were selected is unclear. They seem to have been in place as early as 1906 when one of the names suggested for *The Talisman* was *Garnet and Gold*.[33] The school's immediate predecessor, Florida State College, fielded a championship football team in 1904–05; its uniform colors were purple and gold. The FSC Class of 1905 selected crimson as its class color. Possibly Murphree or the FFC administration combined the recognizable colors from FSC, purple and crimson, to achieve garnet. Members of a Tallahassee family connected with the college since prior to 1900 believed the colors originally represented sunrise and sunset, a delightful though perhaps apocryphal thought.[34]

As for a college song, well, there really was none. Dr. Samuel Tucker had composed lyrics for a Florida State College song and set them to the tune of "The Battle Hymn of the Republic." When the Florida Female College superseded the earlier institution, he merely changed the fifth stanza from "May thy loving sons and daughters still revere thy noble name" to "May thy loving daughters honor and revere thy noble name," thus creating a gender-specific song for the new school. The revision failed to arouse any school spirit among the young ladies.

Belatedly, students and administrators attempted to regenerate the missing enthusiasm for life on campus. In 1909, they planned and presented the first official student ceremony, a "Freshman-Junior Wedding," formally uniting the two classes. Invitations read "Mr. and Mrs. Leap Year Class request the honor of your presence at the marriage of their daughter, Miss Blonza Freshman, to Mr. Walter Dean Junior." One of the freshmen, selected for her beauty and dressed in full bridal attire, joined symbolically with a "groom," a member of the junior class decked out in a tuxedo. The ceremony was followed by a wedding supper and dance (girls danced with each other) held in the Domestic Science Department.[35]

CHANGES

Spring of 1909 held changes with far-reaching ramifications for the college. Those connected with the institution had complained for four years of the unsuitability of the name Florida Female College. The local newspaper pointed out that the school itself had no gender; only the students who slept in its dormitories and attended its classes were female. But the legislators had bestowed the name, and only they could change it. In the absence of legislative action, the Tallahassee *Weekly True Democrat* reported the activities of the "Florida College for Women" during the 1905–06 school year. Students referred to their school as "Florida College for Women" as early as the November 1906 issue of *The Talisman.* The college catalogue reflected some ambivalence in the matter. It referred first to "Florida Female College," then "State College for Women." Finally the Legislature of 1909 declared that Florida Female College would henceforth be known as Florida State College for Women (FSCW) "since the best English usage is opposed to the present title; and, besides, the present name seems to be objectionable to a great many of the friends of this institution."[36] At the same time, the University of the State of Florida became simply the University of Florida (UF).

As an adjunct to the action taken by the legislature, Board of Control Chairman P. K. Yonge requested that the presidents of both institutions oversee the design of seals and creation of mottos for their respective schools. Murphree apparently turned the project over to his Art and Classics departments.[37] Classics professor Bondurant had withdrawn from campus life some weeks earlier. Clarence E. Boyd, Bondurant's replacement, did not arrive in Tallahassee until mid-September. The art teacher, Inez Abernethy, spent the summer in Europe. Responsibility for creating the seal may have been left ultimately to members of Abernethy's art class, or there may have been a contest. At any rate, Agnes Granberry, an art student and member of the Class of 1912 who later became an assistant instructor in the Art Department, originated the seal's motif.[38]

Her final design depicted three torches side by side (perhaps adapted from the crossed torches on the Florida State College seal) with a banner woven through them at midsection. The words *Vires, Artes, Mores* (strength, skill, customs) imposed upon the banner defined the triple purpose of the college—to educate the student physically, mentally, and morally, and thus produce *Femina Perfecta*, the completed woman. The college would give the girls strength and courage to compete, skills to execute their chosen work, and customs and traditions to establish standards for their lives. A *Flambeau* editorial of April 21, 1923, offered the following commentary: "In the strength and in the skill we obtain from her, the traditions of our accomplishments will be established— traditions she will be proud to bear." The new seal appeared in the spring of 1910 in the center of a small plaque used to recognize the winning teams in basketball competitions between the Stars and Crescents.[39]

The event that had the most significant impact on the young college came about as a result of a move to oust Dr. Andrew Sledd from the presidency of the institution at Gainesville. This culminated in his resignation and Murphree's appointment as the new head of the University of Florida.[40] Although his wife and children had been born in Tallahassee and her family still lived there, Murphree accepted with alacrity the new posting to Gainesville.[41]

Faculty members at the college made no public comments about these events, but *The Talisman* devoted two pages to the change in leadership. The editorial rightly credited A. A. Murphree with the success of the women's college to date, saying in part that "chiefly to him may be attributed the harmony which has always existed between students and faculty, faculty and President." Under his leadership the school firmly established for itself a significant and permanent role in Florida higher education.

∽

The Murphree years ended on June 2, 1909, when Governor Albert W. Gilchrist awarded each liberal arts graduate a diploma and a silver teaspoon with "Compliments of Albert W. Gilchrist, Governor of Florida" engraved in the bowl. The reverse side had the graduate's name, the occasion, and the date. The college also issued diplomas to 60 women who had graduated from state schools before 1906. In that way the state reestablished the legitimacy of degrees conferred before the passage of the Buckman Bill.[42]

Chapter III
Conradi and Company: 1909-1920

J ust as selection of the site for the women's college had been of secondary concern to members of the Board of Control in 1905, so also was replacement of its president belatedly considered. After some dithering, the members selected Dr. Edward Conradi, virtually unknown to them, as Murphree's successor. Conradi described his meeting with the board:

> I was questioned extensively, for they did not know me nor did I know them. The subject of my birthplace came up and they asked me, when they discovered I was from Ohio, if I got along all right with Southern children.[1]

The chairman then asked him to leave the room. When he returned, the members announced that they had "decided to elect a Southern man for the presidency of the College." Conradi replied that he had expected little better from Southern thinking, and added that, under the circumstances, he would be happier north of the Mason-Dixon Line. As he left the room, the chairman asked him to wait in the lobby, which he did. Shortly thereafter, he was called back into the meeting room and offered the presidency of the newly named Florida State College for Women. Conradi considered the offer carefully and demanded assurance that the college would always receive facilities and financial support equivalent to those of the university in Gainesville. When granted that, he accepted the position.[2] Not only did the board renege on the promised equity, but it also immediately compromised an existing one. Until then, the presidents of both institutions had received the same annual salaries, first $2,500, then $2,750. Now the board set Murphree's salary at $3,000 and Conradi's at $2,500.[3] Their action should have forewarned the new president of the struggles to come.

DORMITORIES, "ET AL"

Florida State College for Women faced the future confidently, but its physical plant was still mired in the past. Since 1905, the campus had acquired only the Lincoln Academy property, Bryan Hall, and a few acres surrounding that dormitory. Between East Hall and the junction of the Old Quincy Road with West Jefferson Street was a little pond surrounded by bedraggled stalks of corn. North of Bryan Hall, land covered with tangled shrubbery sloped toward the section of Park Avenue that continued onto the college grounds. An unpaved driveway circled College Hall, then ran past East Hall and in front of Bryan Hall to end at Park Avenue.[4]

The changes in leadership at the college and university had drawn sufficient attention so that the legislature empowered a special committee to inspect and make recommendations for state educational institutions. The delegation noted that College Hall rested on pipe clay, also known as Fuller's Earth, a type of material that expanded and contracted with moisture. As a result, the exterior of the building "[was] cracked in many places and [had] the appearance of being dangerous." An engineering survey confirmed the report and condemned the structure. The college desperately needed the hall for classes, so the architects braced the exterior walls at each end of the building with a crosswork of iron rods, and then approved its use for another term. They strongly recommended, however, that the building be abandoned as soon as possible.[5]

Once again the college found its back against a wall, only

this time the wall was not on fire—it was cracked. At the same time that the architects condemned and then reprieved College Hall, they submitted plans for a structure that would become "the central building and dominant feature of a quadrangle of buildings to be erected later on as the needs of the college shall demand." The administration planned to use the shored-up College Hall until a new structure was completed on a site immediately behind it. After two architectural revisions, so that plans and prices matched, a contract for the new building went to Nicholas Ittner of Atlanta.[6] By December 1909, the campus resounded with noise as workmen felled pine trees on the site of the new construction.

On March 8, 1910, the city's schools and businesses closed, and a huge crowd assembled at College Hall. Governor Gilchrist addressed the gathering, and the college choir performed traditional favorites including "The Star Spangled Banner" and "Columbia," as well as the "College Song." Then members of the Grand Masonic Lodge of Florida laid the cornerstone for the new Administration Building.[7] Conradi ceremoniously placed a square copper casket into the cornerstone cavity. The casket contained a brief history of the college written by A. A. Murphree, who disappointed students and faculty alike when he failed to attend the ceremonies.[8] It also held a supplemental paragraph drafted by Conradi, a list of current students, teachers, and class officers, a copy of the college catalogue,[9] a copy of *The Talisman*, and a copy of the University of Florida catalogue. The soon-to-be-graduated Class of 1910, twelve members strong, added a class prophecy and locks of hair snipped from each girl's head.[10] For the remainder of that spring, classes in the old building and construction on the new building continued side by side. When workers finally demolished College Hall late in the summer, college Business Manager J. G. Kellum purchased the light aqua marble steps from the front entrance. He later incorporated them into his own home, which he built in 1914 on the southeast corner of Copeland and Clinton Streets.[11]

Once completed, the Administration Building solved all the space problems at the college. Or did it? The long-awaited auditorium accommodated 1,000 people, four times the capacity of the assembly room in the old building. A Lyon and Healy organ, purchased in 1907 for use in the old chapel, shared space on the stage with a new Steinway grand piano.[12] The remainder of the structure comfortably housed the Department of Home Economics, the Music Department, the School of Art, and the School of Expression. But the more successful the college became, the more students it attracted, and the more residential space it required. Even with all of East Hall used for living accommodations, every room in the two dormitories was filled, and a number of students lodged in town at approved homes. The overcrowded dining room caused mealtime difficulties, and the cramped kitchen facilities presented a constant threat of fire.[13]

Between 1908 and 1916, however, Florida's financial outlook improved daily. Governor Gilchrist traveled extensively to promote the state, encouraging people to come to "Florida the Marvelous."[14] Thanks to publicity and modern transportation facilities, mainly railroads and some highways, the state's population increased rapidly. Henry Flagler extended his railroad to Key West; Jacksonville, the largest city and automotive gateway to the state, had a population of just over 28,000 persons. In an optimistic mood that reflected the state's expanding economy, the 1911 Legislature appropriated funds and the Board of Control architects submitted plans for a new L-shaped dormitory and adjacent infirmary for the college. As usual, all construction bids exceeded the anticipated cost. Eliminating the separate infirmary and scaling back the dormitory plans brought building estimates into accord with available money.[15]

Construction on the residence hall went as scheduled. The three-story brick building located north of Bryan Hall included a basement, a kitchen, and a recreation room for students' use on the first floor and a parlor and matron's office on the second floor. The west wing of the third floor housed an infirmary. The remaining space was given over to shared bedrooms sufficient for approximately 130 students.[16] An arcade connected the new dormitory to Bryan Hall, the Atrium of which was still the only guest reception area on campus. The college named the hall for Mrs. Mary Reynolds, the first Lady Principal, who had died in 1909.

On February 3, 1913, girls moved into their new quarters in Reynolds Hall. A resident of Bryan Hall, comparing her accommodations to those of Reynolds Hall, concluded that Bryan was prettier on the outside but Reynolds "won" on the inside: the bedrooms in Reynolds had bookshelves and better furniture. Upon completion of the new dormitory, students' reactions were varied: "We are really living in our new dormitory and find it very beautiful and very comfortable, but there seems to be very little more room than there was before."[17]

To further alleviate the campus crush, a new single-story Dining Hall (seating 550 persons comfortably) and a connecting two-story kitchen and bakeshop soon rose behind the brick dormitories. In a departure from the norm, O. C. Parker of Tallahassee was awarded the construction contract after only one revision of the plans drawn by architect Edwards and his new associate, William Sayward. On the outside, the new Dining Hall resembled all the other brick structures on the campus. Once inside, however, diners discovered that exposed beam ribbing in the ceiling created a surprising impression of grandeur. The room duplicated the dining hall at Winthrop College in Rock Hill, South Carolina, while Winthrop's dining hall imitated that at Christ College, Oxford. A two-story rear wing, perpendicular to the Dining Hall, housed the kitchen, dishwashing room, bakeshop, refrigeration rooms, and storerooms.[18]

The Middle Florida Ice Company delivered ice for perishable foods such as meats from local dealers, fish and oysters from wholesalers at Carrabelle, St. Marks, and Apalachicola, and poultry from farmers in Leon and adjoining counties. An extensive college garden in the area immediately west of the kitchen provided fresh produce for the boarding department at considerable financial savings.[19] Produce grown there included beets, potatoes, squash, melons, carrots, several varieties of greens, onions, and lots and lots of cabbage.

Milk, served at every meal, caused unexpected problems. Local dairy farmers refused to maintain large enough herds to provide sufficient quantities of milk for the college's seasonal demand because they had difficulty selling the excess during the summers. Conradi and Kellum solved the problem by purchasing 25 milk cows and establishing a college dairy. Leon County dairymen and dealers then purchased the minimal surplus milk from the college.[20]

CONTINUED GROWTH

Two events having an impact on the growth of the college occurred in 1913. The first involved regulations for public school teachers. Other states had for several years accepted degrees from their own state colleges as certification. Beginning in 1913, New York and Pennsylvania issued teacher certifications to FSCW graduates on the basis of their college diplomas. Florida, however, still required an aspiring teacher to pass a certification examination even if she or he possessed a college degree from a state institution. During their 1913 session, state legislators passed a law granting teaching certificates to liberal arts graduates without further testing, provided they had devoted at least one-fifth of their college work to teacher training. As a result, a greater number of students enrolled in education classes.[21]

The second event concerned accreditation of the college. In 1905, the Board of Control had established completion of the 11th grade (a total of 12 high school units) as an admission requirement for the College of Arts and Sciences at both the college and the university and had provided sub-collegiate departments at both to teach the equivalent of the 11th grade. By 1913, all counties in the state had either four-year high schools or the means of supporting them. Conradi and Murphree acted in accord to raise the minimum entrance requirement to four years of high school (15 units).[22] With these new standards in force, in 1915 Florida State College for Women became the first state women's college admitted to the Southern Association of Colleges and Secondary Schools.

FSCW's enhanced reputation for scholarship now attracted more applicants than ever. Including those enrolled in the State School for Teachers, 413 girls attended FSCW during the 1912–13 session; by 1915–16, the number rose to 818. Reluctant to turn any girls away, the college accepted out-of-state students, but housed them in approved rooms near the campus.[23] In spite of the obvious result of the school's good reputation and popularity, namely overcrowded conditions, the 1917 Legislature earmarked all available building funds for the University of Florida. Before any projects at Gainesville could get underway, however, the United States' entrance into World War I altered attendance projections for the men's school. The Board of Control transferred most of the university's appropriations to FSCW, and the college immediately authorized construction of not one, but two new buildings—a three-story residence hall and a structure intended specifically for classroom use.[24]

Both contracts went to O. C. Parker, who confidently projected a September 1918 completion date for the new dormitory, to be located west of Bryan Hall. However, wartime shortages of building supplies and transportation delays caused construction to proceed more slowly than anticipated. By mid-July, with all available rooms reserved and a waiting list, the college prohibited registration of out-of-state applicants and accepted only those Florida students who had exhausted all possible educational programs in their home counties. To render the dormitory livable, the contractor eliminated most of the proposed east wing and the arcade connector to Bryan Hall. Since the Bryan Hall Atrium served as a reception area for the entire campus, students living in the new dormitory went out of that building, around the corner, and into Bryan Hall to receive guests.[25] The oddly truncated structure, with its crenelated roof line matching that of Bryan Hall, was named for former governor Napoleon Bonaparte Broward. Three weeks into the fall semester, students assigned to Broward Hall lamented:

> Be it ever so unfinished, there's no place like Broward Hall. What do we care if we have no doors to our rooms, no lights to see by, no beds to sleep on, as long as there are four walls to contain our toothbrushes and pictures.[26]

The college had been so anxious to make use of its financial windfall that it had unwisely undertaken two buildings at once. While the contractors worked doggedly on Broward Hall, the Education Building slowly took shape northeast of the Administration Building. The new classroom structure would provide space for the State School for Teachers, college high school, psychology laboratories, manual training laboratories, and all education classes. In spite of war-related slowdowns that delayed arrival of windows for the building, plaster work continued and floors were laid.

The college finally occupied the Education Building in the late summer of 1919.[27] The driveway in front of Bryan and Reynolds Halls now turned east, curved in front of the new Education Building, and returned to the main entrance at the head of College Avenue, as the city had renamed Clinton Street in 1916. A fountain in front of the Administration Building and brick piers at the main College Avenue entrance, gifts from the graduating classes of 1915 through 1918, enhanced the entryway to the campus.

The Classes of 1915 and 1917 gave the fountain to the college as their class gift. The Classes of 1916 and 1918 presented brick piers for the sides of the main entrance. The *Flambeau* reported in 1930 that one pier contained a hollow space into which students placed a metal box containing copies of the last will and testament of the two classes, but there is no current evidence to support that. A molded plaque on the pier to the left of the entryway bore the class year of 1916 and a relief of the lamp of knowledge. A similar plaque on the opposite pier bore the class year of 1918 and a depiction of the Cherokee rose, the flower chosen by the seniors of 1918 in lieu of a class tree. Later, the piers were connected by an iron arch that framed the words "Florida State College for Women."[28] A member of the Class of 1918 verbalized the girls' feelings about the gates:

> And we, the girls who have helped to raise
> These guarding gates,
> Now come with hearts that overflow,
> With backward glance and footstep slow,
> To take our places with those who go
> Out at the gates.[29]

Each evening a night watchman stretched a chain from one pier to the other to close the college to outsiders.

FORMATIVE YEARS

Murphree had recognized that a qualified faculty and sound scholarship were absolutely and immediately necessary to establish the college's reputation; Conradi was of the same mind. But the two employed very different management styles. Murphree had handled all administrative and business duties himself. Conradi directed briefly, then delegated the day-to-day business of running the college. J. G. Kellum soon became the school's acknowledged business "boss" and handled all financial and legal matters. After William G. Dodd became Dean of the College of Arts and Sciences in 1913, he served as the school's chief administrator, a "ghost president," involved with every major decision and every student function.[30] Consequently, Florida State College for Women reflected Conradi's philosophical and moral tenets by way of his personnel selections, but derived its tangible success from the effective business and organizational skills of others.

In June 1909, Conradi had barely settled his wife, Augusta, and their young daughters, Elizabeth and Louisa, into temporary quarters in East Hall before he faced his first problem. Since his selection as president, the college had experienced many faculty resignations, necessitating new appointments. On the surface the turnover looked like a rejection of the new administration; upon closer inspection the problem showed little connection to the change in presidents. Those who resigned did so for health reasons or for promotions and higher salaries in other states.

Conradi spent most of the next decade assembling and assimilating his faculty. He made some outstanding selections and some mistakes. He lost some very good teachers because of low salaries. But he chose carefully; several of those who joined the faculty during its formative years remained at the school even after he retired in October 1941.

One of the first faculty members Conradi hired was Lanas S. Barber of Tallahassee. As principal of Leon County and Graded High School, Barber created what the local newspaper called a "public calamity" when he left that position to accept the post of professor of biology and chemistry at the college.[31] He taught biology and zoology at FSCW until 1941, when the Board of Control granted him emeritus status.

Conradi hired Dr. C. E. Boyd to replace campus favorite Bondurant as instructor in Latin and Greek.[32] Boyd remained at the college for three years, during which time he made his classwork "fun" by holding contests every Friday to test students on Latin definitions. Following Boyd was Dr. C. M. Long, whose application Murphree had turned down in 1905 in favor of Bondurant. Apparently the position was not all he expected, for after just one year he yielded his place to Dr. Josiah (J. B.) Game. Game arrived in 1914 and stayed until his death in March 1935. He purchased several acres of land just to the west and southwest of the campus and opened the wooded area, soon known as Game's Woods, to students and faculty for recreation.[33] Over the years he worked with Kellum to acquire for the college much of the property east of what is now Woodward Avenue.

Nathaniel M. Salley accepted the position of head of the State School for Teachers. He and his family moved into the Meginniss house on the southeast corner of Jefferson and Copeland Streets in the late summer of 1910.[34] He, too, became a permanent member of the Conradi faculty, remaining until the late 1930s, and his children spent as much time on the campus as some students.

Dr. William G. Dodd replaced Samuel Tucker as chairman of English language and literature in 1910, when Tucker moved to Brooklyn Polytechnic Institute in New York for a much higher salary. Dodd and his family quickly became active members of the Tallahassee community.[35] He proved extremely popular with the faculty. And although students varied widely in their opinions of him, he championed them at every opportunity. Some girls thought he was "very strict," and many were "scared to death of him." One described him as "that huge and awe-inspiring man." Another was less than awed by him and noted in her scrapbook that "Dr. Dodd, the ladies' man, talked to us and whirled his watch chain and thought he was 'cute' at YW today."[36]

Conradi experienced even more difficulties with modern language instructors than he did with ancient language faculty. By the end of his first year as president, he was dissatisfied with the way German was being taught. The Board of Control made no mention of marital status when Conradi hired A. W. Calhoun, an acquaintance from his years at the St. Petersburg Normal School, to teach German and history. Calhoun was young, single, and extremely popular. He spoke only German in class and expected his students to do likewise. Girls considered his table in the dining room a "curiosity," for members of the German Club sat there and conversed exclusively in German.[37] The 1911 annual saluted him with a limerick:

The German Club has a table!
I wish to add to my fable,
They clatter too much
In horrible Dutch
To eat fast they are unable.[38]

Caddabelle Farr got along quite well at the German table because Calhoun was one of her "beaus." She just smiled sweetly at the teacher and pointed to what she wanted passed, "and it usually worked!" And if party invitations are any indication, mothers of young ladies considered Calhoun one of the more eligible gentlemen about town.[39]

Calhoun received kudos as a German instructor but not as a history instructor because he advocated socialism as an acceptable economic system. Amid news of political discontent in Europe and labor unrest in the United States, Calhoun's espousal of socialistic ideas was decidedly ill-timed. In June 1911, seniors from his history class delivered Commencement speeches that expressed sympathy for the working class. The editor of the *Pensacola News* took offense at the tone of the students' presentations and demanded an investigation of possible socialists ensconced at the college, filling the minds of "pure, lily-like little girls" with "socialism of the rankest brand." Other state newspapers picked up the refrain and stridently demanded Calhoun's resignation.[40]

The Board of Control ordered Conradi to conduct an investigation. Calhoun admitted privately to his friend that he did, indeed, believe in socialism although he denied being a member of the Socialist Party.[41] The instructor resigned early in October 1911, making it quite clear that he did so under duress.[42] He later earned a Ph.D. from Clark University, Conradi's alma mater, and was subsequently fired from a teaching position there for opposing the United States' entry into World War I. After that, he taught at Montevallo in Alabama and Winthrop in South Carolina, both state-supported women's colleges.[43]

On a campus full of females, young unmarried male instructors were extremely popular. Calhoun's successor, J. H.

Garnand, not only attracted attention as a bachelor—he married a graduate of the Class of 1911. After six years in Tallahassee, he and his family moved to New York, where he completed both his master's and doctoral degrees. He next went to Emory and Henry College in Virginia, where he remained until 1961 as head of the Department of Foreign Languages.[44]

Coincidentally, there were two language professors named Calhoun on the Tallahassee campus. The other Calhoun, J. C., had been at the school with Murphree prior to 1905, but chose to move on to the College of William and Mary in 1911. Ludwig Marienburger, a "Prussian born and bred, who thought Count Otto von Bismarck just below God," replaced J. C. Calhoun. The blustery Marienburger resigned after three years, and Dr. P. A. Claassen filled the vacancy. Genial and quiet, Claassen quickly became a favorite with students and faculty alike. He and his wife regularly hosted both French and German Club meetings in their home. Sadly, he died unexpectedly in early December 1916 of acute appendicitis.[45] The campus was stunned; classes were canceled. Conradi took over the late professor's German sections until Christmas vacation. Dr. Emil Saverio, a native of Austria-Hungary, stepped into Claassen's position after the holidays. A year later, as a patriotic response to America's involvement in World War I, the college dropped German from the curriculum and Saverio resigned.[46] He was succeeded by Edmund V. Gage, who taught modern languages other than German.

Between 1910 and 1920, the School of Music evolved from a program conferring certificates to a full college program leading to a bachelor's degree. Ella Scoble Opperman, who joined the faculty as Director of the School of Music in 1911, was responsible for this development. Her arrival on the college's music scene professionalized the program, removing the "finishing school" character it had had under Murphree.

Opperman remained at the college for more than three decades, but members of her department changed frequently over the next few years. One of the more controversial was

Miss Selma Bjorgo, a piano instructor who arrived at FSCW in the fall of 1916. As the United States became more deeply involved in the European conflict that escalated into World War I, Bjorgo, a native German, unwisely refused to temper her nationalistic sympathies. She kept a German flag and Kaiser Wilhelm's picture in her studio, and she openly announced her support of his actions to students as well as faculty. It was not long before the Board of Control "suggested" that she resign.[47]

The college's success led to an expanded curriculum, which created the need for more faculty. In 1913, the departments of Botany and Chemistry, headed by Dr. Jerome McNeill, had so many students that the college separated the two. McNeill remained in charge of the Botany Department until 1916, when Dr. Alban Stewart replaced him. Stewart was quiet and reserved, with a good sense of humor. He settled his family permanently in Tallahassee, first in the Bessie Cobb house on Calhoun Street and later in a house on North Monroe Street. While at the college, he taught bacteriology in addition to botany. Lucy Lang recalled that during Saturday classes Stewart went down the roll and asked everybody one question. "One time he asked one girl, Lila Murrow, what bacteria it was that did a certain thing. She said she didn't know. He said, sure she did—it was very common. She said it was too common to mention."[48]

Conradi engaged Dr. Charles A. Brautlecht to teach chemistry. He was a competent chemist, but he was also one of Conradi's mistakes. Students feared him and lacked respect for him. One girl complained that he called her to the chalkboard to do equations, then harangued and embarrassed her for half the class period before he allowed her to take her seat. He acquired a reputation for difficult exams and for "bolstering grades." In one instance, when the class average on a test fell to 48 percent, he raised all scores by 27 points. Such action caused apprehension and mistrust among students. Shortly before the end of World War I, Brautlecht enlisted in the military. He spent four months working for the government in chemical laboratories, returned to FSCW to finish out the spring 1919 semester, and then resigned.[49] Dr. Horatio Hughes taught chemistry for the next few years.

Until the manner of certification for teachers changed, psychology courses had been included in the Normal School curriculum, and Conradi and Nathaniel Salley had shared the teaching of them. When the State School for Teachers expanded, the college created a separate chair in psychology and hired Dr. E. A. Hayden as professor. His students particularly remembered conducting taste experiments in class: blindfolded and with their noses plugged, subjects found it impossible to distinguish ground cinnamon from flour and ground cloves from pepper.[50] Though a popular and effective teacher, Hayden suffered from severe depression, and over his six-year tenure his moods swayed noticeably.

By 1918, overcrowded conditions affected the organization of the College of Arts and Sciences and caused a split in the Department of History and Political and Social Sciences. Professor Arthur "Pi" Williams continued to teach history, while new faculty member Dr. Raymond Bellamy assumed the chair of the Political and Social Sciences Department.[51] Bellamy's chosen fields, politics and sociology, and his outspoken manner often generated controversy.

During President Woodrow Wilson's administration (1912–1920), federal legislation supporting farm reforms affected the Department of Home Economics at the college. The Smith-Lever Act of 1914 provided federal funding for county agricultural extension agents under the supervision of land-grant colleges. Three years later the Smith-Hughes Act extended agricultural and mechanical education to high schools through federal funding. Those two pieces of legislation increased the need for well-educated home economics teachers, both to serve as county educational representatives and to teach in high schools. An agricultural extension agent would transmit information from FSCW, UF, regional experiment stations, and the Federal Department of Agriculture to the residents of her county. In Florida, agents from each participating county were appointed on the basis of their practical experience in farming and/or homemaking combined with their college training in home economics.

To meet federal requirements and the increased demand for vocational training, the college created a Home Demonstration Extension and offered a short course that included instruction, demonstrations, and contests. At first, all who wished to attend could do so; eventually, the program was held for 4-H girls specifically. These actions generated an interest in home economics that led the college to create a separate School of Home Economics in 1917 and to authorize a related bachelor of science degree. Agnes Ellen Harris, who had been director of the program since she joined the faculty in 1909, became dean of the new school as well as head of the extension program. When the extension work was made part of the General Extension Division of the University of Florida in 1919, she resigned and moved to Texas.[52]

By the end of the decade, most of the Conradi faculty members were in place. In 1913, the Board of Control had appointed Arthur Williams vice president of the college, delegated the responsibilities of administrative secretary to mathematics and physics professor Elmer Smith, and named William Dodd as Dean of the College of Arts and Sciences. Nathaniel Salley directed the State School for Teachers; Ella Scoble Opperman was Dean of the School of Music.[53] The School of Home Economics had only an acting dean, but a permanent director was soon hired. Others entrusted with the education of Florida's young ladies included Miss Rowena Longmire and Drs. J. B. Game, E. A. Hayden, Alban Stewart, Raymond Bellamy, L. S. Barber, and Horatio Hughes.

FIGHTING SPIRIT

The sequestered nature of the institution kept students fairly well isolated from jarring world events, but sometimes the outside found its way in. Between 1916 and 1919, college

residents experienced many of the same wartime deprivations and German phobias as did the rest of Florida and the
country. Conradi hired the boarding department's first dietitian, Margaret M. Edwards, to cope with food shortages and
conservation efforts. Special first-aid and basic Red Cross
nursing courses were available for all campus residents. Students learned to knit and to can and preserve vegetables and
fruits. Everyone attended Liberty Bond drives and rallies in
the auditorium and collected red postage stamps.[54]

The first real friction between the college and Tallahassee
residents resulted from the country's wartime anti-German fer-
vor. During 1917 particularly, many Tallahasseans felt strongly
that it was wrong for American boys to be fighting in Europe
while Florida taxes paid the salary of "Huns" at the college.[55]
Conradi had been born in New Bremen, Ohio, of German
parents. Though he was a Yankee, his ancestry had been of
little import to local residents until the United States became an
active participant in World War I. Then he and two other college employees, Emil Saverio of the Modern Languages Department and Julius Steinfuhrer, the campus gardener, were verbally
attacked and their loyalty to this country repeatedly questioned.
Public pressure and statements in the press finally drove Saverio
and Steinfuhrer, neither of whom were United States citizens,
to present signed loyalty statements to Conradi and the Board
of Control in order to keep their jobs.[56] Both eventually resigned,
Steinfuhrer in February 1918 and Saverio in June. Steinfuhrer
returned to his job as college gardener in 1921.[57]

Conradi maintained a dignified silence through most of
the vilification, but he did what he could to dispel the resentment. He declined an offer from a German-American organization to present a scholarship to the college because he
feared it might be part of a pro-German campaign.[58] He also
served as chairman of the Leon County Four Minute Men, a
group of local businessmen whose concise but rousing
speeches encouraged Liberty Bond sales and generally bolstered the war effort.

Conradi's active support of the American war effort might have alleviated public distrust had politicians not interfered. Florida governors Broward (1904–1908), Gilchrist (1908–1912), and Park Trammell (1912–1916) had maintained cordial, or at least polite, relationships with the college. Governor Sidney J. Catts (1916–1920) operated differently. During an acrimonious gubernatorial campaign, he had promised new appointments for the Board of Control and the institutions of higher learning. The presidency of a state college or university seemed a suitable reward for a loyal supporter, and Conradi's position was the chosen plum. Murphree was not as vulnerable because the alumni of the university voted, and an attack on their president might arouse politically dangerous opposition. Besides, Conradi's German heritage offered a logical excuse for his dismissal. Board of Control Chairman Joe Earman, a Catts' supporter, admitted that FSCW had "prospered under his [Conradi's] presidency," but nevertheless he instigated an investigation in an attempt to label Conradi a German sympathizer. Shortly thereafter, Earman audaciously proclaimed, "There ain't going to be any politics in any way, shape or form connected with the Higher Institutions of Learning in Florida if the writer can help it."[59]

Conradi played down the distressing episode in his memoirs:

> In 1918 a man came to my office who said he was an English newsman, and that he had a physical breakdown and so he came to Florida for a rest. He said he just accidentally came through Tallahassee and so he dropped in here for a chat. He began to talk to me about the war. . . .[60]

The blatantly political effort to discredit the president of FSCW failed. Later, when the next governor took office, a new Board of Control chairman privately communicated to Conradi his embarrassment with the past administration, saying:

> This letter should reach you on the morning of the fourth day of January Nineteen hundred and twenty-one, just at the end of a

State Administration which no man could measure. You have lived through it. Please let me offer you my congratulations.[61]

WOMEN'S SUFFRAGE

Conradi and the college successfully withstood charges of a different nature, brought by the Florida Chapter of the National Women's Party. In the United States, nearly equal educational opportunities had become available to women beginning in the 1830s. By the 1850s, educated women such as Margaret Fuller, Susan B. Anthony, Elizabeth Cady Stanton, and Carrie Chapman Catt initiated the fight for women's right to vote. The women's suffrage amendment, later known as the Susan B. Anthony Amendment, was first presented to Congress in 1878, yet most federal and state legislatures denied it passage until 1919. In the mid-teens the National Women's Party, one of several organizations dedicated to achieving suffrage, moved aggressively to force acceptance of the amendment.

FSCW students were keenly aware of the suffrage question by the spring of 1917. Many cheered when William Jennings Bryan spoke in support of prohibition and women's suffrage at the Leon High School auditorium in early April,[62] and quite a few girls visited the Capitol regularly while the male legislators debated the suffrage bill. Conradi, however, always mindful of the tax base of his institution, refused to allow students to voice political opinions. The *Flambeau*, closely monitored by the faculty, cautiously editorialized under the caption "The Suffrage Bill and the College," that

> there is a wide difference of opinion in the college, some feeling that the situation was well expressed by the toast given by a gentleman having dinner at the college, 'Here's to women, who tried to be our equals but God bless them, [they are] still our superiors.' Others who watched the debating on the bill with keen interest deeply regret the fact that since suffrage for all the states is only a matter of time, Florida should be the last instead of the first.[63]

After the Florida Legislature defeated the suffrage bill during its 1917 session, Ruby Leach and Sue Pope, FSCW graduates living in Miami, took issue with the *Flambeau's* ambivalent tone. Leach had been the college newspaper's first editor-in-chief, in the spring of 1915, and both she and Pope were now employed as journalists and feature writers by the *Daily Metropolis* in Miami. Pope also belonged to the National Women's Party. The two young graduates sent a provocative letter to Emily Badcock, the 1916–17 editor-in-chief of the school newspaper, decrying the apolitical stance adopted by FSCW and declaring:

> "The Suffrage Bill and the College" conveys the impression that the majority of the college girls are anti-suffragists, wishy washy, spiritless and wavering. This cannot be true because of the very fact that the girls are in college. You doubtless are well enough informed to know that the arguments advanced against the higher education of women (50 years ago) are now being advanced by unthinking people against suffrage for women.
>
> The insulting toast quoted in your article must have been given by some backwoods cracker who has never associated with intelligent women. We hope that none of the girls sat around in simpering approval of the almost maudlin words.
>
> Can you not in some way get the life work of Susan B. Anthony, and her noble struggle against prejudice and injustice, before these students who are still willing to have men think for them?[64]

As if that were not challenge enough, Pope and Leach practically dared Conradi to censor their actions:

> Dear Dr. Conradi:
>
> We are inclosing [sic] a copy of a letter which we are sending by the same mail to Emily Badcock, editor-in-chief of the *Florida Flambeau*, protesting against the article which appeared in that paper, April 28, which seemed to insinuate that the college sentiment is against the question of woman's suffrage. Will you use your influence to see that it is given publicity?
>
> For our own information we would like to know who now

dictates the policy of the paper. Is [it] a school organ or is it controlled by the editorial staff?[65]

Whether the Miami journalists were naively swept along by more politically adept suffrage crusaders, or whether their remarks reflected conflicts with the administration that occurred during their years at FSCW is difficult to determine. Conradi chose to publicly ignore the girls' query and allowed the situation to cool over the summer. Apparently his strategy succeeded because when school resumed the *Flambeau* printed a discreetly worded request from Pope asking students to form a Suffrage Club to support the suffrage campaign planned for the 1919 legislative session. Under a new editor, the college paper circumspectly took a stand and advised the girls to do the same:

It seems beyond doubt now that women's suffrage is inevitably coming. To some it will be a right for which they have long hoped and worked; to some it will be a duty which the world calls upon them to shoulder. It surely seems that this is a question to which 490 young women cannot be indifferent. We not only welcome, but invite discussion of this question in the *Flambeau.*[66]

Oddly, no further comment regarding suffrage appeared in the *Flambeau* until early April 1918, when once again an editorial solicited student opinions and noted that one senior, Grace Dupree, had already voted in another state. Dupree had recently moved to Florida and transferred to FSCW for her senior year. She and her mother had both exercised their right of franchise in the State of Washington, where women had achieved the vote in state and local elections in 1910. The Miami duo of Pope and Leach learned of Dupree's voting experience through the *Flambeau* article, contacted her, and appointed her their "agent" on campus to present the National Women's Party program to Conradi. They asked her to obtain student signatures on a petition to be forwarded to the U.S. Senate. Rather than act on her own initiative, Dupree consulted Conradi, who declared himself to be in sympathy with the "cause," but said:

> It has always been the policy of the school to refrain from taking an open stand, *as a body*, on questions either purely or semi-political and . . . in accordance with this policy, . . . I do not believe it wise or best for the school that such a stand should be taken by the student *body* on this matter.[67]

The National Women's Party soon had chapters throughout Florida, and Tallahassee fell within an active Third Congressional District. The group aggressively challenged Conradi's attempt to keep students and FSCW politically neutral regarding the issue. The next missive to Dupree on the organization's letterhead displayed names familiar to the college community.[68] Officers of the local chapter, organized in March 1918, included Caroline Mays Brevard and Mrs. J. G. Kellum, wife of the business manager. Another name was that of Helen Hunt, first vice-chairman of the party's Florida State Committee, who, for various reasons, had been denied her diploma from Florida Female College in 1908 and had become a thorn in the side of the administration in her quest to obtain it.[69]

Pope and Leach continued their efforts to sidestep Conradi and obtain FSCW's public support of women's suffrage. Eventually Pope admitted that she was attempting to use the students to influence Florida's senatorial delegation:

> Senator Trammell and Senator Fletcher have sent down the word that Florida women are asleep—that in only one section (the southern east coast) do they seem to want to vote. My idea of having the college pass the resolutions was to convince them that modern women of all sections do want to vote.[70]

When Pope's efforts failed, the National Women's Party stepped up the attack with a formal "Resolution and Protest" that cited "recent action of the president and faculty of the FSCW in prohibiting all discussion among its student body of the present vital question of suffrage for women and of the pending suffrage amendment to the United States Constitution."[71]

Conradi refused to be pressured into a political false step that might jeopardize his position or FSCW's reputation. He responded, "To both the faculty and the students the whole thing seems ridiculous nonsense because it is so foreign to the atmosphere of the college."[72] The *Flambeau* rallied with a resounding endorsement of Conradi's devotion to developing the "finest intellectual, social and moral spirit in the college." The commentary cited the Student Government Association, the YWCA, the Athletic Association, and the paper itself as indications of student initiative and independence.[73] Although the writer only alluded to faculty supervision of these activities, and the editorial made absolutely no mention of women's suffrage, the college came out of the fray unscathed. Proof that the National Women's Party attack was politically motivated and even spiteful appeared in later correspondence from Pope:

> Dr. Conradi prevented it [discussion of suffrage] for the reason that the *Metropolis* gave and for the reason, too, that he is not exactly modern in his methods, as is shown by his refusing the girls inter-collegiate athletics. His objection to bloomers was the strongest argument which he found to give us against this.[74]

∞

This decade was one of remarkable growth and tumult for Florida State College for Women. Physically, four buildings were added to the campus—two dormitories (Reynolds Hall and Broward Hall), the Administration Building, and the first structure intended solely for classes, the Education Building. The number of faculty members increased from 18 to 58. Confronted by problems that arose from the popularity and expansion of the college, an unstable national economy, World War I, and state-level political machinations, the president and administration of FSCW never lost sight of their *raison d'etre*, the academic and social education of the young ladies of Florida.

aught between the era of finishing schools for young
ladies of means and the era of growing acceptance
of a solid liberal arts education for women, Florida
State College for Women declared in its 1924 catalogue that
the school's "peculiar service" was the training and enrich-
ment of the young women of the state.[1] To accomplish that,
Murphree had turned the cultural aspects of campus life over
to his Lady Principal, Mrs. Mary Reynolds. As director of dormitories, her role had included being a stern but caring parental
substitute whom anxious mothers and fathers could trust and
an advisor to the president concerning nonacademic activities. FSCW lost Reynolds's valuable services in 1909, shortly
before Conradi arrived in Tallahassee, when she suffered a
broken hip in a carriage accident. Despite her strong personal
desire to return to "her girls," her physical health deteriorated. In mid-October she checked into Johns Hopkins Medical Center in Baltimore, where she died several weeks later.[2]

"TISSIE"

Conradi, in his first year as president and without an experienced Lady Principal or Dean of Women to consult, tended
to overprotect his charges. New to Tallahassee and North
Florida, he was alarmed by the number of unsuitable (to his
mind) persons that congregated in town on Saturdays. That
was market day in the city, when most of the local farmers

and 'colored' residents gathered at the Rascal Yard at the corner of Adams and Jefferson streets to conduct business and gossip. He decided to hold classes on Saturday rather than Monday, to be certain students remained on campus on that day. Local merchants quickly took notice of the Monday holiday and advertised specials that encouraged the young ladies to shop at P. W. Wilson's or Van Brunt and DeMilly's, or to have lunch in town at the Busy Bee or the Savoy Cafe on "the college girls' day off."[3]

In the summer of 1910, Conradi hired Mrs. Sarah Landrum Cawthon of DeFuniak Springs to fill the position of Dean of the College Home. Mrs. Cawthon was the widow of a professor at the old Normal School in DeFuniak Springs, and had taught kindergarten in that city for a number of years.[4] Affectionately referred to as "Tissie," Mrs. Cawthon quickly became the students' guiding spirit. She knew each girl and offered motherly advice or reassurance when one of them was troubled or felt blue. She counseled them about personal hygiene, appropriate behavior, proper dress, and other qualities that she and Conradi felt they needed to succeed in polite society. With Tissie Cawthon overseeing the personal aspects of their daily lives, girls began a metamorphosis from schoolgirls to more mature college students. But they remained girls in the eyes of the FSCW administration.

DAILY LIFE

In the five years since its founding, the women's college had established a daily routine for its residents. A rising bell sounded throughout the dormitories at 6:30 A.M. Monday through Saturday. Students then had 45 minutes to bathe, dress, and get to the dining room, where breakfast was served promptly at 7:15.[5] Mandatory attendance at the first meal of the day assured that students got out of bed, dressed, and ate a substantial meal before going to early classes. Typical breakfast choices included two shredded-wheat biscuits with cream and sugar, muffins, meat, and two eggs or two buckwheat pancakes and syrup.[6] After breakfast the girls returned to their dormitories to tidy up for room inspection.

Beginning in January 1910, Monday was a holiday from classes, but it was hardly a "free" day. Students attended compulsory chapel in the Administration Building at 8:40 A.M., then used the remainder of the morning for mending, laundry, and general housekeeping. Kathlyn Monroe described Monday as the day when "every girl washes her hair, then finds the most convenient place to dry it." For many girls that meant sitting in the sun or hanging their heads out the dormitory windows. Soon the *Customs and Regulations* booklet forbade such unseemly activity. Monday afternoons were times for special entertainments or activities, such as cutting and chewing sugar cane in Kellum's cane patch, watching a flower and folk dance exhibition presented by one of the gym classes, or attending a matinee at the Daffin Theater in town.[7]

On Tuesday through Saturday mornings, the first class of the day met at 8:00 A.M., followed by chapel at 8:40. Four more class periods came after chapel. Girls returned to the dining room at 1:10 P.M. for the midday meal. Afternoon classes convened at 2:00 and 3:00 o'clock. Everyone had some classes every day. The evening meal was served at 6:00 P.M., followed by a social period until study hour at 7:15. First light flash, the warning that bedtime was near, occurred at 9:45, the second flash at 9:55, and lights out was at 10:00 o'clock.[8] Over the years, the college rearranged the times for meals and chapel to better suit a changing curriculum and gradually moved light flash to a later hour.[9]

Saturday evening dances in the gymnasium were the highlight of the week even though the FSCW administration forbade students to dance with members of the opposite sex, on or off campus. Sometimes girls from town attended the dances and remained on campus as "spend-the-night" guests. Freshmen invited to their first campus dance found little to be excited about, knowing there would be no boys present. Imagine their surprise when they arrived and found a number of handsome young men in attendance. Those "men" belonged to the Cotillion Club, founded in 1911, whose all-female membership dressed and played the part of boys at dances. Sometimes they wore suits or even tuxedos; other times they were attired as the male counterpart to a costumed partner, as when Grace Lothridge attended a Halloween party as an Irish lad and her partner, Coris Shands, dressed as a colleen.[10] Strange as it now seems, the administration endorsed Cotillion Club activities yet refused to allow girls who acted a male part in a play to appear on stage wearing trousers. It was considered unseemly for young ladies to appear in public in men's attire.

Sunday mornings were reserved for church attendance, of course, but afternoons were mostly unscheduled. Some young ladies received dinner invitations from church members and spent the time with those families. In fair weather many girls enjoyed well-chaperoned treks into the surrounding countryside for picnics. Sometimes they walked to the railroad station on Gaines Street to watch the afternoon train pass through. The administration also welcomed guests to the campus on Sunday afternoons.[11]

Close friendships naturally developed among girls living in the restricted campus environment. Students commonly experienced adolescent crushes, and they openly referred to each other as "crush," "rave," "pash" (passion), "smash," or "flame."[12] In this era of innocence, little sexual awareness was involved. As the *Flambeau* explained:

> A "crush," Websterially speaking, is a violent compression or collision. That isn't what it means in a girl's school. But probably Webster didn't know much about girls! Anyway, a "crush" occurs when you see some lonesome little underclassman, with sad brown eyes and down-turned lips, and you smile at her with an expression a la gumdrop in your eyes, and say "Hey" in syrupy tones, and she falls for it.
>
> After that, the "love of a vase" on your study table is always filled with violets. When you're in a play you're always sure to receive flowers grown in Tampa or Jacksonville. Then Crush will

also take you to the Tea Room for milk, and to the corner store for potted ham, and sometimes she takes you to the picture show in a taxi. When you're in a hurry she helps you dress. And because of these hundreds of acts of love, you begin to realize what a regular brick she is, and what a worthless specimen you are.

To be sure, you can to some degree compensate for the debt you owe by kissing her goodnight, and by giving her advice. But very often you stand indifferently before this person who watches your every act with admiring and doting eyes. She has adopted you for her pattern. Are you a fit subject? Think it over.[13]

The more mature and usually more independent students sometimes poked fun at themselves for being caught up in the phenomenon. This missive, typed on a sheet of *The Talisman* letterhead, came from the editor of the *Flambeau*:

Dearest [ ]: I love you more than tongue can tell. For you my longing heart breaks and palpitates and overflows. I sob when you speak to me not. I pine for you like a poisoned bed-bug. I turn to you as the golden sun-flower turns to the orb of day. I need you as I need my false teeth. What care I if your hair is false—if your limbs are offen the old apple tree—if your eye is glass! Be still, thou young and kittenish heart. Yours till the stars grow cold. Flossy[14]

Both students and faculty accepted crushes as a normal part of college life. The faculty accurately interpreted these relationships as admiration for someone older and presumably wiser than the student herself; they accepted them as harmless and possibly helpful emotional experiences for girls testing their independence.[15]

DINING HALL FORMALITIES

Communal dining offered yet further opportunities for socialization and instruction. All dormitory residents and many unmarried faculty members ate their meals in the Dining Hall. The college had always provided what it considered a balanced, nutritional diet for boarders, and for the most part students seemed satisfied with the institutional fare. Before 1914, the kitchen served meals Southern style, with a heavy dinner at midday and a lighter supper in the evening. When the new Dining Hall replaced the East Hall dining room, students voted to have the more substantial meal at night.[16]

Dining assumed a set pattern in the new facility. Each of 40 tables seated ten, with a faculty member, matron, or senior classman at its head. Other faculty members had separate tables. A large bell, suspended on a pulley wheel high in the ceiling at the west end of the kitchen, announced mealtimes. Seats were chosen by drawings or assigned, sometimes weekly, other times monthly or for an entire semester. Business Manager Kellum placed a piano at the back of the room, and a music student or faculty member accompanied the girls as they sang a blessing before the evening meal. Students stood behind their chairs until faculty members were seated, then took their own seats.[17]

As time went by, girls arrived late for meals much too often, making a shambles of dining formalities. In the spring of 1916, the Student Government Association implemented the practice of closing the doors to the Dining Hall ten minutes after the breakfast bell sounded and fifteen minutes after the midday and dinner bells rang in order to teach the students the importance of timely arrival and consideration for others.[18] Would-be diners who appeared after the doors closed simply forfeited that meal.

The college expected students to exhibit exemplary behavior at mealtimes. Those not familiar with dining etiquette quickly learned by observation and association. Table settings on linen tablecloths always included silver flatware, engraved with the initials *FSCW,* and a vase of fresh flowers from the college garden. Each girl provided her own white linen napkins. At the end of a meal, a guest replaced her folded napkin on the table if she expected to return for the next meal; if not, she left her napkin unfolded.[19]

Though the Dining Hall format was necessarily strict, some

girls found ways to bend the rules. Students were expected to come to breakfast dressed for the day, but many a night-gown hem slipped out from under a topcoat during the early meal. Most diners wore class attire at lunch and took more care with their grooming for evening and Sunday meals. Holidays such as Halloween, St. Valentine's Day, and St. Patrick's Day entailed special table decorations and menus, and often girls dressed in costumes.[20] April Fool's Day was a favorite time for the dietitian to have some fun with a nonsense dinner, served on dessert plates and eaten with spoons or served backwards from dessert to appetizer.

A number of girls received free room and board in exchange for waiting tables, a scholarship arrangement inaugurated by Murphree in 1907.[21] Students granted these full scholarships served three meals a day on Monday through Saturday and two meals on Sunday; they also had to maintain a certain grade average. Each dining room girl arrived one-half-hour before the meal, sometimes helped prepare salads or fruit dishes, and set two tables (20 places). When diners arrived, she poured water and milk, served food and dessert from trays and rolling carts, then went to her own table to eat. After the meal she cleared her tables before she resumed her daily class routine.

RULES, RULES, AND MORE RULES

Students at women's colleges in the North as well as the South traditionally came under close supervision. Matthew Vassar told a colleague in 1861:

> It is just as important that we have our Scholars under our own control as the Colonel of a Brigade when going into battle. . . . An essential element of our Institution is the perfect control of the pupils during the period of their instruction in the College; anything short of this is a yielding up of our immediate guardianship, while the responsibility remains—happen what may to these young thoughtless creatures in a moral point of view the College must incur the Odium.[22]

As late as 1915, Conradi, and to a great extent many Florida parents, still adhered to Vassar's sentiments. Social regulations cited in the FSCW catalogues between 1905 and 1920 closely duplicated those noted in the 1857–1863 catalogues of, among others, Wesleyan Female College of Cincinnati, Lindenwood College in Missouri, and Mary Sharp College in Tennessee.[23] Florida State College for Women ensconced girls in dormitories, then regulated and monitored their activities 24 hours a day. By its own admission, the administration at FSCW went beyond supervision and ventured into surveillance of girls entrusted to its care. The catalogue informed prospective students that they were "required to submit to such regulations as will insure faithful study and exemplary conduct." It warned, "the president and faculty will exercise such supervision over the students as, it is hoped, will effect all needed restraint without partaking of the character of espionage."[24]

Strict rules governed off-campus activities, all of which required a chaperone who was either a specified faculty member or an approved upperclassman. Regulations allowed only one visit to town per week. Before leaving campus, each student "signed up" in a log book in Bryan Hall. She noted her destination, the persons in her party, the time of departure, and the anticipated time of return. She "signed off" when she arrived back on campus. Groups of ten, arranged prior to 3:00 P.M. Saturday and adequately chaperoned, could attend one Saturday night movie per month, after which they often went *en masse* to the ice cream parlor. Girls purchased their movie tickets in the dormitory matron's office.[25]

Night matrons, later referred to as "moles," carried flashlights and patrolled the darkened hallways hourly after last light flash, making regular bed checks. Students were either in their own rooms, had special written permission to spend the night in another student's room, or were in the Infirmary. This elaborate system enabled the administration to keep track of each girl, not only for the school's reputation and parents' peace of mind, but also for the student's safety in case of emergency such as an accident or fire in a dormitory.

The school permitted girls to associate with young men only under strict supervision. Matrons answered and monitored telephone calls closely. If a boy called a young lady resident of the campus, the matron told him she was not in and asked him to leave his number. The matron then decided whether to include the telephone number on the message passed on to the girl. Students who received calls used the matron's telephone to return them, and did so in her presence.[26]

Such cloistering of students encouraged curiosity among residents of the city. In 1912 and 1913, young men and boys regularly wandered onto the campus during the week or gathered along Clinton Street on Monday afternoons to ogle the girls. Such "ungentlemanly massing" justified Conradi's fears and his close regulation of off-campus contacts with the opposite sex.[27]

"Students [were] expected to recognize and speak to gentlemen friends, but not to carry on conversations or have treats with them when in town." If the college administration had received written permission directly from the parents involved, it permitted seniors to have a male caller once each week, and juniors once each month. A suitable date consisted of a chaperoned gathering in the Bryan Hall parlor or Atrium.[28] Mrs. Cawthon met all prospective callers; anyone whose behavior or reputation fell below rigorous standards appeared on a blacklist and became ineligible to associate with students.

Young ladies who ignored or "forgot" the dating rules courted restrictions and even expulsion. Faculty committees and later the Student Government Association restricted errant students to their dormitory rooms (except for class attendance, chapel, and meals) for two-to-six weeks for committing such transgressions as "walking with a young man, accepting refreshments and talking with a young man in the drug store." Others were "shipped" (expelled) for more serious offenses, such as riding at night with a young man without specific permission to do so and without a chaperone in the vehicle.[29]

As the number of students increased, myriad rules drafted by administrative committees with no input from students caused supervisory headaches. Hoping that the girls would respond more positively to peer pressure than they had to arbitrary authority, Conradi warily allowed a committee of class representatives to "govern" during exams and quizzes in the spring of 1912.[30] Though the president considered this a form of student government, it actually consisted of only a few seniors and juniors appointed to monitor possible cheating and to report suspects' names to the faculty. But it was a start. The following spring (1913), with the support of Professors Dodd and Smith and the encouragement of Tissie, students presented Conradi with a unanimous request for self-government. The result was the inception of the Student Government Association. The faculty nominated candidates for the offices of president, vice president, secretary, treasurer, and president of each dormitory (East Hall, Bryan Hall, and Reynolds Hall). After a school-wide election, the new officers served out the remainder of that semester, approximately three weeks.[31]

In the fall the Student Government Association formally assumed its duties. Students belonged to the organization by virtue of being enrolled at the women's college. The full membership met in the auditorium, usually immediately after chapel, on a called-meeting basis. The officers constituted the Executive Committee, which met at the behest of the college administration, but at least once a week. President Conradi, Vice President Williams, Miss Longmire, and Mrs. Cawthon formed an Advisory Council that directed the student committee in its consideration of policy and reviewed all actions before they became effective. Unfortunately, the Executive Committee members trusted themselves to make rules, but they had little faith that their fellow students would follow them. They immediately put each girl on her honor to report personal tardiness or absence from breakfast, but just in case the honor system failed, they ordered the student at the head of each dining table to report any absences from her table.[32]

Peer pressure notwithstanding, the Executive Committee quickly learned what the old Faculty Discipline Committee had known—that whether intentionally or unintentionally, many students broke rules. Since each girl received a copy of the college's rules and regulations at the beginning of the school year, the committee refused to accept ignorance as an excuse for wrongdoing. Quickly frustrated with most students' lack of concern about the rules and regulations, the well-meaning officers formed a subcommittee that met frequently, sometimes every afternoon or evening (or both), to consider the many, many cases of alleged misconduct. The subcommittee investigated a profusion of charges against fellow students, restricted girls to campus, lectured them individually on moral or ethical issues, and reported to the full Executive Committee and its Advisory Council.

Conradi and the Faculty Advisory Council reviewed and approved or disapproved all Executive Committee actions. In one case, three students observed and reported what they considered to be the inappropriate behavior of another student and a young man from Tallahassee. The committee restricted the guilty student, a senior, for the remainder of the school year and barred her from participating in Commencement. When she was informed of her sentence, the young lady requested another hearing in the Advisory Council's presence, at which time she appeared to be genuinely penitent. Conradi overruled the student committee's decision and reinstated her Commencement privileges. The young man was blacklisted.[33]

Over the next few years the Advisory Council conscientiously supervised Student Government Association officers while the officers in turn enthusiastically meted out punishment for relatively minor transgressions. The Executive Committee campused girls for up to four weeks for impertinence to YWCA officers, for flirting with boys who were standing at the windows of the dormitory, for visiting a friend in the dormitory during study period, for alleged misconduct in church, and for "ragging" (dancing to ragtime music) on a week night. Although ragging was allowed on Saturday nights, only the two-step and waltz were acceptable during the week. In December 1917, six girls received two-week restrictions for cutting breakfast more than twice during the semester. At the same time, a case of cheating on a test, a serious breach of ethics, garnered the guilty party only a lecture from the Student Government president, after which the guilty student apologized to her class and was allowed to take another test.[34]

The Executive Committee's jurisdiction ostensibly reached not just those students who lived in dormitories but also those who lived off the campus in houses rented for college use and those who lived with their families in the city. By early 1918, Mrs. Cawthon admitted that the enforcement responsibilities were much too broad and suggested that the administration revise the Student Government Association's constitution. She particularly favored elimination of compulsory church attendance, which she felt was unenforceable, but the requirement remained.[35]

The college modified the constitution, but the new regulations still adhered to an honor code and contended that every student had a duty to report any wrong conduct to some member of the Executive Committee.[36] Of four new committees created, only the Welfare Committee, concerned with changes in the campus social or domestic life, offered a positive outlook. The others presupposed wrongdoing by students and relegated student government to little more than espionage. The Campus Committee inquired into all cases of misconduct on campus. The Library Committee investigated and reported any mutilation of books or magazines. The Censorship Committee watched girls for misconduct away from campus, or at any public function on campus, and reported any student who left campus without permission. How the committee members knew if the student had permission or not was unclear, and many girls presented authorization for their activities when brought before the Executive Committee.[37]

After World War I, the Student Government Association gradually shifted its focus from petty infractions to the overall quality of campus life. The Executive Committee assumed responsibility for seating assignments at meals and allowed students some choice in dining companions. The officers successfully petitioned the Advisory Council for open motion-picture privileges on Saturdays and Mondays, and convinced the administration that optional breakfast attendance, at least during the last two weeks of school, did not endanger the health of students. The Advisory Council acknowledged the more mature attitude of the students and responded in kind. They allowed girls to walk off-campus after dinner, until time for the 7:45 P.M. study period, without special permission and even conceded that cutting breakfast was a less serious offense than talking to boys in the drug store.[38]

ATHLETICS

In 1909, token student resistance on campus revolved around the extracurricular, but closely regulated, athletic program. The ban on intercollegiate and public athletic contests heralded the demise of the original Athletic Association begun in 1905. The girls found it difficult and uninspiring to excel only for each other. In the absence of any competitive spirit, they lost interest in athletics in general. Even the campus basketball rivalry, now between Stars and Crescents instead of Prickly Pears and Cockleburs, failed to satisfy them. As unofficial coaches for athletic activities, faculty members Arthur Williams and Elmer Smith encouraged their colleagues to rescind the ban on public contests; in the fall of 1910, a slim majority voted to do so. Before Williams and Smith could schedule a game, Conradi bowed to minority pressure and put a stop to the plans. Student dissatisfaction with his capitulation simmered until spring, when the administration finally resurrected the Athletic Association and allowed students some voice in their extracurricular games.[39] Then the basketball teams of Stars and Crescents resumed their contests.

Dubose Elder, Director of the School of Physical Culture and Expression, brought FSCW's athletic program back to life in 1913 when she proposed Field Day, a college-wide celebration of physical fitness. Since the ban on public contests extended only to males not associated with the faculty, the college invited the ladies of Tallahassee to attend the premier event. The day-long competition showcased all collegiate athletic activities, including tennis, basketball, swimming, gymnastics, and track events such as broad jump, distance throws, and relay races. All students in the college and in the State School for Teachers and all children who attended the Kindergarten or Model School participated in Field Day activities.[40] The day's success convinced the college to make it an annual event.

The following year Field Day contests took place over two days. By 1915, students pressured the faculty to allow all interested citizens, not just women, to attend the athletic meet. Swayed by the suggestion that a public field day would be a good advertisement for the college and aware that many local merchants who donated prizes for individual events were presently prohibited from viewing those events,[41] Conradi and Cawthon invited a few non-faculty males to attend. Invitations read:

> The Athletic Association of Florida State College for Women invites you to be present at their Third Annual Field Day, April 12 and 13, 1915. Men admitted by card only. Present this at the gate.[42]

At Field Day, points were awarded for first, second, and third place in the various events. After two days of competition, the class with the greatest number of points received an

FSCW banner; the individual who accumulated the most points won a garnet sweater with a gold "F" on the front and became the college's "Best All Around Athlete." The Physical Culture Department conducted the events in accordance with accepted track and field standards, so students who excelled received nationwide and even worldwide recognition. In 1920, Nell Carroll hurled the discus 85'4" to break the national women's record, and became the first freshman to win the Athletic Association letter sweater.[43]

Thanksgiving was only a one-day holiday at that time, and campus residents celebrated the day in Tallahassee, either in the Dining Hall with other students or at the homes of local friends. In 1912, the administration held a basketball game on Thanksgiving morning in an attempt to further encourage school spirit. Since Stars and Crescents played their games in the spring, the Athletic Association selected new teams for this contest. Seniors had their own basketball team that year and elected not to participate, so a team composed of juniors and freshmen opposed one of sophomores and sub-freshmen.[44] The new teams were enthusiastic but nameless.

The Thanksgiving basketball game immediately became *the* event of the fall semester, and in 1913 the seniors opted to play. That year seniors, sophomores, and sub-freshmen joined forces against post-graduates, juniors, and freshmen. In 1914, members of the even-year classes (juniors and freshmen) wore their green and yellow class colors to chapel on the Saturday morning before Thanksgiving. A spontaneous pep rally ensued. On the following Wednesday, odd-year class members (seniors, sophomores, and sub-freshmen) carried canes wrapped with ribbons in their individual class colors of red, white, and purple. On Thanksgiving Day the odd-year classes claimed an easy victory (26–5) and celebrated with a march into town before they returned to a traditional turkey dinner in the recently completed Dining Hall.[45] Normal School students, still considered separate from the liberal arts students, watched the game from the sidelines.

The *Flambeau* reported that "the two Famous Basketball Teams of the six college classes" each began the 1915 fall semester with pep songs and team cheers. Post-graduates, juniors, and freshmen—that session's odd-year team—chose for their insignia the red, white, and purple winners' colors from the previous year. The even-year team once again sported their class colors of green and gold and waved a banner with "SSS" (seniors, sophomores, sub-freshmen) boldly displayed. The odd-year team repeated its victory. After the celebratory parade into town, students, faculty, and guests retired to the Dining Hall, this year decorated inside in colors of green and gold and outside in red, white, and purple. On the Saturday following the festivities, the college newspaper formally named the teams "Odds" and "Evens" and declared them successors to Stars and Crescents.[46]

The popularity of the Odd/Even basketball game rendered moot the question of intercollegiate athletics at FSCW. The Odd team formally adopted victory colors of red, white, and purple, while the Even team chose green and gold. The *Flambeau* referred to the Odd team as "garnet" (a blend of red and purple) and the Even team as "gold," the college colors. The faculty encouraged students' enthusiasm and even established their own loyalties. Conradi and Mrs. Cawthon always supported the seniors, so they rooted for Odds one year and Evens the next. Dean Dodd consistently backed Odds; "Pi" Williams, Drs. Game and Brautlecht, and Miss Longmire always supported Evens. Because open Field Days had been so successful, the college not only welcomed townspeople to the annual Odd/Even basketball game, but they also charged admission.[47]

Students permitted absolutely nothing to interfere with Thanksgiving Odd/Even contests. In mid-October 1918, in the midst of a devastating nationwide influenza epidemic, 39 persons died in a single day in Jacksonville. The illness was less deadly in Tallahassee, but serious enough to close all churches and theaters for fear of spreading the illness. Dean

Dodd officiated at Sunday morning services on campus, and Monday night the Daffin Theater presented a special showing in the college auditorium of the movie "Johanna Enlists," starring Mary Pickford. Amidst such evidence of extraordinary precautions, the *Flambeau* scoffed at rumors that the games would be canceled because of the flu. "Nothing short of a German invasion could keep the Odds and Evens from their annual war," the paper proclaimed.[48]

The students truly considered the contest a war. For days prior to Thanksgiving, teams participated in "Color Rush," the object of which was to "capture" buildings by affixing the team colors to the highest point. Each team raised its token above the previous one, until finally fishing poles bedecked with ribbons of red, white, and purple or green and gold protruded rakishly from rooftops. The administration hesitated to squelch the girls' enthusiasm but feared things had gotten out of hand. To forestall faculty intervention, the Athletic Association devised a more subdued and ladylike plan for displaying team colors. In 1919, that organization decreed that, for decorative purposes, the fountain, presented to the college by the Classes of 1915 and 1917, was "forever Odd," and henceforth only Odd colors adorned it. The entrance arch and brick piers, a gift from the Classes of 1916 and 1918, became "forever Even," and sported only green and gold from that time forth. Color Rush began with the rising bell, when selected runners dashed from their rooms to tag the Administration Building, the Education Building, and the dormitories at designated target points. Evens decorated the Dining Hall in even-numbered years, and Odds did the honors in odd-numbered years.[49] Once initiated, Odd/Even rivalry eclipsed all other competitions on campus.

Athletic zeal at the women's college peaked during the 1919–20 session. An ecstatic Athletic Association organized the "F" Club to encourage further pursuit of athletic superiority. Only members of the association who had earned an "F" for varsity (intra-class contests), Field Day, or tennis excellence belonged. The *Flambeau* acknowledged the role of athletics in campus life and each week devoted "an important place in the college paper" to coverage of the various activities.[50]

WORLD WAR I

The United States' entry into the First World War in April 1917 affected students and the campus in numerous ways. War-induced shortages of building materials exacerbated the already long-delayed construction of needed dormitories and classroom space. To best use its available space, the college returned temporarily to Monday classes while also continuing those scheduled on Saturdays. Since the dormitories depended on coal to heat water for bathing, and all buildings relied on it for warmth, nationally sponsored fuel conservation measures caused further problems. During the war, regional coal suppliers met government requisitions before they filled smaller, private orders. Because of that, the college experienced difficulty acquiring the coal it needed and found itself forced to purchase one ton at a time from distant sources. Delivery, dependent on railroads affected by wartime schedules, was unpredictable. To cope with the situation, Kellum ordered the heat turned down in all buildings, especially in dormitories at night. As luck would have it, Florida experienced some of its most frigid weather between 1917 and 1919. The winter of 1917 was one of the coldest ever in the state. In Tallahassee the temperature fell to 15 degrees on February 2, a record for that date that still stands. In January 1918, the mercury dropped to 16 degrees. Icicles hung for two days from the upper basin of the new fountain in front of the Administration Building. To keep warm, roommates pushed beds together and huddled under blankets heaped with stacks of clothing.[51]

In the Dining Hall, Miss Edwards saw to it that campus residents, like most patriotic Floridians, observed one wheatless and two meatless days per week. Students and faculty worked in the college garden, cultivating more vegetables than ever before. Cabbage in particular grew abundantly. Edwards dutifully served it in some fashion at almost every meal, and diners became heartily sick of it. There were cheers all around when the February 1917 freeze temporarily wiped out the crop. Later that year 75 bushels of peanuts raised on the college farm appeared on dinner plates in various guises.[52] Rumor had it that the eggs, now served only every other morning, were powdered. Cereal, bread, and cocoa were regularly available and thought to be the real thing. Lunches usually included meat substitutes such as sweet potatoes from the garden, cheeses, and soups. Fried fish was served occasionally for dinner, and the hogs raised on the farm furnished plenty of pork. For dessert the dietitian served pudding, using eggs and milk from the college dairy. The cooks economized on sugar by substituting honey whenever possible, and they encouraged residents to do likewise.[53]

Patriotism abounded on campus; students readily contributed their own time and energy to the war effort. The *Flambeau* inaugurated a world news column and for the next two years printed weekly coverage of the war. Girls sang or hummed patriotic tunes as they walked to classes or went about the grounds. American flags waved from the windows of Reynolds and Bryan Halls and the Administration Building. Some campus activities were deemed nonessential. For the duration of the war, the Junior Class canceled the Spring Prom, traditionally presented to the seniors every year. Class members donated the money they would have spent on decorations, an orchestra, and refreshments—approximately $75—to the Red Cross as a gift from the seniors.[54]

More than 300 students joined the Tallahassee Red Cross, prompting that chapter to make the college an auxiliary. Members of the organization transformed the YWCA lobby below the Atrium in Bryan Hall into a Red Cross workroom, where they met between classes to roll bandages and make surgical dressings. All students, whether members of the Red Cross or not, participated in a five-hour training course in first aid and elements of Red Cross nursing presented by college physician F. Clifton Moor. In a single month, Red Cross-sponsored sewing classes on campus turned out 100 pairs of pajamas for hospitalized servicemen. In keeping with the organization's request that Americans knit garments for soldiers, the local chapter distributed pamphlets with instructions for knitted sleeveless jackets, scarves, and socks; similar knitting patterns appeared in the *Flambeau*. Students eagerly picked up their needles and contributed their share of the 24 million military garments knitted for the army and navy. The girls met weekly in the Bryan Hall sun parlor for several hours at a time and knitted while they took turns reading aloud books and reports about the war. Instead of serving sweet refreshments, they conserved sugar by offering slices of fruit.[55]

Every Friday the faculty presented a special program devoted to helping students understand the war. Conradi lectured on the German philosophy responsible for the conflict; Dodd spoke on the connection between German literature and the hostilities. Williams put a Hammond's Large Scale War Map of the Western Front on a table in his classroom. As the war progressed, he marked Allied positions with small flags, and students referred to the map as they read daily newspaper bulletins. Just prior to the armistice in 1918, a paper shortage curtailed the library's access to national newspapers, so Williams posted maps and daily reports on a bulletin board in the Administration Building and gave talks in chapel every Wednesday on the war's progress.[56]

Community support for the war effort did much to relax students' off-campus restrictions. Perhaps because he was under pressure to prove his loyalty to the United States, Conradi allowed college residents to participate in most patriotic events in Tallahassee. When a Liberty Bond meeting was held downtown, students marched there and took part. Conradi led the entourage, followed in turn by the mayor carrying the college flag, seniors in caps and gowns, and the remainder of the classes. Later that evening students and townspeople gathered back on campus in front of the little gymnasium and lit "bonfires for liberty." On several occasions the entire student body joined in "community sings for unity" on the front lawn of the Capitol. Conradi even permitted campus residents to entertain 750 soldiers en route from Texas to Jacksonville and Camp Joseph E. Johnston. While their troop train was serviced, the men marched to the college where the president, students, and local citizens sang patriotic songs and visited with them for the remainder of that afternoon.[57]

At 5:00 A.M. on November 11, 1918, the campus awoke to shrill whistles and alarms. Few students reacted until they heard the fire bell clanging. Then they jumped out of bed and ran across the campus to (they thought) watch East Hall burn. When they saw no smoke, they realized that the clamor signified the end of the war. At 5:30 the city fire truck, carrying a coffin that contained the symbolic remains of Kaiser Wilhelm, waited at the front entrance to the college. Wearing sleepwear under coats or hastily donned outerwear, four lines of girls marched behind the truck to the corner of College Avenue and Adams Street, where waiting Tallahassee residents heaved the coffin into a roaring bonfire. Students joined in singing until they were hoarse, then returned to the Dining Hall for a late breakfast. Conradi announced a holiday. The war was over. Later, the Federal Division of Women's War Work commended FSCW for its many wartime endeavors.[58]

TRADITIONS

During this decade, 1910–1920, rife with growth and constant change, Conradi wisely allowed students to establish several enduring rituals, the most important of which were athletic contests between Odds and Evens. Other traditions, even those begun before Odds and Evens existed, eventually coincided with or bolstered Odd/Even festivities. When first performed in 1909, the Freshman-Junior Wedding had captured the girls' imaginations; the two classes repeated the ceremony annually. After the first year, the president or another faculty member officiated at the services and "join[ed] together this man and this woman in 'classimation' which is a temporal estate instituted by the freshman and junior classes."[59] Wedding invitations attested to the creative talent lavished on this ritual and the impact of Odd/Even designations. With the advent of the athletic rivalries between the classes, the formality took on particular significance. The ceremony introduced new students to the adversarial roles of Odds and Evens. In early years, Ima Green Freshman wed Oby A. Junior, or Jess A. Freshman wed Loy Al Junior. As Odd/Even symbolism unfolded, Miss Ima Odd married Mr. Hezza Oddtoo, and Miss Eve Ann Freshman married Mr. B. Wise, Jr.

Along with Field Day, another spring semester event was the May Day Festival. In years past, the college had celebrated springtime with a lavish pageant that was usually historical or Shakespearean in nature. In 1916, the students and administration agreed that the Red Cross and other relief organizations could better use the money usually spent on such activities, so they planned an old-fashioned but inexpensive May Day gala instead. The event consisted of a program combining elements of expression, music, art, dancing, and gymnastics. It also included a May Pole dance and the crowning of the most popular girl in the senior class as May Queen. The festivities took place among the pines behind the Administration Building, and the audience sat in the sunken gardens in front of Bryan Hall.[60]

In 1915, the president of the University of Indiana delivered the FSCW Commencement address. Enthusiastic students wrote to that school for a sheet music copy of its Alma Mater to use in the graduation program. They then appealed to Dean Dodd, known in town and on campus for his musical prowess, to draft a similar song for FSCW. Dodd composed the music and words for a new "College Song" which the school then adopted as its Alma Mater:

With spirits light, we're singing tonight;
We're come with a right good cheer,
Our hearts a-glow, our love to show
To our Alma Mater dear.
Long may she live, her blessing to give,
And long may she famous be;
And far and wide may we show our pride
In the FSWC.

So long may she bind, our Mother so kind,
The hearts of her children true,
By love's own tie that ne'er shall die,
But shall live the long years through.
May we, one and all, with love recall,
In the years that are to be,
The mem'ry of the golden days
At the FSWC.

Chorus:
Then pledge her, one and all together,
In a cup to the garnet and the gold—
In fair or stormy weather,
Our love shall never grow cold.
We'll sing her praise to every nation
And wherever we may be,
We'll spread the fame and drink to the name
of the FSWC.[61]

STUDENT PUBLICATIONS

Between 1910 and 1920, further signs of institutional identity emerged in new student publications. *The Talisman*, begun in April 1906 and still printed bi-monthly under the auspices of the Thalian and Minerva Literary Societies, emulated both a newspaper and an annual. The Class of 1910 published the school's first authentic yearbook and dedicated it to the late Mrs. Mary Reynolds. The class called it *Flastacowo*, an acronym for FLoridA STAte COllege for WOmen. Succeeding senior classes through 1915 continued the publication. The Classes of 1916 through 1918 committed their money to the fountain and the entrance gates in front of the Administration Building. A member of the Class of 1916 explained why her class had abandoned the yearbook by saying "long after the annual would have grown yellow with age, the gates will stand firm and strong, inviting us all to pass through the portals to the temple of wisdom."[62] The Classes of 1919 and 1920, constrained by war shortages and inflation, also opted to forgo publication of an annual. The *Flastacowo* reappeared in 1921.

The yearbook's hiatus coincided with the first issue of a weekly student newspaper that replaced *The Talisman*. On January 23, 1915, the first issue of the *Florida Flambeau* appeared. According to Ruby Leach, Class of 1915 and the newspaper's first editor, she had complained to Milton Smith, editor of the *Tallahassee Democrat*, about the sparseness of college news in his paper. He hired her to write two columns per week about campus activities at 50¢ per column. When the faculty realized from reading her columns that there was enough going on at the college for a newspaper, Conradi presented the idea to the students, and they agreed. Student Lucille Freeman, who said she simply took a dictionary and ran her finger slowly down the "f"s until she came to "flambeau," a flaming torch, proposed the publication's name. "Pi" Williams teased that she liked the name because "there's a beau in it."[63] The second edition of the paper explained the choice more seriously:

> Look at the great seal of our Alma Mater—three primal ideals enumerated for which our college stands. For each ideal stands its symbol, the classical torch, which our dear mother hands on to succeeding generations. Let us hope that each shining emblem symbolizes a greater light than ever was on land or sea.[64]

Faculty sponsors carefully supervised and passed judgement on all student publications, especially the *Flambeau*. Dodd scrutinized each edition before it went to the printer. At first the staff cautiously worded its editorials and seldom ventured into the realm of commentaries. After a year or so, an editorial occasionally voiced an opinion contrary to regulations but consistent with common sense. Such was the case when the paper reported student objections to housekeeping inspections on Mondays, when they had no classes. But the *Flambeau* never dared to challenge the administration outright until after World War I. Just as the Student Government Association gained strength and focus from wartime, so the paper evinced more student concerns and drew attention more often to campus problems. By 1920, an editorial boldly challenged the faculty's habit of skipping required chapel services. It asked, "Where are the professors in chapel? We meet every day at 12:00 noon in the auditorium for a few minutes of devotion, yet a majority of the teachers are conspicuous for their absence."[65]

⌘

In the aftermath of the activism inspired by World War I, the campus ostensibly returned to normal. After that conflagration, however, few other than Warren G. Harding professed to know for certain what normal was. FSCW's administration found it extremely difficult to recapture the sense of unquestioned authority that had fostered students' earlier adherence to the school's outdated restrictions and regulations; outside influences had produced a more aggressive student body. The college girls now considered themselves mature women and resented the minutiae of constant supervision.

1903 *Argo*

Albert Alexander Murphree was the first president of the women's college and began its liberal arts tradition. Jennie Murphree Hall was named for his wife, a 1905 graduate of Florida State College.

ca. 1900, postcard, Alumni Association

College Hall after an 1891 remodeling enveloped the original Classical Revival building of 1855 with red brick and towers. It stood in the area of Westcott fountain and circle and was razed in 1910.

ca. 1929, FSU Special Collections

Bryan Hall, erected in 1907, is the oldest remaining building of the women's college. With the addition of Reynolds Hall in 1912 and Jennie Murphree Hall in 1922, the three were known as dormitory row.

1916 FSCW *Bulletin*

Bryan Hall parlor and Atrium became the social center of campus upon its completion, replacing East Hall in that regard. The Mission-style furnishing and decor were cited by the administration as examples of FSCW's modernity.

1916 FSCW *Bulletin*

The Administration Building was erected in 1910 immediately behind College Hall, which was then razed. After a major restoration in the 1930s, the building was renamed for James D. Westcott, Jr., an early benefactor.

Alumni Association

Among 1909 graduates, the first after the name-change from Florida Female College to the more seemly Florida State College for Women, were Annie Dorcas Broward, Effie Doane Pettit, May Alice Moore, Mary Eugenia Van Brunt, Margaret Taylor Bradford, and Ella Lee Manning.

ca. 1925, Florida State Archives

Dr. Edward Conradi was the longest-serving president of FSCW, from 1909 to 1941. He assembled the faculty and staff that brought national prominence and recognition to the institution. Conradi withstood many political and academic storms by simply waiting patiently for the weather to clear. It usually did.

Sarah Landrum "Tissie" Cawthon was titled Dean of the College Home, a position she held from 1910 to 1925. "Tissie" supervised the students' nonacademic lives and was the campus arbiter of good taste and social values. Cawthon Hall is named for her.

1913 *Flastacowo*

1913 *Flastacowo*

Behind this 1913 gym class stood FSCW's most unusual building. Originally a Negro school and church, it was purchased in 1905 and used as a gymnasium until 1929. From then until the end of FSCW, it housed the School of Music offices. The FSU School of Social Work next used it for several years.

1911 *Flastacowo*

Stars (above) and Crescents (below) replaced Cockleburs and Prickly Pears in a second attempt to develop an intramural rivalry on campus. An earlier brief experience in intercollegiate basketball in 1907 with Stetson and Rollins had been halted when the student body became too intensely involved.

1911 *Flastacowo*

1915 *Flastacowo*

The Broomstick Regiment drilled on the playing fields of FSCW as World War I spread through Europe. The young ladies of the college sought meaningful ways to share the national burden in both World Wars.

ca. 1918, Alumni Association

The wrought iron arch and gates were not yet in place when this photo was taken of the new brick piers presented by the Classes of 1916 and 1918. The high point of the modest Tallahassee skyline was the water tower.

1915 *Flastacowo*

The Flastacowo *featured the inaugural front page (Vol.1, No.1) of the* Florida Flambeau. *The newspaper quickly became the voice of the students and was usually ahead of the administration on issues from women's suffrage to coeducation.*

ca. 1920, Florida State Archives

ca. 1930, FSU Special Collections

The south wing of the Old Dining Hall was built in 1914 and connected to Broward Hall by a covered arcade. The north wing, added in 1923, brought the seating capacity to 1,000. The room's design was inspired by the dining hall of Christ College at Oxford. With coeducation it became the Suwannee Room cafeteria. In recent years, an interior warren of temporary offices and modular cells has obscured its magnificent wooden arches and Gothic appointments.

1933 *Flastacowo*

William G. Dodd joined the faculty as head of the English Department in 1910. In 1913, he also became Dean of Arts and Sciences and filled both positions for most of the next 31 years. He was FSCW's main academic force.

John G. Kellum, Business Manager from 1907 until 1945, kept the college fiscally sound and growing despite inadequate funding. His shrewd business deals extended the college's 13.5 acres to holdings constituting today's main campus plus farm acreage used in some of the golf course and Innovation Park.

1931 *Flastacowo*

Arthur Williams joined the Florida State College faculty in 1903 and remained at the new women's institution. In 1913, he was appointed vice president of FSCW. Known affectionately as Mr. Pi by generations of students, he died in 1937. Years later, FSU renamed the History Building for him.

1932 *Flastacowo*

ca. 1906, postcard, Alumni Association

East Hall stood on the site later occupied by Science Hall and still later by the Diffenbaugh Building. In the earliest years, East Hall was the social hub of the campus. Though its social role had diminished, it was still a major dormitory on the Sunday morning in 1920 when it burned to the ground. Because of the day and time of the fire, most residents were in church, and no one was injured. However, 28 girls lost all their possessions.

1920, Alumni Association

ca. 1925, Alumni Association

The Education Building, erected north of Westcott circle, was the first building constructed solely for classroom use. Over the years it housed classes in education, psychology, social work, industrial arts, and some grades of the elementary school. Today it is the Psychology Building.

1924 *Flastacowo*

Science Hall was the phoenix that rose from East Hall's ashes in 1922. It served FSCW's Chemistry Department and School of Home Economics before giving way to the Diffenbaugh Building in FSU days.

1922 *Flastacowo*

The 1922 May Court made a fashion statement in garden hats and lace frocks. Because May Day occurred too late in the school year to make the Flastacowo *deadline, editors frequently had the queen and her court secretly photographed ahead of time without the elaborate costuming. This memorable record of high style at FSCW in the early twenties was the result.*

1923 *Flastacowo*

The Freshman-Junior Wedding, with juniors in male roles and freshmen in female roles, began in 1909 as a way to create bonds between the two classes. A new Dean of Students discontinued the traditional event after 1925 as out-moded.

1923 *Flastacowo*

1923 *Flastacowo*

Odd/Even intramural rivalry, begun in 1914, was well established when these two 1923 teams (Evens top, Odds bottom) met on the basketball court. Out of the Odd/Even rivalry grew leadership honoraries, elaborate student productions, and a year-long series of contests in major and minor sports. Odd/Even activities remained a significant part of campus life throughout FSCW's history.

1926 *Flastacowo*

Posed on a city fire truck is FSCW's 1926 fire department. Each dorm or housing unit had a fire captain who reported to the campus fire chief. This group organized fire drills and checked to make sure students followed instructions.

ca. 1928, Florida State Archives

This 1928 aerial taken from the south shows only the west wing of the Library completed, while Gilchrist (far left) is still under construction. Westcott circle (far right) serves as an orientation aid.

ca. 1930, Florida State Archives

ca. 1930, FSU Special Collections

The central and east sections of the Library are considered architect Rudolph Weaver's masterwork. Recognizing the significance of a library in academia, Weaver lavished Collegiate Gothic ornamentation on his design. The high vaulting and arching beams created interior spaces of particular grace. It was named Dodd Hall to honor FSCW's long-time Dean of Arts and Sciences, William G. Dodd, after FSU's Strozier Library was built in 1956.

ca. 1930, FSU Special Collections

A memorable inscription above the entrance to the Library, "The half of knowledge is to know where to find knowledge," has been the subject of recurring and intense research, to no avail until now.

1922 Flastacowo

Membership in the Village Vamps was proof that a girl was a real campus cutie. Members practiced their charms serving as ushers for a variety of recitals, concerts, and dramatic presentations.

1931 Flastacowo

Cotillion Club was formed in 1911 to provide dancing partners because men were not allowed at dances on campus. In the late twenties and thirties, as men were invited to more and more dances, Cotillion's mission shifted to teaching ballroom dancing and the latest steps.

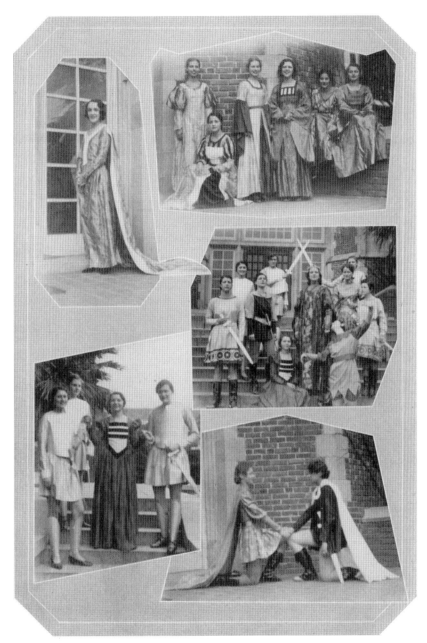

1931 *Flastacowo*

Fealty was one of several annual pageants costumed in an eclectic mix of Classical, Medieval, and Renaissance styles. In the mid-thirties, Fealty was merged with Torch Night into a single expression of loyalty and allegiance to Alma Mater.

1930, Florida State Archives

The Silver Jubilee Parade celebrated FSCW's first 25 years with exuberance. The alumnae Class of 1920 won the second place prize for this entry.

1932 *Flastacowo*

Orchesis was organized in 1926 to explore dance as an art form and to provide opportunities for performance in the group's annual presentation. Membership was determined by tryouts.

Spirogira was the Odd leadership honorary formed in 1924, proudly (for the Odds) the first of the Odd/Even rivalry. The skull and crossbones was its symbol and the Jolly Roger's black and white its colors.

1931 *Flastacowo*

Esteren, with its green and white colors and steaming cauldron, was the Even leadership honorary begun in 1930. Most of the symbolism and secret rites of both organizations were simply designed to keep the other club mystified and guessing.

1931 *Flastacowo*

1932 *Flastacowo*

Organized during the 1919-1920 school year, F Club encouraged and recognized athletic abilities. To qualify, a student had to make at least two Odd/Even teams in one school year. The club and its "goating" of provisional members was a highly visible part of campus life.

FSCW's Ann Harwick won the javelin event in a 1922 national track and field meet. After the college, its students, and generous Tallahasseans raised $1,500 for her expenses, she represented Florida on the American team at an international meet in Paris. She won medals in two events, but did not compete in the javelin because of "over-training."

1922, newspaper clipping, Alumni Association

 Part Two

etween 1920 and 1930, Florida's economy fluctu-
ated. A land and development boom alleviated the
early postwar inflationary conditions and later aggra-
vated a financial decline that presaged the Depression. Advan-
ces in modern technology, spurred by the recent war, put
automobile ownership and family vacations within reach of
most American workers, and improved highways and railway
transportation encouraged travel for leisure. Where better to
spend those relaxing times than the subtropical climes of Florida?

To accommodate tourists, the Atlantic Coast Line Railroad
added a second route to its original one running from Richmond, Virginia, to Tampa, Florida; this one went via Jacksonville.[1] The Florida East Coast Railway doubled its line from
Jacksonville south to Miami. Seaboard Air Line Railroad
extended tracks and depots to West Palm Beach and Miami.
Public and private enterprise, optimistically participating in the
prosperity of the Coolidge years (1923–1928), laid down a system of roads and highways in the state. Projects such as the
Gandy Bridge from Tampa across the bay to St. Petersburg,
and the southernmost segment of the Tamiami Trail between
Fort Myers and Miami, made both coastlines readily accessible.[2]
Many tourists who traveled the peninsula remained as residents of the state. Florida's population rose from 968,470 in
1920 to 1,263,540 in 1925, and reached 1,468,211 in 1930,
increasing the number of residents by 51.6 percent. The state's

educational institutions struggled throughout the decade to keep up with that growth.

CAMPUS EXPANSION

Between 1922 and 1930, Florida State College for Women acquired most of the contiguous property that today comprises the campus east of Woodward Avenue. The college accomplished this feat primarily through actions taken by President Conradi, Business Manager J.G. Kellum, and Classics Professor J.B. Game, with timely assistance from local businessmen. Game had purchased a sizeable amount of land west of the campus from the Wallace family when he first arrived in the city in the mid-teens, and he had built his home at what later became the intersection of West Jefferson Street and Woodward Avenue. In 1921, he and another landowner, R.O. Eagle, requested that the city open Woodward Avenue from West Jefferson Street to the Old Quincy Road (at the present intersection of Call and Woodward streets, just south of where the Student Union is located today). Game, Eagle, and the city shared the cost involved in this undertaking.[3]

In the summer of 1923, Game and Kellum urged the state to eliminate completely the section of the Old Quincy Highway that cut a diagonal swath across property still held by the Wallace family and to further extend Woodward Avenue in its stead.[4] The state complied, but Kellum and Conradi feared that the resulting property, subdivided into lots, would be sold and improved before the 1925 Legislature had an opportunity to appropriate money for its purchase by the college. Accordingly, ten Tallahassee entrepreneurs entered into a contract with the Lewis State Bank whereby the bank purchased the tract for $9,500. At the same time, the businessmen signed a note at eight percent interest to guarantee the availability of the land until the next legislature met and authorized the expenditure for the college. To ensure the availability of an adjoining segment of land owned by Game and Edward M. Windham, Conradi and Kellum cosigned a promissory note for $20,000 and placed it in the Lewis State Bank vault until the same legislature could approve it.[5] These extraordinary transactions involving employees of the college, local businessmen, and the bank went unquestioned amidst the frenetic land acquisitions occurring in Florida at the time.

COLLEGE FARM

The college farm, originally established in the early teens as a garden behind the Dining Hall, soon became an integral part of campus life. As the college's business manager, Kellum oversaw the farm's development and gradually increased the size of the operation whenever the budget allowed. In 1915, he purchased 20 hogs, useful both for the pork they provided for meals and for garbage disposal. The garden produced corn to feed the hogs—and the students. The ultimate purpose of the farm, however, was to maintain a dairy herd to supply milk for the boarding department.[6]

By 1917, the farm included more than 150 acres. The following year Kellum built a milking barn and purchased 45 cows. Board of Control member P. K. Yonge gave the college a Jersey bull, named Gay Nancy's Tormentor, for breeding.[7] In 1920, Kellum hired J. P. Love of Gainesville to manage the farm and dairy operation. Love and his family moved into a house that sat under a cluster of oak trees where Strozier Library now stands. In 1923, the college added poultry and eggs to its farm production; Mrs. Love managed that part of the operation. For the next several years, the farm supplied an average of 100 gallons of milk and 20 to 25 dozen eggs per day for the dining room.[8] Kellum continued to increase the farm's acreage until 1930, at which time it consisted of approximately 250 acres of land lying to the west and north of the occupied campus area. By then the college property stretched from Copeland Street on the east to beyond

Woodward Avenue on the west, and from West Call Street on the north to West Jefferson Street on the south.

CAMP FLASTACOWO

In addition to the campus and adjoining farm acreage, the college owned land at Lake Bradford, southwest of town. A number of Tallahassee residents maintained cottages and boats at the popular recreation site, and friends of the college frequently opened their cabins to the students. In 1915, faculty and staff members purchased, in the school's name, approximately six acres of property with 200 feet of lake front.[9] A few lakeside property owners wanted to keep individual holdings small, but both Tissie Cawthon and Conradi felt strongly that the college needed more than the standard size lot to assure privacy for the girls. To get around residential objections, Conradi purchased, ostensibly for his private use, a lot adjoining the college property. He told his family, "I'm buying this for the students, but I have to take [it] in my name and let things settle, then I'm going to turn it over to them."[10]

Though undeveloped, the lake quickly became a favorite destination for Monday outings. Students enthusiastically trekked the five-mile distance to the site for cookouts, boating, and swimming. In May 1918, the Athletic Association sponsored the college's first water sports day, an event much too expansive to hold in the little pool under the gymnasium. Girls walked to the lake after breakfast, ate lunch near the water's edge, and in the afternoon took part in aquatic contests. Since the college property lacked improvements, local businessman Lewis M. Lively, owner of the Middle Florida Ice Company, allowed the girls to change clothes at his cottage nearby. In 1920, members of the Board of Control inspected the Lake Bradford site and approved further development of the recreation area. Shortly thereafter, Conradi transferred ownership of his lakefront lot to the college.[11]

Meanwhile, Tissie solicited contributions statewide for the camp on the lake. She also met with students on Sunday evenings after YWCA to discuss ways of earning money for

Camp Flastacowo, the name chosen for the facility by the Student Government Association.[12] Each girl pledged to earn the considerable sum of two dollars during the summer for the camp fund. Many recently enfranchised young ladies contacted their state senators and representatives during the 1921 legislative session and asked them to solicit contributions from persons in their districts. Even Jules Elliot, security guard and general campus handyman, contributed proceeds from the sale of his handmade knitting needles.[13]

By May 1922, the camp fund totaled $3,148.88, and the Board of Control's architectural firm drafted and delivered blueprints for a camp house. The original building contained only sleeping and dressing room areas and bathroom facilities, so the campus dietitian provided food for lunches or packed supplies for outdoor meals. Despite the unfinished state of the camp house, during the 1923–24 school year more than 900 students and faculty members used it.[14] Between 1923 and 1930, the college added sleeping porches and kitchen facilities to the camp house, but the building still lacked electricity; girls prepared meals on wood stoves and ate by the glow of kerosene lamps. When the college added a wharf and boathouse, the Athletic Association provided canoes and rowboats painted in the school colors. As the lake area became more populated, the college fenced off its site and hired a full-time caretaker, who lived in a cottage on the grounds. In 1930, Kellum used money from a student recreation fund to purchase an additional 40 acres of adjoining property.[15] Camp Flastacowo became an integral part of life at FSCW.

Residence Halls

During the late teens and twenties, as Florida communities grew in size and wealth, the number of high schools in the state increased proportionally. At the same time, more families realized the importance of higher education for their daughters as well as their sons, and determined to send their girls to the tuition-free (for Florida residents) state college for women. The administration, already aware of the trend and concerned with the housing shortage on campus, decided not to advertise in the summer 1920 issues of national or statewide publications. Officers of the college who usually traveled the state recruiting students remained in Tallahassee that year. Even so, eager students reserved all available dormitory rooms by mid-July. College officials juggled overcrowded housing facilities on the campus and in nearby homes as best they could, allowed sororities to rent or own their chapter houses, and continued to refuse dormitory space to out-of-state applicants.[16]

The 1919 Legislature had provided funds for extensive additions to the four existing dormitories (East Hall, Bryan Hall, Reynolds Hall, and Broward Hall), but post-war inflation had boosted the price of building materials to a level far beyond expectations. The financial shortfall halted labor on the west wing of Reynolds Hall and the south wing of Broward Hall, robbing the college of living space for approximately 60 girls for the 1919–20 session. Lack of accommodations forced the college to turn away many applicants,[17] but it took another dormitory fire before the legislature acknowledged the school's need for additional residence halls.

East Hall, the last remaining pre-1905 building on campus, had suffered numerous minor fires between 1916 and 1920. Usually these had started when sparks from the chimney fluttered down to the wood shingle roof and ignited stray pine needles. None had involved injuries or significant loss of property. After each incident, repairs and additional fire protection efforts had restored the building to habitable status. However, both administration and students recognized the fragile condition of East Hall. On several occasions girls declined election as dormitory officers because they were afraid to live in the building, a requirement for the Student Government positions.[18] The inevitable occurred on Sunday, October 31, 1920. Just before noon, a man rushed into the First Baptist Church downtown, interrupted the sermon, and cried, "All students had better come! East Hall is on fire!" Everyone hurried up College Avenue to the campus.[19]

Miss Mamie Andrews, matron of the dormitory, ran from church and flagged a motorist to take her to the college, where she set about helping the firemen. Twelve girls in the residence hall at the time thought the alarm was a fire drill, so they took their time exiting the building. When they reached the front doors, they met firemen who hurried them outside and out of danger. Firefighters saved very little from the second floor because the flames spread so quickly, but they did salvage clothing and furniture from the first floor. Within an hour only smoldering beams and piles of rubble remained on the site of the old building. Volunteers collected various items scattered around the area and carried them to the auditorium, where the YWCA secretary sorted and tagged them. After dinner that evening, East Hall residents were allowed to search through the articles for their personal effects.[20]

Twenty-eight of the 85 girls residing in the dormitory lost all their possessions. Led by members of the Elks Club, residents of Tallahassee immediately responded to the girls' plight and contributed more than $750 along with material goods. Conradi secured a house near campus for 17 East Hall residents, moved 12 more to the recreation area in Reynolds Hall, and dispersed the rest throughout the three brick dormitories. Some rooms now housed three or four girls in quarters that barely provided enough living space for two.[21]

Students had daily expected the building to burn, and they took the fire in stride. Jeanne Compton noted its passing humorously:

> "What's that column black of smoke?"
> Asked J. G. [Kellum] from the farm.
> "It's rolling up so thick and black
> It fills me with alarm."
> And running from the dairy barn
> He breathed in accents rather warm,
> "May that old fire-trap be darn!"
> It's Old East Hall a-burnin' in the mornin'.[22]

Ann Onn adopted a more thoughtful tone with her poem, "L'Envoi."

> The bells will ring in East no more,
> The girls go crowding in and out
> A ruin and memory now.
> A dream to weep and laugh about,
> But on a dark and chilly night
> A phantom building rises there,
> Ethereal and light as air.
> The trees and starlight seen right
> through
> And maids in white, ethereal too,
> Of other years, long past from sight.
> The pine trees sigh and chant and sway,
> And then the vision fades away.
> A host of hearts for Old East Hall a-mournin'![23]

Through a bit of political legerdemain,[24] the college used the insurance money received from the East Hall fire to complete the Reynolds Hall addition begun so optimistically in the summer of 1919. Students named the annex Elizabeth Hall in the mistaken belief that Elizabeth had been Mrs. Reynolds's first name. Fifty girls, many of whom had slept on cots in the recreation room since the fire, moved into the new section. The wing remained a separate entity until 1928, when the college renumbered its rooms to correspond to those of the main dormitory, and Elizabeth Hall ceased to exist.[25]

Addition of the wing's 25 rooms improved the housing situation only slightly. Campus residence facilities still accommodated only 30 students more than they had in 1918. The legislature appropriated emergency money for completion of the south wing of Broward Hall, adding another 12 rooms. Conradi and Kellum predicted that the college would need at least 150 more double rooms over the next two years.[26]

The West Hall fire of 1906 had provided the impetus for construction of Bryan Hall; in 1921, Florida lawmakers authorized construction of a dormitory to replace East Hall. Located just beyond Reynolds Hall, the new facility continued the northward march of buildings from Bryan Hall and complemented the architectural style of earlier campus structures. Southern Ferro and Concrete Company began construction in November 1921, and finished the brickwork on the three-story building in May 1922. The Board of Control named the dormitory Jennie Murphree Hall, honoring Jennie Henderson Murphree, who had died in Gainesville the year before. Mrs. Murphree, wife of A. A. Murphree, had graduated from Florida State College in 1905 and held a duplicate diploma from Florida State College for Women. Her daughter Martha was a member of the Class of 1924.[27]

Both contractor and school officials confidently predicted completion of Jennie Murphree Hall in time for the start of classes in September. Based on the expected availability of living quarters, the college accepted more than 700 resident students for the fall term, and assigned 160 of them to rooms in the new dormitory. But as opening day neared, the building still lacked windows and doors. The contractor installed temporary windows made of white sheeting, and Kellum added screens to protect the girls from insects. Rough waste lumber doors kept intruders out and students in at night. Residents shivered through November and part of December before permanent windows and doors were finally installed. Girls who lived in Jennie Murphree Hall accessed the Bryan Hall Atrium, still the only public reception area on campus, through a three-story arcade between their dormitory and Reynolds Hall immediately to its south.[28]

By late 1922, inflation eased and the state's economic prospects improved. Local and statewide support for higher education in general, and the women's college in particular, kept pace with financial development. Editorials in state newspapers vociferously opposed the State Budget Commission's attempt to cut $28,000 from the school's biennial appropriations in 1923. In the opinion of most journalists, "women make the mothers of the land, and no restrictions should be placed on the means of their intellectual development." Governor Cary Hardee rejected the commission's unpopular recommendations and maintained the school's budget of $529,500 for the biennium. The sitting 1923 Legislature, noting the general attitude of its constituents, not only ignored the Budget Commission's actions but also granted the college an additional $200,000 for new construction.[29]

Though Conradi used the majority of that money for a free-standing library to replace the woefully inadequate space on the second floor of the Administration Building, the remaining appropriations financed a west wing to Jennie Murphree Hall.[30] Architectural specifications called for red tile on the roof to match the original section of the hall, but building boom demands for George Merrick's Spanish-style development of Coral Gables had boosted the price of that material exorbitantly.[31] The contractor substituted a rubberoid material used for pre-tile waterproofing but not intended for prolonged exterior exposure. This allowed 142 students to move into the wing in September 1924. The following year the contractor properly tiled the roof.[32]

The number of students continued to increase over the next several years, but appropriations for housing facilities remained frustratingly elusive. The dormitories, always constructed with economy rather than quality in mind, required constant upkeep and repair. Bryan Hall's gravel roof leaked constantly, and ceiling plaster frequently fell on residents. The dormitory's casement windows were so out of alignment that girls had permission to leave them open during fire drills. In rooms too small for optional furniture rearrangement, radiator pipes mounted on walls dripped relentlessly on beds placed beneath them.[33]

Because of the dismal housing conditions and the growing number of students, Conradi and Kellum proposed that the Board of Control assess each dormitory resident an additional $40 per year for a dormitory construction fund. The board declined; the housing situation remained critical.[34] By

1928, more than 800 students lived in the dormitories, 400 roomed in private homes, and approximately 150 resided in sorority houses. An off-campus matron visited the girls living in private homes in an attempt to exercise some control over them, but she faced an impossible task.[35]

Though much of the growth engendered by the Florida land boom occurred in the southern part of the state and along the coasts, other areas benefited from the general population surge. In Tallahassee, local landowners converted wooded tracts just outside the city's business area to exclusive real estate developments. One such example was Dr. Game's property immediately west of the campus boundary, where he created a highly restricted residential section called College Park Subdivision Number 2. To accommodate his development, the city laid out West College Avenue, West Park Avenue, and Wildwood Drive beyond the western boundary of the college.[36] The following advertisement appeared in the Tallahassee *Daily Democrat*:

> Any property close to the college, properly priced, is an absolutely safe investment. Choice lots available in College Park Subdivision 2. A house on any of these lots will always sell or rent at maximum price. Water, gas, and electricity already on West College and West Park Avenue. See C. K. Allen, Real Estate, or owner, Dr. Game.[37]

The possibility of houses all around the campus portended a supervision nightmare for college administrators. Conradi, who believed that effective security was possible only if all students lived in residence halls on campus, urgently requested an appropriation for a new dormitory. While Broward Hall was under construction in 1918, a site plan had indicated that any further dormitory expansion would be to the north and east of Bryan and Reynolds Halls. So far, Jennie Murphree Hall, to their immediate north, conformed to that plan. But Rudolph Weaver, successor to Board of Control architect William Edwards, directed campus expansion in another direction in 1925 when he located the next residence hall to the west of Broward Hall. His plans for a T-shaped dormitory included an ornate lobby to serve as a private reception area, separating residents from Bryan Hall—until then the hub of campus life.

Between the time Weaver executed his plans for the new dormitory and the time construction began, the pace of development in South Florida occasioned a 200-to-300 percent rise statewide in the price of building materials and labor. The $100,000 appropriation, adequate for completion of all three wings in 1925, enabled D. Thomas and Son of Memphis, Tennessee, to construct only one wing of the building in 1926. The Board of Control named the new dormitory Gilchrist Hall after former governor Albert Gilchrist, who died while the residence hall was under construction. The governor had left $10,000 to the college to provide scholarships for needy students—but this fact was unknown to the board when it selected the name.[38]

To combat the rise in building costs, the board authorized the administration to raise room and board charges from $175 to $200 per year in September 1926. That same month South Florida real estate values collapsed; tropical breezes about which salesmen had rhapsodized turned into two deadly hurricanes, the last of which struck the Gold Coast on September 17 and 18. Amidst flooded streets, uprooted trees, ruined roofs, and automobiles thrown about like toys, a five-masted steel schooner rode high and dry in the street at Coral Gables, testimony to the area's vulnerability. The hurricane continued inland and nearly demolished settlements in the Lake Okeechobee region. South Florida businessmen downplayed the damage, but would-be land purchasers reconsidered their planned investments in the state.

Five months later the State Budget Commission cautioned Conradi that a drop in cotton prices in the Panhandle and a winter freeze that damaged much of the citrus crop meant a decline in property taxes over the next year or so and a concurrent decrease in funds available for campus expansion.

That news discouraged the president, who had contended that the college needed a minimum housing appropriation of $1,100,000 for the 1926–28 biennium. He had based this estimate on completion of Gilchrist Hall, construction of another residence hall in 1927, and construction of two more in 1928.[39]

Conradi knew that additional on-campus housing was imperative. More than 300 girls had lived in private homes during the past session. However, since the school insisted that residential households adhere closely to prescribed campus regulations, supervision of the students living in the various off-campus homes fell heavily on the landlady, a responsibility most found difficult and even annoying.[40] Many nearby householders who had welcomed students as roomers in the past ceased to do so because of the administration's inability to maintain close control over the girls.

Resigned to further delays in dormitory expansion, Conradi pointed out to the Board of Control in his biennial report that enrollment and housing capabilities were directly connected. No matter how many prospective students applied for admission, only those who found suitable living arrangements attended and consequently paid board to the state. Confronted with that reality, the board located enough money to complete Gilchrist Hall and convert the attic floors of Jennie Murphree and Reynolds Halls to living quarters.[41]

The final section of Gilchrist Hall opened in September 1928. The entire dormitory cost the state $258,000. When compared to $46,000 for Bryan Hall in 1908, the rise in construction costs over the 20-year period seemed excessive. However, Gilchrist was the most up-to-date building on campus. Each of its rooms had two lights and double base electrical outlets, a sure sign of modernization. Kellum must have expected the future residents of the new dormitory to be tall and slender because the mattresses he ordered measured 3' by 6'3". The dormitory's two matrons shared a suite with a private office, as well as a kitchen and a laundry. Residents had access to four small parlors and one large living room for entertaining. Reynolds, Broward, and Jennie Murphree Halls lacked parlors or public areas and used those in Bryan Hall, but the separate social rooms in Gilchrist Hall proved so popular that similar areas were created in each of the older dormitories the following summer.[42]

With the completion of Gilchrist Hall, the school reached an enrollment plateau of 1,642 students: 1,116 lived in residence halls, 238 lived in sorority houses, 168 lived in 23 approved off-campus houses, and 120 resided with their parents or guardians. Women's colleges nationwide had garnered increased attention and attendance since the end of World War I, and Florida State College for Women was rapidly becoming one of the leading educational institutions in the country. Conradi noted that most "high-class colleges for women" faced the same housing dilemma as FSCW, and feared that lack of resources threatened the school's reputation. According to Conradi, "the enrollment is always the extent of our capacity. If the capacity increases, the enrollment increases."[43] But, despite his concerns, a decade elapsed before the college built another dormitory.

SUPPORT BUILDINGS

Ideally, deployment of scholastic buildings on campus would parallel construction of residence halls, but that did not happen. Postwar inflation caused the college to postpone indefinitely improvements to the kitchen and construction of a free-standing infirmary, originally scheduled for the summer of 1919. Two years later, however, the legislature provided emergency appropriations for completion of both projects.

Prior to the opening of the Infirmary in September 1921, any student who required more than cursory medical treatment either went home or went to the hospital in Bainbridge, Georgia. The new Infirmary maintained offices for a college physician and three assistants, reception, consultation, and treatment rooms, and a modern operating room with an adjoining two-bed recovery room. At last the administration felt that it offered "sick students the conveniences and the comforts of a first class hospital."[44] The building also offered two sleeping porches with 24 beds each. Medical science at that time endorsed the beneficial properties of fresh air, so students diagnosed as depressed, anxious, or generally in poor health retired to the Infirmary at last light flash for supervised sleep on the porches. Arcades connected the medical facility directly or indirectly to every residence hall on campus.[45]

With the opening of the Infirmary, the college hired its first full-time resident physician, Dr. Anne Young, who held regular office hours for consultations.[46] Dr. Young's responsibilities included the general well-being of all those enrolled, whether they lived on campus or not. She reviewed the medical histories of each student and advised faculty members concerning emergency situations that might arise in their classrooms. Two local doctors, an X-ray specialist and an ear, nose, and throat specialist, were on-call.[47]

Dr. Anne Sharpe replaced Dr. Young in 1925. During the three years Dr. Sharpe served as college physician, she dealt with an influenza epidemic that closed down the campus. In mid-December 1928, more than 125 students reported to the Infirmary suffering flu-like symptoms.[48] Dr. Sharpe, aware that three million cases of influenza were predicted nationwide by Christmas, recommended that the school close for the holidays immediately, one week earlier than scheduled. The administration acquiesced in an attempt to stem the spread of the illness. Their precautions came to naught, however, for the girls not infected at the college came in contact with the virus over the holidays and brought it back to the campus on their return. Before the epidemic was over, so many students were stricken that the Infirmary commandeered the connecting arcade and the second floor of Reynolds Hall, as well as the recreation room on the floor above, to treat patients.[49]

Earlier signs of crowded conditions had been apparent in 1922 when 777 students sat down to eat in the Dining Hall, which had been designed and built to hold 550 persons. For the previous 18 months, at least 12 students had been seated at tables meant to seat ten. An addition to the north side of the Dining Hall, funded at the same time as the Infirmary, expanded the dining capacity to 1,000 in one huge room;[50] a lower section added needed storage space. Covered arcades from Bryan, Reynolds, and Broward halls connected each to the Dining Hall. On the day the addition opened, the college celebrated with a Halloween dinner of creamed chicken on toast, green peas, creamed potatoes, and pumpkin pie with whipped cream for dessert. The college even held its 1924 Commencement exercises in the enlarged dining room. New campus dietitian Anna May Tracy scheduled breakfast that day for 7:00 A.M. to be sure the room was cleared in time for the ceremonies. By 1925, the college needed both the upper and lower levels of the building for dining.[51]

In the fall of 1920, Conradi insisted that the state provide more classroom and laboratory facilities for the college. He wanted a structure similar to the Education Building to house the Chemistry and Home Economics Departments. After the 1921 Legislature provided the necessary funds, Southern Ferro and Concrete Company began construction on a new classroom building on the site of the ill-fated East Hall.[52] When the structure, named Science Hall, opened early in 1923, the Home Economics and Extension Departments moved from the Administration Building into the first and second floors of the new facility. The Chemistry Department occupied the third floor. The physics, botany, bacteriology, zoology, psychology, and geography programs remained in the Administration Building or the Education Building.

As planned, the college used a major portion of its 1921 legislative appropriations for a library building. Once again the Board of Control rejected as too high all original bids for the new structure. The college eventually awarded a compromise contract for a single wing of the proposed building. When completed, the two-story, 108' by 40' section, located south of Bryan Hall and west of the Science Building, housed a reading room and a few smaller side rooms used for classrooms. It still lacked a main entrance and stack rooms.[53] The extent of the library collection, which comprised 25,500 volumes, 250 monthly and weekly magazines, a number of departmental journals, and 16 daily newspapers, surpassed the building's capacity even before it opened. More distressing was the fact that frequently when students arrived to work on assignments they found all seats occupied.[54]

Conradi, who usually acquiesced to board decisions without public protest, vented his frustration with the building program for FSCW shortly thereafter. He soundly chastised the Board of Control for its shortsightedness, particularly with regard to construction of the Library:

> A building which is such a fundamental part of every activity of the College should be built properly and adequately in the first place and not patched together piece-meal. The west wing, which has been built, the central part and the east wing here recommended to be built, all together make the first fundamental part of the Library Building as planned in the first place. Later, as the College grows, wings can be added to this in the rear. But this first essential part should be built as a whole. Not to do so means loss in efficiency, unnecessary expense in making temporary adjustments and would give the main building a patched up outward appearance which should never be permitted.[55]

His uncharacteristic outburst may explain why the central and east sections, designed by Rudolph Weaver in 1928 to complement the existing section, entailed the most elaborate exterior architectural elements and ornamentation of any building on campus. When completed in early 1929, these areas afforded spacious stacks with a total capacity of 130,000 volumes, meeting rooms, seminar rooms, offices, and miscellaneous areas for library needs such as receiving, unpacking, checking, and cataloging. A visitor to the new Library climbed granite steps and passed through a recessed Gothic archway decorated with colorful terra cotta replicas of the insignias of Nicholas Jenson and Aldus Manutius, 15th-century printers.[56] An anonymous maxim, "The half of knowledge is to know where to find knowledge," was rendered in gold leaf and framed above the doorway.

Over the years this inscription elicited curious comments from all who saw it. New members of the library staff searched in vain for the maxim's origin. Louise Richardson, Director of the Library from 1922 until 1956, worked directly with the architect and contractor during the building's construction, yet remained publicly mum on the subject. Privately, she responded to a colleague's query that one of the workmen made the comment as he and Weaver, the architect, stood observing the work in progress. Weaver liked the sentiment so well that he decided to put it on the facade of the building.[57]

In the first half of the 1920s, every building on campus seemed too small. The 12-year-old auditorium in the Administration Building no longer accommodated the entire student body at one time. The school's remarkable growth had rendered its seating capacity of 1,000 woefully inadequate.[58] Freshmen left school a week early in the spring of 1923 to make room for friends and relatives of the graduates at Commencement. To make matters worse, a wall near the stage area developed an ominous-looking crack, disturbingly similar to those that had appeared in the old College Hall. Edwards and Sayward filled the crack with cement and advised that it posed no further danger to the building. Kellum, however, continued to monitor the walls, and when the crack reappeared, he measured it daily. Eventually the ground around the building began to crack, and the architects ordered another geological survey of the campus.[59]

The report reiterated the 1909 findings that the hill under the Administration Building was underlaid with soft, spongy "pipe clay" that expanded when saturated. Where the clay deposits neared the surface, the expansion and subsequent contraction caused walls to crack. The report suggested that the architects fill in around the foundation with more clay or cement to keep the ground under the building dry.[60]

With that done, the construction firm of Parker and Yeager began enlarging the auditorium.[61] It came as no surprise when only the preliminary work was accomplished with the funds available. The walls remained unplastered, and the stage needed a curtain and simple settings for dramatic presentations. The biggest problem, however, was a shortage of permanent seats. With the room's capacity increased to 1,800, guests sat on folding chairs. Eighteen months later, bids at last went out for interior finish work.[62]

The college was finally able to use the auditorium again in May 1926. In the interim, students and faculty held chapel services and meetings in an outdoor theater southwest of the Library. Julius Steinfuhrer, restored to his position as college gardener in 1921, took advantage of the natural slope of the ground for seating and planted shrubbery that served as screens and a backdrop for an elevated stage area.[63]

In 1925, the college planned a third classroom building, originally intended to house the Industrial Arts Department and the Commerce Department. Conradi wanted this structure to include a small assembly room capable of seating 300 to 400 persons. Because of cost fluctuations in the Florida construction industry in 1925 and 1926, the architects did not submit plans for this particular building to contractors until 1927.[64] At that time, a statewide building industry slump made materials readily available, and contractors were looking for jobs. The first half of the building, located between Science Hall and the Library, was completed in seven months. The Board of Control named the new structure Social Science Hall, but the campus community referred to it as the History Building. Typical of construction on the campus in this decade, its 12 classrooms and four conference rooms failed to meet the administration's requirements and provided little relief for the crowded conditions.[65]

As a result of the collapse of the land boom in 1926, Florida entered the Depression three years before the rest of the country. Retail sales that had peaked at more than $5 million during the real estate heyday dropped by half over the next six years. After 1927, property values in Leon County and Tallahassee plummeted with those in the rest of the state. The county issued building permits in 1926 valued at more than $1,000,000. That amount dropped to slightly more than $600,000 in 1927. In the first three months of 1928, the total reached only $93,000. Despite a resulting decrease in property taxes statewide and a related decline in the state's general revenue, the legislature attempted to make funds available to the state's two collegiate institutions.

HOME MANAGEMENT HOUSE

The Smith-Hughes Act of 1917 had offered federal funds to educational institutions for training future teachers in home extension work; universities or colleges in turn provided a house where home economics students lived for a semester and gained personal experience in day-to-day home management. Until 1923, FSCW rented various nearby residences for use as practice houses,[66] but both students and teachers found the arrangement unsatisfactory. In 1923, the college purchased a house and tract of land behind Broward Hall and remodeled the dwelling for use as a practice house. Two faculty members, Elizabeth Doane and Leila Venable, moved into the domicile, but before any students had a chance to use the facility it burned down.[67] Faced with the possible loss of federal funding for the home extension program at FSCW, the Board of Control ordered plans for a practice house drawn up early in 1926. Unfortunately, the board's belated efforts coincided with the boom-induced rise in the cost of building materials. Bids for the small structure ran $10,000 more than allotted, and the board tabled the project. In 1927, the federal government insisted that the program meet its requirements or lose its funding; the legislature appropriated additional funds for the facility.

The Old-English-style house, now referred to as the Home Management House, opened in February 1928 near the corner of Copeland and Call Streets.[68] A dozen or more students at a time lived in the house with one or two resident teachers. On a rotating schedule, they planned menus, shopped for supplies and prepared meals, and hosted formal dinners for college officers and Board of Control members.

Physical Education Building

By the 1920s, the college had outgrown the tiny white church building purchased in 1905 for use as its first gymnasium. Conradi referred to it as "hardly an excuse for a name." The curriculum mandated physical education, yet the old gymnasium offered no lockers and no shower facilities. A well-appointed athletic field was laid out by O.C. Parker in 1922, just north of the dining room. Nearby were two tennis courts, basketball courts, a track with hurdles, pits for high jumping and broad jumping, areas for javelin and shotput, and a little wooden shed to house athletic equipment. But inclement weather caused class cancelations for lack of indoor space. The gymnasium director even asked permission to use a tent to protect students during rainy spells.[69]

Structurally, the old building was simply not able to support many exuberant students. During Thanksgiving week in 1925, a contingent of Odds returned to the little gymnasium after their lantern parade and held a pep rally that literally brought the house down. In the midst of all the wild cheering, a stove (used for heat) on one wall and a piano on the opposite wall began to slide towards each other as the floor gave way.[70] Grace Fox recounted:

> The cheerleaders were on top of the piano and they were really getting the pep going. And the floor gave way, and every Odd claims to have been right in the middle where the floor went down.[71]

In September 1928, architect Rudolph Weaver presented plans for a new athletic building, to be the largest structure on campus to date. The college solicited bids, but the state provided funding for only the west and south wings of the T-shaped edifice. J.L. Crouse of Greensboro, North Carolina, submitted the low bid of $284,000. His application for a building permit, filed in early 1929, boosted the value of construction in Leon County to $376,000 for the year.[72] The college anticipated a year of construction and expected to use the new gymnasium for the fall session of 1929. However, financial problems plagued the subcontractors on the project. Crouse managed to complete the building by late December 1929, some four months behind schedule, after taking over the plumbing work himself.[73]

The south wing of the building housed a 40' by 70' swimming pool. Students picked up their gym suits or bathing suits and towels from a distribution room in the lower lobby. The west wing held the main activity room, called the "big gym" (60' by 113'). Its floor was laid out for basketball and included a balcony for spectators. Holiday Odd/Even games were played there. Dressing rooms, lockers, and showers filled the area beneath the gym floor. In the basement beneath the locker rooms and showers was the campus laundry. Located on the far west side of the campus, the building seemed extremely distant from the dormitories and classrooms. It wasn't long before Conradi found it necessary to remind teachers to dismiss their classes on time "since the new Gymnasium was so far away from other buildings."[74]

※

By 1930, the college owned more than 300 acres, including 250 acres of farm land. The estimated value of the physical plant was $3,000,000. The Depression brought even tighter educational budgets to the state, and with the exception of a heating plant, authorized in mid-1930 and completed in 1931, and an addition to the History Building, major construction ceased until 1938.

lorida State College for Women, like its home state,
came of age in the "Roaring Twenties." Its curriculum and physical plant expanded to accommodate some of the rapid growth and development of the
state itself. In 1924, the Association of American Universities placed the school on its approved list of colleges and
universities, giving students and graduates national recognition as well as standing in all foreign educational institutions. Florida State College for Women was the first tax-
supported women's college in the United States to receive
this recognition.[1]

During the first half of the decade, the college administration wrestled with financial inadequacies, unable to understand
why the legislature refused to share the growing prosperity so
evident elsewhere in Florida and the nation. Salaries consis-
tently below those at most Southern educational institutions—
and, more to the point, particularly below those at the University of Florida—created morale problems among faculty
members. Nevertheless, growth and development brought
additional instructors, who in turn brought different and sometimes more progressive ideas to the campus.

A greater number of faculty members and students meant
a loss of the close-knit, family atmosphere of previous years.
More often than not during this decade, the outside world
intruded on the cloistered atmosphere so essential to the

administration's total control of the campus. As a result, FSCW faced one disturbing situation after another.

ADMINISTRATION

When FSCW opened in September 1920, its nominal charges were higher than in 1905. Students paid an annual registration and library fee of $7, an infirmary fee of $8, and a damage and laboratory deposit of $5. Board, which included sleeping quarters, meals, fuel, and light, had risen from $100 to $175 per yearly session, yet out-of-state tuition remained reasonably priced at $20, payable in advance. Since the School of Music still charged separate fees for twice-weekly private lessons offered in pipe organ, piano, violin, or voice and paid its faculty from these fees, music education costs had risen over the years to meet the increased salaries. The same was true of the School of Art and the School of Expression, which also offered private lessons.[2]

In 1920, practically every county in the state had at least one standard high school, with the result that the sub-freshman class at the college had only six students at the 11th grade level. With that in mind, the Board of Control discontinued the high school departments at both the women's college and the men's university as of the 1921–22 sessions.[3] The college administration followed that action with a change in general scholastic organization for the 1922–23 school year. Revised divisions included the College of Arts and Sciences, School of Education, Normal School, School of Art, School of Expression, School of Music, School of Home Economics, Summer School, and the Extension Service. A Business Department, established in 1917 at Conradi's suggestion, prepared young ladies for careers as stenographers, secretaries, bookkeepers, and commercial subject teachers in an area that was rapidly expanding for women. The school awarded both one-year certificates and two-year diplomas to those students who completed the program.[4]

Partly because of the shortage of trained nurses during

World War I, the School of Home Economics added a bachelor's degree in nursing. The college worked with hospital schools designated by the American College of Surgeons to provide future nurses with a more liberal education than was possible in hospital training programs alone, while not having their college years interfere with their medical training. Students spent their first two years at FSCW, the next two years in an accepted hospital, then a fifth year at the college, after which they received a bachelor's degree in nursing.[5]

SCHOOL OF EDUCATION

The State School for Teachers had evolved into the School of Education, and since 1916 had conferred a bachelor of science degree on its four-year graduates and a Licentiate of Instruction (L.I.) on its two-year graduates. The state automatically awarded certification to those students who held a bachelor of science degree in education, and considered them qualified to teach at the high school level as well as to serve in an administrative capacity at all levels. Receipt of an L.I. degree also conferred certification and permitted graduates to teach first through tenth grades. The college retained its two-year L.I. program primarily for financial considerations; those students not sure of funding for four years took the two-year Normal School course. While the L.I. degree remained the standard choice for those unable or unwilling to spend the time or money in pursuit of a four-year degree, the bachelor of science degree in education soon became a preferred option. The number of students enrolled in the two-year program rose from 107 in 1922 to 229 in 1924, but the number of students who received a bachelor of science degree in education grew from 13 in 1922 to 155 during the same time.[6]

Because of the more stringent requirements set forth in the School of Education, both for admission and graduation, the gap between Normal School students and those students enrolled in the liberal arts program gradually narrowed. By 1923, seniors in the Normal School and sophomores in other curricula, all in their second year at the college, voted to join each other in social activities and athletics. After 1923, the Sophomore Class incorporated the Senior Normal Class, and removed any perceived scholastic or social distinction between Normal and academic students.[7] At that time, officially or not, the Normal School ceased to exist, and all future teachers entered the School of Education.

The Model School, an integral segment of the teacher-training program, originally offered classes in kindergarten and grades one through four for local children. Prospective teachers observed the training teacher's techniques, then under his or her guidance tried their own teaching.[8] Maud Schwalmeyer, director of the Model School, introduced her teaching hopefuls to their peers by having each of them come to the front of the classroom and respond to a question. According to one of her students, "Miss Maud had the idea that if you couldn't come up and face the group, you would never make a teacher. I think she may have been right. But honestly, she scared us to death."[9] She assigned each student a particular class each week, and for one-half hour every day the student actually taught the assignment. L.I. students repeated this procedure for their entire two years of training; candidates for bachelor's degrees in the School of Education participated during their last two years of school.[10] This process became known as "practice teaching."

In 1919, the Model School held fifth- and sixth-grade classes in a single classroom of the new Education Building. Over the next three years, high school classes were added to the training department schedule. By 1924, what the School of Education now referred to as the Demonstration School consisted of five sections scattered over campus in three different buildings: kindergarten, grades one through three, grades four through six, three junior high grades, and three senior high grades. The 1925 Legislature answered a plea for a single building for the school,[11] but because of financial constraints, the state parceled out the needed funds. Consequently, construction lagged and space remained inadequate as late as 1928.

In 1927, the State Department of Education accredited the upper grades of what then became known as Florida High School, but many students still transferred to Leon High School after they completed the sixth grade. The elementary grades were awarded accreditation in 1928. The Demonstration School interacted with the college, and the young students often appeared in appropriate roles in college plays, shared the Odd/Even enthusiasm of their practice teachers, and adopted the green and gold or red, white, and purple of their prospective graduation year.[12]

Summer School

When the Buckman Bill established the men's university at Gainesville and the women's college at Tallahassee in 1905, each institution held an independent Summer School on its campus. Originally, the summer session provided training for teachers already employed in the county school systems. The terms ran six or eight weeks in length, depending on the whim of the State Board of Education. In 1913, the legislature established permanent Summer Schools at the University of Florida and at Florida State College for Women. The Dean of the School of Education at each institution automatically served as Director of the Summer School under the supervision of a board composed of the State Superintendent of Education, the president of the university, and the president of the college. Since the Buckman Bill failed to mention gender with regard to summer school enrollment, both men and women attended summer sessions on both campuses. When W. S. Cawthon became Superintendent of Education in the summer of 1922, he charged the regular officers of each school to administer their own summer programs. The coeducational aspect of the shorter sessions remained in force, with one dormitory set aside on each campus for members of the opposite sex.[13]

The fact that, until 1922, the state allotted only half-pay for Summer School instructors reinforced the idea that the summer programs were less professional than the regular sessions. This salary disparity caused many faculty members to take summer positions out-of-state, and the college was unable to replace them with equally qualified teachers on such a paltry pay scale.[14] Even though salaries remained dismally low, after 1922 heads of the various departments continued in their positions through the summer, ensuring that the schools offered the same high caliber courses all year.

Most persons still attended summer classes for certification rather than as part of a college degree plan. Gradually, the number of pupils who worked toward a degree only during the summer increased, and many regular students applied summer work toward their graduation. In 1926, a total of 45 students finished their college work in the summer; one earned a master's degree, 18 received bachelor's degrees, and 26 were awarded L.I. degrees.[15] Summer school also gained more acceptance when regular expenses increased at the college and dormitory space became more difficult to secure during the regular school term.

By 1923, the cost of room and board had risen to $200 per annual session. It dropped by $25 the next year but returned to $200 in 1925. Out-of-state tuition jumped to a staggering $100 and remained there.[16] A paradox existed regarding out-of-state students: the college wanted their tuition as well as board but begrudged the space they took from prospective Florida registrants. Despite the extra cost and the necessity of locating accommodations off-campus, 74 young women from 14 states other than Florida enrolled as regular students for the 1923–24 term, not quite ten percent of the total enrollment of 964. Dean Dodd of the College of Arts and Sciences believed that $100 was far too little for out-of-state tuition. However, when he proposed that the state impose a larger amount in order to control the enrollment, his suggestions fell on deaf ears. In early 1926, the Board of Control attempted to restrict admission to Florida residents, but the state's Attorney General feared repercussions from such a practical proposal and negated the action.[17]

The school's popularity continued to attract studious young women. September 1927 arrived along with 1,324 students from 17 states. Based on registration figures for 1927–28, FSCW ranked seventh in enrollment among all women's colleges, public and private, in the United States.[18] In 1928–29, it moved up to fourth, behind Hunter, Smith, and Wellesley; Vassar was fifth. By opening day in 1929, more than 1,600 students attended classes, and Conradi reported that the number was still climbing.[19]

FACULTY

Fifty-eight faculty members held positions at FSCW in the fall of 1920. Only seven, including President Conradi (who taught very little), had doctorates; 11 held master's degrees.[20] Arthur Williams of the History Department and Elmer Smith of the Mathematics Department remained vice-president and secretary of the institution respectively. William Dodd still held his position as Dean of the College of Arts and Sciences, and Ella Scoble Opperman continued as Dean of the School of Music. Nathaniel Salley, after an altercation with the Board of Control over his participation in local politics nearly cost him his job, stayed on as Dean of the School of Education and head of the Normal School.[21]

Though relatively pleased with his faculty, as enrollment increased Conradi felt the need for more teachers with at least one year of advanced training beyond a bachelor's degree. Once again the bottom line was financial; low salaries presented a major stumbling block to the school's ability to hire well-qualified professionals. In 1922, the Board of Control set Conradi's salary at $5,000, on a par for the first time with that of A.A. Murphree at the University of Florida.[22] Conradi thanked the board for the raise and noted that when compared with 70 other state institutions in the nation, FSCW was one of six that paid the lowest salaries to its department heads. In fact, faculty members at the college received less money than did those in like positions at the university, and even at that institution salaries averaged less than $1,500.[23] By 1926, salaries remained at levels established five years earlier, when the state treasury was relatively impoverished.

A faculty committee composed of Arthur Williams, J.B. Game, Nathaniel Salley, and Alban Stewart transmitted a formal complaint to the Board of Control via Conradi's biennial report. Concurrently, a similar committee at the University of Florida presented its case. Either the time was right, the University of Florida's argument carried weight, or both, for the board established guidelines for salaries at the two state institutions. The presidents each received $7,500; professors earned $3,500–4,500, plus $500 more if they served as deans; associate professors earned $2,900–3,400; assistant professors earned $2,300–2,800; and instructors, usually those with little or no graduate training, received $1,700–2,200. The 1927 Legislature appropriated funds for any raises necessary to meet these levels and for the employment of several additional teachers at both schools.[24]

Prior to that legislative action, the college had lost several faculty members as a result of low salaries, and also two through death. Psychology and philosophy professor E. A. Hayden, battling depression, committed suicide in October 1921. The college community had barely recovered from the shock of his death when tragedy struck again. In March 1922, voice instructor Emma Boyd, Director of the Glee Club and a vivacious young lady in her early twenties, visited an Indian mound about seven miles northwest of Tallahassee. She and her two companions, Mary Lewis and Gertrude Levy, tunneled out an archway and then foolishly crawled into the cavity. The arch caved in, trapping Boyd and Levy, but the latter managed to struggle free. Boyd suffocated before help arrived.[25]

Many faculty members appointed by Conradi in the 1920s remained at the college to guide it through the Depression years and another world war and into its transition to coeducation.[26] One of the most well-known of those was Katherine Montgomery. "Miss Katie" came to FSCW as a freshman in 1914. She served as president of the Athletic Association during her senior year and received a bachelor of arts degree in 1918. She taught science in the Normal School for two years, then became an instructor in physical education while the college program was still part of the School of Physical Culture and Expression. As an originator of FSCW traditions as well as their beneficiary, she tried to make of each student a *femina perfecta*.[27] From 1923, when Conradi appointed her Director of Physical Education, until the end of the decade, students took two or three physical education classes each week under her supervision. The college's entire athletic program, based on class contests and Odd/Even rivalries in every sport, developed under Miss Katie's direction. She so completely adopted the administration's early disapproval of interscholastic competition that she later referred to games between schools as "inter$chola$tic" sports.[28]

Anecdotes about Katherine Montgomery attest to her popularity and significance on the campus. One story concerned the delayed completion of the new gymnasium. In anticipation of the building's projected September opening, the newly created Department of Physical Education scheduled swimming classes and hired a teacher. When the pool was still not ready in October, nor in November, Miss Katie purchased enough wash basins for each person in a class to have one. Though unable to swim, students filled their basins with water and practiced proper breathing techniques. Another account related the dismay of students who found a single question on their final exam in kinesiology: "List the muscles, in the order in which they come into movement, used by a woman carrying a 20-pound child up a flight of 15 stairs."[29]

Louise Richardson came to the college as Librarian in 1919

but left in 1920 when the administration refused to raise her salary from $1,100 to $1,200. She returned two years later and made the college her permanent post.[30] While Richardson's stern demeanor intimidated some people, no one ever questioned her competence or her authority with regard to the Library. She rarely made an exception to an established rule and never considered special privileges. She supervised construction of the first wing of the Library in 1923 and did the same with the final phase six years later. During her tenure she started a library science program to train county school librarians, the only such program available in the state prior to 1947.[31] Until 1926, she worked with only one full-time assistant, Clara Hayden, widow of the psychology professor, whom Conradi appointed to the library staff after the death of her husband.[32]

When Dining Hall Matron Mrs. Yonge retired in 1916, Conradi hired dietitian Margaret Edwards. Edwards managed the kitchen and dining room so efficiently that the college was able to "set a better table than ever before" over the next two years, without increasing boarding charges. However, she resigned in the summer of 1918 to go into the military.[33] For the next four years, rising food costs and a continual turnover of dietitians hampered the efficiency of the boarding department.[34] Then Conradi hired Anna May Tracy, a graduate of Battle Creek, Michigan, Sanitarium and the Lewis Training School in Washington, D.C.

When Tracy arrived at FSCW in 1922, plans were underway to build a new kitchen. The original kitchen had coal stoves, which she insisted be replaced with electric ranges. This required extension of electricity to the kitchens and included replacement of ice boxes with electric refrigeration units. Under her auspices, the college was one of the first state institutions to use frozen foods, including frozen orange juice. Tracy prepared all the menus and coordinated the work of 40 employees and two assistant dietitians as they daily prepared meals for more than 1,000 persons. She and Kellum personally selected the girls who received dining room scholarships, and she trained and supervised their work.[35]

Several other faculty members began long associations with the college in the early 1920s. One was Dr. Herman Kurz, hired as an assistant professor of botany in 1922. His Saturday field trips around the area taught many students to recognize and appreciate the local flora. On one such excursion, instruction fell victim to a waist-high patch of wild blueberries. Kurz told his charges to "forget the field work—just go ahead and eat!"[36] In the classroom, Kurz used small cards to call roll; at the same time he asked each student a question about the day's assignment, then marked on the card whether she answered correctly.[37] Another instructor in the scientific field was Ezda May Deviney, who assisted Lanas Barber in teaching zoology and later became head of that department.

Dr. William Hudson Rogers, associate professor of English, arrived on campus in 1922. The debonair Rogers acquired a reputation as a campus heartthrob, for he looked the part. In his tweed jacket, with his pipe in his mouth, he strode rather than walked about the college grounds; students swooned in his wake. When he played tennis in immaculate white trousers, "the track gym class immediately formed a line of admiring spectators."[38] His ability in the classroom matched his appearance, and students clamored for a seat in his classes on Robert Browning.

Between 1924 and 1926, the College of Arts and Sciences separated its heretofore combined programs in mathematics and physics, in economics and sociology, and in political science and history; geography joined the now independent History Department. Elmer Smith elected to remain as head of the new Department of Mathematics. The college hired Dr. Harold Richards to teach physics and astronomy. Lucy Lang remembered when Richards and his wife, Hazel, planned a party for the astronomy class in connection with an eclipse of the moon. Richards set up a five-inch refractory telescope near the fountain in front of the Administration Building, and class members went outside at intervals to observe the stages of the eclipse. Back inside the building, each student used a stylus to write her name through wax spread over a sheet of copper, then watched as Richards etched the sheet with acid. Mrs. Richards provided hot cocoa and marshmallows to toast over Bunsen burners.[39]

Dr. Bessie C. Randolph, whose penchant for wearing scarves occasioned good-humored teasing among the students, stepped into the Department of Political Science. In the History Department, Dr. Kathryn Abbey joined Venila Lovina Shores, who had been at the college since 1922. Dr. Olivia Dorman joined J.B. Game in the Classics Department in 1924 and later became Dean of Students. In 1926, Dr. Arthur Seymour was added to the Language Department as instructor of French and Italian, becoming one of 111 faculty members at the college.[40]

Between 1927 and 1929, using funds appropriated by the 1927 Legislature, the administration employed several new teachers who spent the remainder of their professional lives at FSCW. These faculty members determined to a great extent the character of the school during its last years as a women's college. They included Mark DeGraff and Ralph Eyman in the field of education; Earl Vance in journalism; Robert Cotterill in history; Guy Diffenbaugh in English; Coyle Moore in sociology; Henry Becker in geography; Viola Graham in physiology; Paul Heinlein in experimental psychology; and Anna Forbes Liddell in philosophy.

Dodd hired Forbes Liddell on the recommendation of her mentors at the University of North Carolina, where she had earned her bachelor's and doctoral degrees. As a committed supporter of women's rights, she trained her students to think for themselves.[41] Dorothy Bulloch recalled that

she gave us a topic to write on, and gave us a reading list on the subject; books to check in the library. So we went to the library and read and read and read, then wrote our papers. Well, of course we were repeating what we had read. We all got "D-". That was not what she wanted. So we would take the topic and write it out, then do our reading. After that, we got "A"s.[42]

Coyle Moore, hired to assist Dr. Raymond Bellamy in the Sociology Department, arrived on campus just in time for the faculty meeting at the opening of the Fall 1928 session. The interests of this new associate professor of sociology contrasted significantly with those of Bellamy, and their ideas clashed frequently. Bellamy described Moore as "almost coarse in his mannerisms," and went on to say:

> He put up a big show of being rough and tough. He [called] his students Skillet-Head, Lame-Brain, and other such names, and he acted as if he were just about to chew them up. Actually he had a deeply sensitive nature and was very close to his students. He soon learned about their financial situation at home . . . and he often loaned them money, or even gave it to them without anybody else ever knowing anything about it.[43]

Bellamy also credited Moore with bringing new life to the Sociology Department by introducing extension work and correspondence courses, affiliating with various welfare organizations, and generally giving a more progressive outlook to the subject matter.

DECADE OF DISSENSION

Conradi delegated many of his official duties to the college's business manager, J. G. Kellum, or to Dean William G. Dodd. Those two had their hands full dealing with financial shortages, overcrowded conditions, and faculty selections. But the president personally guarded the reputation of the college. That was a major reason for carefully sequestering students on campus and closely supervising them off campus. If something of a scandalous nature occurred, the administration dealt with it carefully lest the press misrepresent or the public misinterpret the circumstances. Conradi handled one occasion in particular with extreme care.

In 1920, a group of Shriners attending a convention in Tallahassee created a disturbance on campus when they tried to get students to celebrate with them, but Conradi successfully contained the incident. When the North Florida Shriners planned another convention in Tallahassee in 1921, most Tallahasseans looked forward to the upcoming visit as an exciting and financially rewarding event. Businessmen decorated the downtown area and planned a gala street dance on Adams Street. According to the *Democrat*, the city expected a "splendid, magnificent, blues-busting, mirth-provoking program" from the conventioneers.[44] Conradi, concerned that another confrontation between Shriners and college administrators might occur, asked Dr. O.G. Kendrick, one of the college doctors and head of the local Shrine organization, to see that the men stayed off the campus.

The revelry began when a contingent of Shriners from Jacksonville arrived in Tallahassee at 3:00 A.M. on Saturday. They went immediately to the Leon Hotel, where they joined local Shriners for breakfast, initiation rituals, and a parade. As the morning wore on, a good number of them who had begun their adventure at the Jacksonville railway station some 14 hours earlier, motored out to the college, where classes were still in session. They swarmed over the campus and into the buildings, disrupted classes, and created general confusion.[45]

Though reluctant to make the episode public, an angry Conradi nevertheless felt compelled to take some action. The Faculty Senate lodged a private protest with the Jacksonville Shriners, relating how the visitors had

> forcibly dragged the president from his office; forcibly carried away from the campus in automobiles some of the men teachers; placing the young women students, against their will, in cars and carrying them about the streets of Tallahassee; forcibly pulling and jostling young women students and teachers about the halls of the college buildings; subjecting the young lady students to

rough handling by men on whose breath the odor of liquor was plainly perceptible; attempting to force into the mouth of young lady students and teachers the nose of a bottle containing quinine and milk, in some cases while the student was forcibly held on the grass.[46]

After Nina McAdam, a scholarship student from Miami, frankly described the incident to her parents, the Miami *Metropolis* printed her letter:

Here came all the Shriners pouring into the building and playing and shouting to beat their own band. They went into all the class rooms and declared a holiday, and if the girls wouldn't leave, they just dragged them out by main force. One teacher locked the door and they took off the hinges. They certainly were rude and vulgar. All day long they rode around here and grabbed up girls and made them ride with them. Most of the girls were thoroughly disgusted for they acted so much like wild men, most of them over 50, too. So last night the student body met and decided to write them a letter, saying that we thought they had overstepped the bounds of propriety and had damaged the dignity of the institution.[47]

Conradi encouraged students to present their own letter of protest (composed with faculty guidance) to the local Shrine organization. He hoped the people of Florida would interpret the trespass against the students as unfortunate but unavoidable, thereby making the college administration seem innocent and outraged, rather than inept. The *Flambeau* printed the Shrine reply to the students in its March 5 issue:

Your letter to Dr. O.G. Kendrick, president of the Tallahassee Shrine Club was read today at the first meeting of the Divan of Morocco Temple held since the recent ceremonial at Tallahassee. It is the unanimous sense of the Divan that any such rowdyism be severely condemned and that apologies be respectfully offered to your student body and to the State College for Women. The Divan regrets exceedingly that any Shriner should at any time act in any manner unbecoming a gentleman, and we will

> bring this whole matter before the next regular meeting of Mo-
> rocco Temple to be held in March. Further than this action of the
> student body it is understood that the faculty has communicated
> with T. E. Jordan, Potentate of Morocco Temple, and that resolu-
> tions have been placed in his hands.[48]

Thus the public learned of the incident, but both FSCW
and the Shrine organization exited the predicament grace-
fully. No mention of the fiasco ever appeared in the Jacksonville or Tallahassee newspapers. Neither did any mention of
Shrine ceremonials appear in the Tallahassee paper over the
next several years. As a result of the unfortunate events, however, the Tallahassee Chamber of Commerce and several businessmen exhibited a decidedly cool attitude toward the college for a number of years.[49]

Purity League

A more serious attack leveled against Conradi, science
professors at FSCW, and even the University of Florida filled
newspapers statewide in 1926 and remained in the public
forum for three years. It began as a well-meaning attempt on
Conradi's part to hire the best faculty possible for the college.
For several years he had wanted to divide the teaching
responsibilities for philosophy and psychology and add a program of applied psychology and educational measurements
to the curriculum.[50] When psychology professor Hayden died,
Conradi hired Dr. Basil Blaine Bassett to teach philosophy
and Dr. Paul F. Finner to teach psychology and direct a psychology laboratory. However, Conradi and Dodd found
Bassett's performance unsatisfactory and decided not to
reappoint him at the end of the summer session.[51] In his place
they employed Dr. Walter Scott McNutt, who not only held a
Ph.D. but also was an ordained Presbyterian minister in the
Presbytery of North Florida.[52] Though hired to teach philosophy, McNutt spent much of his time during his first year on
classes in education and general psychology. Both Salley in

education and Finner in psychology gave Dodd unfavorable reports of his work.[53]

In his second year, McNutt taught only philosophy. His students complained that "his work in class showed little or no evidence of organization or certainty of purpose."[54] He spent much of the class time relating how learned he was and often made the observation that certain philosophical writers took their ideas from him. He seemed oblivious to the fact that those men had written their books 30 years earlier. By the second semester, students remarked openly that his class was a good place in which to bring personal correspondence up to date. One girl related that on her parallel reading assignments for one of his courses she listed only fictitious books and authors, and he made no objection to her choices. Louise Richardson reported that she repeatedly rebuked students for referring to the teacher as "Boob" McNutt. Dr. Alban Stewart of the Department of Botany and Bacteriology flatly refused to allow Ruth Schornherst, one of his major students and his lab assistant, to take a course with McNutt.[55]

Conradi and Dodd cautioned McNutt at the end of the 1924–25 session that, if he failed to overcome his classroom difficulties during the next year, they would not recommend him for reappointment. In March 1926, Conradi advised McNutt that he planned to ask the Board of Control to drop him from the faculty at the college. According to the president, McNutt threatened to "show up some things of the college."[56] He enlisted the assistance of fellow Presbyterian L.A. Tatum, a relative newcomer to Tallahassee and an elder in the very church Conradi and his family attended. Together McNutt and Tatum mounted a campaign that dovetailed with anti-evolutionist activity in the state and nation.

In the first half of the 1920s, North Florida provided fertile ground for the growth of religious fundamentalism. William Jennings Bryan, spokesperson for the national movement, made Miami his permanent residence in 1921.[57] As a moderate fundamentalist, he provided leadership for conservative,

Southern Protestant Floridians. In furthering the fundamentalist cause, he sparked a national drive for laws to protest the teaching of evolution, with positive results mainly in the South. In Florida, he worked behind the scenes and managed to get the 1923 Legislature to pass a resolution that declared:

> It is improper and subversive to the best interests of the people of this State for any professor, teacher or instructor in the public schools and colleges of this State, supported in whole or in part by public taxation, to teach or permit to be taught atheism, agnosticism, or to teach as true Darwinism, or any other hypothesis that links man in blood relation to any other form of life.[58]

Conradi made no public comment regarding the resolution. A. A. Murphree at the University of Florida claimed he agreed with his close friend Bryan, but he stipulated that he did not object to the theory of organic evolution, only to its being taught in a manner that upset religious faith.[59] Because the resolution lacked legal penalties for noncompliance, it failed to discourage the teaching of evolution. Two years later, when anti-evolutionists attempted to strengthen the proclamation and impose legal restrictions on those who imparted such heresy, Bryan had shifted his attention to the Scopes Trial in Dayton, Tennessee. He died shortly thereafter; the Florida bill never came out of committee. A Clearwater realtor and good friend of Bryan's took up his mantle and, in November 1925, announced the inauguration of a campaign to ban the teaching of evolution and "German philosophy" in tax-supported schools. He appealed first to Governor John Martin and then to State School Superintendent W. S. Cawthon to either delete all references to evolution from Florida texts or remove the offensive books entirely from the schools.[60]

Fundamentalists McNutt and Tatum entered the anti-evolution fray in April 1926. The lame duck philosophy teacher, while remaining in the background, gave Tatum information about textbooks and reading assignments used by several professors, including Sociology Department Head Raymond

Bellamy, whom he believed had prejudiced Conradi against him. Though McNutt's name was never publicly connected with any of Tatum's activities, Conradi and later Murphree became convinced that he ghost-wrote the script for the ensuing events. Tatum, armed with half-truths and his own sense of righteousness, appeared before the Board of Control and charged that through the use of several books promoting "German kultur" and others that were, according to him, satires on American religion, "there is being taught, and every effort made to implant into the minds of the students, ideas altogether foreign to Southern tradition and chivalry."[61] He left the books, their objectionable passages clearly marked, with the board members for their perusal.

Tatum returned to the next board meeting to make certain that the members had read the pertinent sections in the books he had left with them. He drew their attention to various passages from Freud's *The Interpretation of Dreams* that contained sexual connotations. He then took special care to point out that Van Teslaar's *Psychoanalysis* contained five lectures concerning Freud and psychoanalysis that had been translated from German and delivered by a Fellow in Psychology at Clark University, Conradi's and Bellamy's alma mater.[62] To tie his crusade to that of the 1925 Florida Legislature, he quoted Van Teslaar as saying "psychoanalysis represents but an extension of the theory of evolution, an application of the principle of evolution to the study of the mind." He concluded his presentation with the remark, "Florida State College for Women is sadly in need of a genuine house cleaning, including therein removal of its present president."[63]

Conradi replied that none of the professors at the college taught as true "any theory that is in conflict with the biblical story of the creation of man." As to the textbooks declared objectionable, most were "used in . . . state universities, women's colleges, denominational colleges and universities, and privately endowed colleges and universities throughout the country." The Van Teslaar book, no longer used at FSCW, consisted of a collection of articles by 12 different writers, only five of which were assigned reading.[64]

The matter simmered for several months with no overt action until the spring of 1927, when another proposal to ban teaching of evolution was introduced in the legislature. Educators in the state's public and private colleges and universities condemned the bill. President Murphree of the University of Florida, a staunch fundamentalist, declared that his faculty consisted of Christian gentlemen, "no one of whom would permit the use of books . . . that would undermine the moral life of a young man or shake his faith in the Bible." He opposed the bill on the grounds that it subjected Florida to ridicule. Hamilton Holt, president of Rollins College, signified his opposition and revealed that he had refused a large endowment offered to his institution when the donor had demanded that he exclude evolution from the curriculum.[65] Most state newspapers implied that the proposed legislation was ill-advised at best. No comment came from the women's college. The bill passed the House but died in the Senate Education Committee. Instead, the senate adopted a politically flexible resolution that provided for a committee to scrutinize state texts and report to the Board of Education, which would then remove all those deemed "detrimental to good morals and clean thinking." Outraged, the *Florida State News* declared that most of the legislators were incompetent to teach grade school, let alone censor college texts.[66]

The turn of events delighted Tatum. Now aided by several deacons from the local First Baptist Church, he renewed his attack against evolution. He created and headed the Florida Purity League, dedicated to ridding all state libraries of objectionable publications and all state schools of "dangerous teachers."[67] In August 1927, Tatum requested that the two state schools remove certain works from their libraries, among them Sigmund Freud's *General Introduction to Psychology*, H.G. Wells's *Outline of History*, D.H. Lawrence's *Sons and Lovers,* and George Bernard Shaw's *Man and Superman.* Conradi and Murphree refused to remove the books completely, but agreed to restrict their use to faculty members and certain students, in order to decrease the possibility of their abuse "as a result of the unfortunate advertising they have received from Mr. Tatum."[68] The Board of Control and the Board of Education formally approved the presidents' actions and endorsed their positions.

Tatum continued his attack, determined to open the public's eyes to the scandalous situation that he believed existed. He contended that

> the greater percentage of books in use in our State institutions of higher learning in the State of Florida, as well as throughout the nation, are the product of infidel writers [and] the same holds equally true as to instructors in these same institutions.[69]

He printed bulletins containing much of the material to which he objected, and distributed them statewide. He continued to add works to his book list. Murphree died unexpectedly in 1927, but before his death he effectively removed the university from the fray. In order to make the volumes in question accessible to professors, who "need to combat the evil propaganda now being broadcast over the country," he placed the materials in a locked recess of the library. According to Carl Van Ness, Archivist at the University of Florida, many years later when the library underwent renovation and restoration, the books were found in their locked closet, and no one knew why they were there.[70]

Conradi initiated his own investigation, determined to prove what he already believed, that a disgruntled faculty member had instigated Tatum's attack. He demanded that every science professor deliver to his office a list of text books and required reading assignments used over the past several years. As the president made accusations based on misunderstandings and mistaken identities, the campus atmosphere became decidedly uncomfortable. Unintentionally illustrating the absurdity of the prevailing mood, Classics professor Game wrote to Conradi,

> I [Game] was calling on Professor Williams and his family on the evening of Sept. 19. As my close personal friend of many years, Professor [Williams] told me that you [Conradi] had told him [Williams] that Professor Finner had told you [Conradi] that Dr. Kendrick had told him [Finner] that I [Game] had prepared the list of Library books which had been under investigation.[71]

Game then confronted Dr. Kendrick, who admitted:

> When I [Kendrick] made the statement that [one of the deacons] told me you [Game] had given information to Mr. Tatum, I was mistaken, for I find upon asking him again that he says it was Dr. McNutt, and not you at all.[72]

Conradi ordered Librarian Louise Richardson to search the library for any and all books that appeared on Tatum's list, an exercise that Richardson reported took an additional 52 hours of her time.[73] Meanwhile, the president addressed the college Scientific Society and stressed the essential harmony of science and religion.[74]

Tatum escalated his attack by spreading a rumor that Bellamy had told his summer school class that "the white race of the South would in a very few more generations become imbeciles unless they intermixed with the [N]egro race."[75] The students themselves squelched that rumor quickly with a signed resolution to the effect that such a charge was "an absolute untruth" and the entire hullabaloo "a gross misrepresentation of facts as to what is being taught here at the college." The young ladies further stipulated that

> we resent the reflection these charges imply against our character, our ideals, and our intelligence as young women, and must here express our utter surprise that men who claim to be gentlemen could persist in making such false charges and casting such

reflections upon our character. It is unthinkable that any group of young women with character and intelligence would peaceably accept such teaching as is charged by the accusers.[76]

The Purity League was quickly becoming an embarrassment to the state. The Florida Presbytery disassociated itself from Tatum. Conradi and Bellamy requested, received, and advertised confirmation from publishing houses that most leading universities used those texts singled out by the league. The Tallahassee Chamber of Commerce, not one of the college's most enthusiastic supporters in the recent past, publicly stated what others were thinking about the Purity League:

> We are not in sympathy with your propaganda against the Florida State College for Women, Dr. Edward Conradi and the faculty of the college. It is our opinion that your propaganda is distasteful to the vast majority. Not only to the people at Tallahassee, but to those of the State of Florida who are at all familiar with it. The students and faculty of FSCW are many times welcome with us. We believe them to be a body with ideals and intelligence of the highest type, and we deplore the continued attack upon them.[77]

Friedreich von Falkenberg, city editor for the *Florida State News*, brought the whole sorry episode to a conclusion with two very sensible suggestions to Conradi. First, he implied that since the Purity League was attempting to sell its pamphlets, an action contrary to copyright laws, if the college conveyed this information to the publishers of the reference books cited, those publishers would undoubtedly take legal action. Second, he conjectured that Tatum could probably be prosecuted "under the statute which prohibits the publication and dissemination of obscene literature," with reference to the excerpts he had reprinted (out of context) from the books he found objectionable.[78]

In the fall of 1928, the college offered two courses in Bible and religious education, taught by Arthur Williams and Dr. J.B. Game.[79] Nothing further was heard from McNutt,

Tatum, or the Purity League in Florida. However, a column in the *Chapel Hill Weekly*, some four years, later opened with "The tirade launched last week by L. A. Tatum against the University and the North Carolina College for Women. . . ."[80]

❧

To the administration, the 1920s probably seemed an endless stream of adversity. Nevertheless, the need to explain questionable positions and to respond to various challenges shaped the future of the college. The people of Florida, their elected representatives, and both supporters and detractors of the state educational system learned that in many instances FSCW and its administration could define and would stand firm for what it believed to be in the best interests of the young women of the state.

T he changing social mores of the 1920s surprised and dismayed the college administration. The greater number of students in itself caused problems for dormitory matrons and housekeeping staff, who now found it extremely difficult to remember all the names and faces of those under their supervision. New inventions such as radios brought the outside world right into the residence halls. An unwelcome proliferation of automobiles gave students easy access to locations beyond the observation of college authorities. Long before parents, faculty, or administrators were willing to make policy adjustments, students adopted new styles and attitudes. With or without permission, they stepped into the modern age. While they remained loyal to the institution, they spoke out against perceived injustices more frequently than had the young ladies of years past, and they willingly challenged those customs and regulations that they considered to be unfair, outmoded, or overly restrictive.

COMING AND GOING

By the 1920s, transportation to and from Tallahassee and FSCW was available via train, bus, or private automobile. Frequently, families who lived within 50 or so miles of the college purchased their first car to transport a daughter to and from Tallahassee, but students were not allowed to keep their own automobiles on campus or in town unless they lived with their families.[1] In September, at Christmas, and in June, railroad lines added special trains or extra coaches to their routes from Miami, Jacksonville, Tampa, and Pensacola. If a train schedule involved a late night or very early hour arrival, the railway companies sidetracked the sleeper cars in Tallahassee so the college-bound passengers could sleep until daylight.[2] Representatives of the school always met the trains and escorted the girls to campus.

For departures from Tallahassee, representatives of both the Seaboard Air Line Railroad and the Georgia, Florida, and Alabama Railroad (known locally as the Gopher, Frog, and Alligator line) sold tickets and trunk tags from the campus business office. A typical end-of-the-year exodus entailed two separate trains from Tallahassee, one at 10:15 A.M. for underclassmen, and another at 11:00 that night for graduates, junior ushers, sophomore sisters, and others who remained for Commencement exercises. The later train included a baggage car, two coaches, one parlor car to Jacksonville, and five sleeper cars to Tampa, Fort Myers, Lakeland, and Miami. By September 1928, Seaboard Air Line found it needed 13 additional sleepers added to four regular trains to convey new and returning students to the campus.[3]

DAY BY DAY

In 1920, a new generation of students matriculated at colleges all over the country. At the various women's colleges in New England, self-assured young ladies

arrived for the fall semester with their hair radically shingled, their skirts shortened almost to the knee and a new and startling vocabulary that included words like libido, repression, and carburetor. They all were ready for a changed world, but once inside the Victorian iron gates of their colleges they were handed copies of rulebooks . . . that hadn't seen any substantial revisions in 50 years. Chapel was still mandatory, curfew was still 10 P.M. on week nights, motoring was allowed only under certain circumstances, and smoking was forbidden.[4]

Those young ladies who enrolled at Florida State College for Women differed very little from their Northern counterparts. In Tallahassee, college officers tried to ignore changing customs and maintain an atmosphere of traditional Southern gentility, but their efforts came to naught. Mrs. Cawthon, Dean of the College Home, counseled her girls on proper dress,[5] but hemlines continued to rise alarmingly, first to nine inches above the ground, then to knee length and above! Dietitian Anna May Tracy, taken aback by the increasingly casual clothing fashions of the decade, posted a notice: "Until established custom approves of bare legs as being in good taste for all occasions, I must ask that you do not come into the Dining Room without stockings on."[6]

Miss Mamie Lewis, a Chi Omega patroness who ardently believed that a lady was well dressed "if when she left a room no one could remember what she had on," offered the sorority chapter "a goodly sum of money" if every member agreed to forgo makeup for one year.[7] Her offer went begging. Mrs. Cawthon's admonitions concerning "the vulgar habit of gum chewing" failed to make much difference at a time when one of the most popular songs in the country was "Does the Spearmint Lose Its Flavor on the Bedpost Overnight?" A few years later gum chewers still abounded and even put their gum on the tile walls as they entered the new Gymnasium swimming pool.[8]

Neither Mrs. Cawthon nor anyone else could combat the popularity of shorter hair. Freshman Omar Davis, recently returned from an extensive tour abroad, introduced the first bobbed hairstyle to the college in the fall of 1919. Soon there were so many short haircuts on campus a rumor arose that Dean Dodd planned to open a barber shop and make bobs compulsory. According to a 1924 *Flambeau* survey, 69 percent of the students wore their hair even with their ears.[9]

The college assiduously upheld its smoking ban, however. Until the end of World War I, there was never any question of tobacco use among young ladies of good character.

During the 1920s, as cigarette smoking became a symbol of the liberated college woman, its increasing popularity became another source of friction between administration and students. The president of the Class of 1920 recalled that, "smoking was simply taboo!" By mid-decade, amidst changing attitudes toward women's smoking, other colleges recognized the difficulty in enforcing or defending a regulation that went against public opinion. Many institutions opted to set aside smoking rooms or areas to avoid smokers sneaking about.[10] The conservative Southern attitude regarding young ladies smoking cigarettes did not change, though, and the FSCW administration refused to consider such accommodations. The college handbook stated the administration's position under "Laws of Honor":

> The individual must subordinate her wishes to the rights of the community, and hence students may not smoke while they are members of the College Government Association.[11]

For "rights of the community" many students read "demands of the administration" and continued to smoke whenever and wherever possible. The college enforced its edict strictly, as one young lady learned when she was put on full restrictions indefinitely for smoking a cigarette while sitting in a car parked on College Avenue. No females associated with the college, students or faculty, were allowed to smoke in dormitories, sorority houses, off-campus residence houses, other college buildings, on college property, or in any public place until well into the 1930s. Male faculty members, in a custom typical of the time, gathered behind the Administration Building between classes to smoke their cigarettes and pipes.[12]

TRADITIONS

As the number of students, particularly from out-of-state, increased, the young ladies were exposed to more divergent attitudes. To combat inescapable outside influences, the college continued to create and embellish insular campus traditions. Most students looked forward to the rituals as a source of security in their new environment. One of these was the celebration of Conradi's birthday. It evolved inadvertently from Mrs. Cawthon's habit of taking several seniors with her on Sunday evenings to call on friends in town, an activity that introduced the young ladies to Tallahassee society and furthered the relationship between town and gown. One evening the group stopped at the Conradi residence on the corner of College Avenue and Macomb Street to deliver birthday wishes to the president.[13]

Two years later, on the evening of Conradi's birthday, the entire student body assembled at the gates and marched down College Avenue singing. They gathered at Conradi's front porch, and each class president called out greetings. By 1924, Mrs. Cawthon abandoned Sunday evening social calls, but with the help of Miss Tracy the birthday celebration flourished. The student body offered a serenade, and the seniors presented the president with a cake baked and decorated in the college bakery. The Conradis invited everyone in for refreshments. Gradually the celebration assumed formal elements. The senior class assumed responsibility for the cake, and the other classes conceived suitable gifts of their own. Each year the juniors presented a book, the sophomores gave candy, and the freshmen brought flowers from the college garden.[14]

Other ceremonies, soon to become traditions, evolved throughout the decade. One, new in 1920, recognized members of the senior class in a special investiture ceremony. The investiture service extended the relationship between classes derived initially through participation in the Freshman-Junior wedding. Early in the school year, seniors donned academic robes for the first time and marched down the left aisle of the auditorium while their sophomore sisters, dressed in white and carrying mortarboards, filed down the right aisle. After all were seated, a faculty member delivered a meaningful address. For this first event, Bellamy, senior class sponsor, spoke on the origin of the cap and gown. Then Conradi moved to the front of the stage and called each senior's name. Side by side, she and her sophomore sister ascended the steps and crossed the stage. The senior knelt in front of the president, and her sister handed him the cap, which he placed on the senior's head.[15]

In 1924, the investiture service introduced a hymn, "Day is Dying in the West," that the college adopted as a favorite grace for the Dining Hall. The ceremony that year drew attention to the remarkable growth of the college, for there were too many seniors (117) to be called individually. Instead, the upperclassmen and their sophomore sisters proceeded in twos across the stage; each duo paused briefly in front of Conradi while he took the cap from the sophomore and placed it on the senior's head. As the college continued to grow, the status of seniors and the ceremony itself lost some of its significance. In 1929, with 209 seniors to be invested, the service became part of a regularly scheduled convocation.[16]

Another tradition that created an attachment to classmates and the campus was Sophomore Week, first devised in the fall of 1917. During this week the older but wiser sophomores introduced the new freshmen to their duties and responsibilities as neophyte collegians. Soon what had started as harmless fun for sophomores turned into an ordeal for freshmen. In 1921, the faculty voiced serious objections to the activities. Loath to let the youngest class escape without some hazing, the sophomores agreed to restrict the harassment to a single day. That year they ordered freshmen to appear on campus

> with hair divided exactly in the middle, the right-hand side arranged as usual, the left-hand side braided into three equal braids and tied with string; faces to be divided down middle with right-hand side creamed and left-hand side rouged and powdered;

wear raincoat belted with organdy sash and bedroom slippers; books to be carried to classes in wastebaskets balanced on heads.[17]

For the remainder of the week, only special "rat caps" on the newcomers' heads proclaimed the observance of Sophomore Week. At 8:00 P.M. Saturday, sophomores carried lighted pine torches around the darkened Administration Building and met the freshmen at the fountain. The girls piled their flambeaus onto a bonfire, which lit the circle for ensuing skits. Then both classes moved to the Dining Hall for a dance— girls only, of course.[18]

This abbreviated version of initiation to college life met with faculty approval. The practice reappeared each fall over the next three years and gained considerable notoriety in cities all over the state. Girls contemplating matriculation at FSCW read descriptions of "Sophomore Day (the day the Sophs reign supreme over the 'Rats')" in their local newspapers.[19] Reports warned that the "poor Rats" of 1923 (Class of 1927) were required to

wear white dresses with pillows stuffed inside and 27 stripes of black crepe paper around the dress (the pillows were pincushion size for a buxom effect, and evoked much hilarity in the flat-chested flapper era); put nail white on lips; plait hair in 27 plaits; back out every door; every time a Freshman met a Soph, she had to coo-coo 27 times; bow 25 times to a Senior.[20]

The news reports, however, were exaggerated. That fall 500 girls, the largest freshman class yet in the college's history, assembled at 9:00 A.M. Saturday wearing their dresses turned wrong side out and backwards, with their faces made up with lipstick for eyebrow pencil and vice versa, and carrying laundry bags that contained their school supplies.[21]

During World War I, the junior class had discontinued the Junior-Senior "prom," the one really big event in the spring social calendar. The event had been the only time that the administration allowed men in many areas of the campus.

However, couples had only "promenaded" on a predetermined, lighted, and chaperoned course instead of dancing. The path usually went around the Administration Building and fountain and back to Bryan Hall; then couples returned to the Atrium for refreshments.[22] Now that same administration exchanged the students' opportunity to entertain young men for an all-female May Day celebration that again focused attention on the presumed sisterhood of sophomores and seniors.

The new celebration took place on the first Monday in May. It began early in the morning with a Southern breakfast of boiled ham, hot biscuits, shoestring potatoes, and coffee served on the lawn in front of Bryan Hall. Following the meal, students in physical education classes performed a Maypole dance. At twilight everyone gathered under the pines behind the Administration Building to crown the May Queen, a senior selected for her beauty. To end this special day, after light flash the sophomores serenaded the seniors.[23]

A considerable transformation in campus life began in June 1925, when Mrs. Cawthon left the college after 15 years as Dean of the College Home. Failing health precipitated her resignation,[24] but Conradi gave the students no reason for her leave-taking; he implied that she was visiting in Virginia. The *Flambeau* noted her absence with sadness:

> The best years of her life have been spent in building up campus and citizenship, a home atmosphere for her girls in college. Every problem that came to them was her personal problem also, and worked out with them at any sacrifice. . . .[25]

The college, and to a very great extent Conradi, had relied on the beloved Tissie as the arbiter of good taste and social values. With her leaving, everyone realized there would be a time of adjustment. But neither the administration nor the students were prepared for the reorganization of daily life that came about when Conradi selected Dr. Mina Kerr, Executive Secretary of the American Association of University Women, as the new Dean of the College Home. Dr. Kerr had received a bachelor's degree from Smith College and a Ph.D. from the University of Pennsylvania, had served as dean at colleges in Wisconsin and Massachusetts, and during the past few summers had lectured in Columbia University's summer school on the problems of deans of women. Though highly qualified for her new position, she lacked an understanding of traditional Southern attitudes regarding women and made the colossal mistake of trying to wrest the college from the grips of its past in several short months. According to Dodd, "Dr. Kerr immediately dropped the word 'Home' from her title and proceeded to officiate as sort of super-Dean."[26]

In the first of her two years at the college, Kerr found conditions too adolescent and took issue with most of the established traditions. Sophomore Day was the first casualty. In what the *Flambeau* called a "joyless time on campus," ceremonial elements of the freshman initiation into college life vanished. Instead, sophomores carried torches from Bryan Hall to the front of the Administration Building, where they met the freshman class. They threw the torches down in two piles, one bonfire for each class. Then everyone proceeded to the dining room for an all-girl dance. Only the jazz music, allowed for the first time on campus and played by the college orchestra, lifted the girls spirits.[27]

Kerr remained oblivious to the discontent she created and continued cutting her swath through the established system. In February 1926, she addressed the Hillsborough branch of the AAUW. After her presentation, she commented to a *Tampa Tribune* reporter that the state allocated only $19 per month for each girl's room and board, an amount she considered too paltry to keep Florida's college women on a level with those of other states. In her opinion, the students were "not adequately housed nor adequately fed because of insufficient financial support."[28] Since more than ten percent of students at the college were from Hillsborough County, Kerr's statements had the potential to do serious damage to enrollment figures. Business Manager J.G. Kellum immediately took umbrage with her comments in spite of their fiscal accuracy. He privately asked Miss Tracy to review her menus and change them, if necessary, to "provide proper and adequate food and also [ensure] that the same is properly cooked and served."[29]

Miss Tracy responded with menus and caloric information that indicated the dining room daily offered each student an average of 2,445 calories. On a typical day, the fare included grapefruit, cream of wheat, cocoa, coffee, and biscuits for breakfast; for lunch, creamed asparagus on toast, fruit salad, jelly (gelatin), and raisin cookies; dinner might be Swiss steak, mashed potatoes, string beans, celery, and chocolate meringue pie. Tracy even supervised special tables for girls who were underweight. The college physician and dietitian jointly determined eligibility for the "get fatters." For an extra 75¢ per week, girls at these tables received an additional dish such as custard, a baked potato, or ice cream and between-meal-snacks such as milk and fruit juice.[30]

Kellum made certain that the press carried Tracy's observations as rebuttal to those of Kerr. But Kerr's remarks concerned enough girls and their families that many began eating lunch and dinner at the Three Torches or the Wisteria Tea Room, restaurants near the college. Conradi eventually forbade all students who lived on campus from taking meals outside the college Dining Hall.[31]

Despite Kerr's ineptitude, not all the changes she wrought were ill-conceived. Because of her influence, graduates of the college became eligible for full membership in the AAUW. She encouraged two outstanding professors and members of that organization, Dr. Kathryn Abbey and Dr. Bessie Randolph, to relocate to Tallahassee and FSCW. She also convinced the administration that its ban on card-playing was outdated, although the dormitory matrons refused to condone such a threat to morals on Sundays. Shortly thereafter the game of bridge surpassed other spare-time activities on campus.[32]

But some things were never the same again. Dr. Olivia Dorman, who had quickly become a favorite of students when she arrived in 1924, stepped into the female leadership void that developed during Kerr's last year on campus and restored some unity to the classes. She helped the sophomores meld some of their Sophomore Day ceremony with more sophisticated imagery to reestablish a meaningful connection between their class and the new freshmen. Sophomores who missed the formal initiation of freshmen into campus life were delighted with the classical connotations of Torchnight, a new ceremony in which members of their class "passed the torch" to the newcomers. The Athletic Association coordinated the ceremony, in which each freshman accepted a burning flambeau from a sophomore and vowed to carry its flame on high. The administration hoped it would become a "tradition to hand the lighted torches of FSCW down through the years from one sophomore class to the next."[33]

The Freshman-Junior Wedding fell victim to Kerr, also. In November 1925, she watched incredulously as a collegiate congregation assembled before a white trellis adorned with greenery and violet chrysanthemums. Standing under the bower, Conradi officiated at the nuptials of Jess A. Freshman and Loy Al Junior. The following fall, a Ceremony of Fealty united the two classes. The juniors, previously the groom and family, still represented the masculine element of the presentation. A junior knight presided over a special cake with a ring baked into it. Each of several freshman ladies cut a slice of the cake; the one who found the ring was named the knight's Lady.[34]

In the fall of 1927, Charlotte Beckham succeeded the hapless Kerr in the position of Dean of Students rather than Dean of the College Home. In spite of the change in title, Conradi hoped that Beckham, a native of Texas with family ties to South Carolina and Virginia, viewed her position as less that of a dean and more that of a substitute mother to the girls, as had Tissie.[35] Instead, Beckham paid more attention to her personal social aspirations than to the socialization of the students. When she did concentrate on her responsibilities as dean, however, she directed student loyalty to the school rather than individual classes, and she encouraged the college to adopt the more modern attitudes introduced by her immediate predecessor.

STUDENTS VERSUS THE COLLEGE

In the fall of 1925, the college resumed Monday classes, suspended in 1910 when Conradi first came to FSCW, but retained those held on Saturdays. This ill-conceived attempt to deal with overcrowded classrooms caused resentment among students, many of whom disregarded the new schedules and skipped classes whenever they felt overworked. To ensure Monday attendance, Conradi required teachers to personally call roll at the beginning of every class and to sign students' excuses when they returned to class after an absence.[36]

At the same time, the administration devised a new grading system that used letters rather than numbers, and assigned quality points relative to course units. An "A" equaled 3 quality points (per credit hour or course unit), a "B" equaled 2 points, and a "C" equaled 1 point. The school required students to have at least as many quality points as units of course work in order to graduate.[37] In other words, a student had to maintain a "C" average or better.

When girls continued to skip classes, particularly on Saturdays and Mondays, the administration decided to cut one quality point for each missed class and to count tardiness as an absence. Under this plan, if a student had an "A" in a class at the end of the term but also had three unexcused absences in that class, she got no credit for the course. To offset this strict new attendance policy, the college instituted a week-long vacation at Easter, something students had requested for several years.[38]

The *Flambeau* surprised the administration by voicing strong opposition to the new cut policy. Reprimanded for outspokenness, the editor modified the paper's tone but not its objections. In the very next issue, the editorial staff informed students that they had no choice but to accept the cut system, fair or not, and offered this advice:

> Girls, please notify your families not to come visit you at any time except Easter, because you cannot serve two masters. You cannot be in classes and with your family at the same time. Classes on Saturday and classes on Monday and no absences allowed literally tie you hand and foot. So write the family and tell them to save the old flivver until you can enjoy it. All work and no play makes the FSCW girl what we don't want her to be.[39]

Since many students felt cutting class was a rejection of the honor code, the basis of self-government on the campus, the brouhaha raised questions about the effectiveness of the Student Government Association. Again the *Flambeau* spoke up for its constituents, claiming that "the only thing student government can do is restrict girls from being out of their homes after last light flash" and suggesting that the college "abolish student government so they were no longer honor bound to abide by ridiculous rules supposedly made by students."[40] The Student Government Association, as established in 1913, elected officers who "acted in consultation with a committee appointed from the faculty." At that time, unaware that the system served the administration as "the method of college discipline,"[41] the girls had been quite pleased with the small measure of autonomy granted them by their constitution. The students of 1925 saw the limitations of the system rather than the opportunities.

Since the administration had felt for some time that student demands were excessive, they now took advantage of the unrest to assume more supervisory control over activities. The administration reordered student government, but changed only the description of the organization, not the disciplinary intent. The new College Government Association was a

> cooperative organization between students and faculty [whose] purpose is to promote the highest standards of honor and integrity in personal conduct; to encourage cooperation between faculty and students in all matters of college government; to enact and enforce regulations and to foster an intelligent interest in college citizenship; and to increase a sense of individual responsibility in every student.[42]

A Judiciary and a Student Senate replaced the Executive Committee; other offices remained the same. Subtle wording changes implied that the faculty had only the best interests of the college at heart and that lack of cooperation cast aspersions on the honor, integrity, and intelligence of fellow students.

The young ladies of the 1920s made no bones about their displeasure with the revision. They pointed out that the name change from Student Government Association to College Government Association implied they were no longer in control of affairs. They particularly objected to having the faculty involved in the management of student organizations "because the faculty does not consult the students."[43]

Beckham and the administration tried to appease campus leaders. Rather than the faculty proposing the slate of student officers for the next year, they permitted the girls to hold a primary election for the first time. They allowed students to serve on faculty standing committees such as the Health Committee, which worked for the best possible health conditions on campus, and the Usher Committee, which provided ushers for all events that took place in the auditorium. Other opportunities for committee service included presenting each organization's books to the appropriate faculty committee for annual audits and assisting the library staff in creating better conditions in that area. Still, the girls felt their contributions were meager at best. Even the student song leader, who led the singing at special gatherings, had her selections scrutinized by members of the faculty before each event.[44]

On the other hand, several changes that occurred during Beckham's tenure encouraged independence on the part of the students. For one, the crusade against six days of classes was eventually resolved in the students' favor. Saturday class meetings ceased in 1928. The campus returned to a more normal Monday through Friday schedule. The *Flambeau* publication day shifted from Saturday to Friday. Wash women picked up clothes on Mondays rather than Tuesdays and returned them to the campus on Fridays instead of Saturdays.[45]

Another meaningful change came about when the faculty allowed the College Government Association to reinstate the Junior-Senior Prom—as a real dance. The college had never permitted students to dance with men, either on campus or in Tallahassee. They were, however, allowed to attend properly authorized and chaperoned dances at the University of Florida. It is unclear what role the locale played in the acceptability of dancing with members of the opposite sex. At long last, in the spring of 1928, the college permitted the students to host a real Junior-Senior Prom. Beckham advised the girls that this action expressed the faculty's trust and confidence in their integrity and good judgement and that "if they behaved themselves this year, maybe the prom [could] be held again next year." With this admonition in mind, young ladies planned their prom, and the various sororities planned open houses and tea dances.[46]

During the 1920s, restructured chapel requirements offered the most telling evidence that the administration was reluctantly but inevitably acceding to changing social values. In 1921, the administration experimented with optional attendance for seniors. The *Flambeau* argued that in order to perpetuate school spirit, the half-hour daily service with speakers and pertinent announcements needed the full support of the students. But seniors, whose attitude toward an activity largely determined the campus attitude, seldom attended chapel except on Fridays, when failure to do so brought a 25¢ fine.[47] The following year saw the return of mandatory chapel for all.

In the spring of 1926, an article in the University of Florida *Alligator* criticized authorities there for trying to force the Christian religion on students. A. A. Murphree replaced that school's mandatory chapel with a "Compulsory Assembly," and Conradi subsequently referred to the FSCW gathering as a "Convocation." In 1927, the administration reduced the number of convocations per week from five to four and required seniors to wear their caps and gowns on Fridays. Members of both the Freshman Commission and Freshman Cabinet, training programs for the College Government Association and YWCA respectively, double-checked attendance. A majority of the girls still resisted, but the college insisted all dormitory residents and any day students on campus at the time attend.[48]

By 1929, the college held convocation only on Tuesdays and Thursdays, but attendance remained mandatory. Each class had assigned positions: seniors sat in the center front, sophomores directly behind them; freshmen flanked the center, and juniors sat in the wings. At the same time, the college recognized that its ability to supervise off-campus morality had decreased as the number of students increased. The administration no longer felt capable of monitoring weekly church participation. Since only 24 of more than 1,500 registered students claimed no church affiliation, the college felt relatively safe in relying on family training to ensure attendance at religious services. Church attendance, once mandatory, was now simply "expected."[49]

SPORTS ACTIVITIES

Athletic exploits continued to play an important part in college life, but as the student body increased in number, only those truly interested in pursuing an active physical program participated on a regular basis. Field Day popularity waxed and waned with the prowess of the participants and the enthusiasm of particular classes. In 1922, the Athletic Association decided to encourage participation in the events by awarding a banner to the class that exhibited the most spirit rather than to a single student.[50]

One outstanding athlete, Anne Harwick, captured the attention of the entire student body. This track star extraordinaire represented the college at a national track meet in New York, where she took first place in the javelin throw with a distance of 127'10". That accomplishment qualified her to represent Florida at the Women's International Track and Field Meet to be held in Paris in August, in correlation with the 1922 Olympics.[51]

The school raised money for her travel expenses. Letters went out to all Florida Chamber of Commerce groups asking for their financial support for the overseas trip. A hurriedly planned basketball game between residents of Broward and Reynolds Halls netted more than $20 from Summer School students. The City of Tallahassee dug into its coffers and added $130 to the travel fund. Members of the Athletic Association sold candy at a local drug store to raise more money. To prove she had the potential to win, Harwick gave a free public demonstration of her javelin throwing talents. Somehow the school managed to raise $1,500 to send its athlete to Paris as vice-captain of the American team. She won a silver medal for the baseball throw and placed third in the 300 meter dash, but ironically she was unable to compete in the javelin event "because of overtraining."[52]

After 1922, interest in Field Day was confined primarily to the younger classes. In 1923, sophomore Katherine Prime broke the world's record in the discus throw (already held by FSCW) and led her class to victory. In her junior year she broke the college and national records for both baseball and discus throws. For the remainder of the decade no records were broken, and Field Day enthusiasm lagged. In an attempt to bolster interest in athletic events, the Athletic Association adopted a new seal, a scroll with three torches on a garnet background with a gold block letter "F" superimposed over the design. Members of the F Club, organized in 1920 to unite "wearers of the F" (those athletes who had won an F for excellence on a varsity [inter-class] team or first place in a field day or tennis event), were eligible for a seal when they earned seven letters.[53] But most students now saved their athletic enthusiasm for Odd/Even events at Thanksgiving.

Competition between Odds and Evens remained keen and Thanksgiving continued to be the focal point.[54] Pep demon-strations presented on Tuesday and Wednesday nights pre-ceding the Thursday morning contests highlighted the holi-day week. Tradition held that the side that took the stage on Wednesday night had the advantage in the next day's game. Regardless of the demonstration night, Evens draped in sheets gathered around a huge bonfire to sing Even songs and hold a general pep rally after the Tuesday presentation—and after light flash. Odds always staged a pajama parade after lights out on Wednesday for their pep rally. In early parades, each Odd had carried a lantern made from a shoe box, red paper, and a candle, and had proceeded from Bryan Hall to East Hall. By the 1920s, a long line of Odds wearing elaborate pajamas over street clothes and carrying glowing Japanese lanterns wound through the dormitories, around the foun-tain, out the gates and down College Avenue to the president's house, where they cheered him with Odd yells.[55]

Enthusiasm for the holiday games ran high. In 1924, Katherine Montgomery added a volleyball game to the day's activities to enable a greater number of students to partici-pate. In 1926, the college officially declared Thanksgiving as Homecoming. Alumnae usually returned for the annual Odd/Even games; Miss Tracy prepared a festive turkey dinner with all the trimmings. Guest tickets for alumnae and parents went on sale at the cashier's office. Dormitories found space for all who wanted to stay the night. Miss Tracy served breakfast on Thursday at 7:30 A.M. and a formal holiday meal at 2:00 P.M. That year Odds won the mid-morning volleyball game, and

Evens won the basketball game. For the remainder of the decade, the college repeated the annual athletic contests on Thanksgiving Day with the exception of 1928, when the unexpected death of Mrs. Conradi cast a pall over the holiday and caused postponement of the games until a later date.[56]

Several changes occurred in the athletic program in 1929. The college created a Department of Physical Education, and the new Gymnasium opened. With space in which to work, Katherine Montgomery established a more formal program for the well-being of students. She retired the gym costumes of navy blue or black serge bloomers, white middy blouses, and long hose. In their place were one-piece cotton broad-cloth suits in a variety of solid-color pastels, and short socks. The college stocked these outfits and issued freshly laundered, heavily starched ones each week or more frequently if necessary.[57]

Beginning in 1923, students received physical examinations at the start of each term. Based on the results, the physical education program assigned a health grade of A, B, C, or D. Those girls who fell into the "A" and "B" categories participated in basketball, volleyball, soccer, hockey, tennis, golf, swimming, and dancing. Those in the "C" range played games that were less strenuous, such as archery, table tennis, chess, checkers, and croquet. About one-fourth of the students fell into the "D" category, usually those who had heart trouble or were greatly underweight; they were supposed to avoid physical exertion.[58]

Montgomery had joined forces with Dr. Anne Young, who believed in the healthful benefits of vocal training, to create "singing gymnasium" for students in the latter two classifications. The girls reported to the School of Music for their weekly required physical education time. With the completion of the new Physical Education Building, "sleeping gym" replaced "singing gym." At the west end of the balcony in the new Gymnasium was a long room furnished with cots, sheets, pillows, and pink wooly blankets. Girls were assigned an hour of rest. One of the physical education faculty members checked attendance.[59]

Since Florida residents came in frequent contact with lakes as well as the ocean and gulf, the college required every student to pass a swimming test in order to graduate. Regardless of health classification, for her own safety each student had to prove she was able to enter the water head first, float, and swim a short distance.[60]

SORORITIES

Sororities existed at FSCW from its inception. Murphree and his faculty approved of and participated in such activities as sponsors and members. The Kappa Alpha chapter of Kappa Delta, founded in 1904, predated the women's college. The Eta chapter of Alpha Kappa Psi (which became the Alpha Eta chapter of Delta Delta Delta in 1916) was installed on the campus in 1907. In April 1908, local sorority Beta Rho, founded in 1905, became the Gamma chapter of Chi Omega. Alpha Delta Pi (originally Alpha Delta Phi), Iota chapter, was installed at Florida Female College in January 1909. These early sororities held regular meetings in the towers of East Hall and Bryan Hall and initiations in lodge rooms in town.[61]

Between 1910 and 1920, such fraternal organizations gained in popularity nationwide, but they faced difficulties at the women's college. Conradi, with his penchant for sequestering the girls, canceled all off-campus initiation arrangements soon after he arrived.[62] For the next decade, all sorority activities took place on campus under the attentive eyes of faculty sponsors. As of 1916, the college still sponsored only the four chapters that had been in place prior to 1910.[63] The president avowed that he fully supported the sororities, yet when the Board of Control considered abolishing the fraternal organizations on the college and university campuses in 1917, both Conradi and Dean Opperman of the School of Music favored the action. Opperman refused to allow a member of the music faculty to affiliate with any sorority.[64]

The 1920s changed the pattern of mere existence for sororities at FSCW. After ten years of dormancy, fraternal organizations on campus entered a period of renaissance and swept the administration along in the wake. In 1920, Sigma Sigma Sigma installed its Rho chapter, and Sigma Kappa established its Omega chapter at FSCW. In October 1921, Pi Beta Phi installed local Alpha Omega (established several months earlier) as its Florida Beta chapter. Within a year, the *Flambeau* devoted two pages of each issue to sorority news.[65]

Alpha Nu was created in 1923 and affiliated with the national Delta Zeta three months later as its Alpha Sigma chapter. In 1924, Phi Epsilon became the Beta Gamma chapter of Zeta Tau Alpha, and Kappa Alpha Theta established its Beta Nu Chapter. Gamma Beta chapter of Alpha Gamma Delta, Lambda chapter of Theta Upsilon, and Iota chapter of Delta Phi Epsilon joined the campus community in 1925. Alpha Chi Omega installed local Delta Phi as its FSCW Beta Eta chapter in 1926. Two years later Alpha Omicron Pi organized the Alpha Pi chapter. In 1929, Phi Mu created the Alpha Epsilon chapter and Alpha Xi Delta incorporated Beta Tau as the Alpha Omega chapter.[66]

By the middle of the decade, the undeclared ban on off-campus meetings had fallen by the wayside. Members of the various sororities gave rush parties at local residences such as "The Grove" and entertained pledges with bridge parties and refreshments in nearby tea rooms as a matter of course. As sorority membership became an ever more important aspect of some students' lives, the college assumed an active interest in the bid process. Rush Week, the first full week of classes each fall, culminated on the following Monday when the chosen girls, notified of their fortune on Sunday, reported to a designated location for bid distribution in the presence of an attorney hired by the college.[67]

As the 1920s drew to a close, 13 national sororities had chapters at FSCW. Four of those, Chi Omega, Pi Beta Phi,

Alpha Delta Pi, and Delta Delta Delta actually owned their
chapter houses; eight others rented houses. The Kappa Alpha Theta chapter first met at the Kellum house just outside
the college gates, then rented a chapter house two blocks
farther east on College Avenue. The Chi Omega chapter house
was located on its current site, but the original structure was
later razed and replaced with the present house.[68] Delta Delta
Delta purchased its lot on West Park Avenue in 1923, next to
property owned by Professor Gage. Early in 1929, the Kappa
Deltas and Sigma Kappas contracted with Hardin Construction Company of Lake City to build houses on the northeast
corner of Pensacola and Copeland Streets and the southwest
corner of West Park Avenue and Macomb Street respectively.[69]
The 248 girls who lived in sorority houses did so under the
same rules and regulations as those enforced in the residence
halls and under the immediate supervision of chaperones
approved by Conradi.[70] Though the president worried about
the proliferation of student activities outside the immediate
confines of the campus, he realized that sorority houses
relieved the crowded dormitories of some of the residential
burden.

HONOR SOCIETIES

A proliferation of honor societies acknowledged the academic development of the women's college during these years.
Alpha Chi Alpha, installed in 1921 and the first national honorary established at FSCW, recognized students who took an active part in collegiate publications and furthered the study of
journalism. Beginning in 1922, the national home economics
honor society, Omicron Nu, recognized those who excelled in
that field. Kappa Delta Pi, international education honor society, came to the campus in 1925. Phi Kappa Phi, emphasizing
scholarship and character in all departments of American universities and colleges, installed its FSCW chapter in 1925 also.
The history honor society, Phi Alpha Theta, installed a chapter
in 1926, as did Beta Pi Theta, French honorary, and Eta Sigma

Phi, Classics honorary. The Spanish honorary, Phi Beta Sigma, followed in the next year. The Class of 1926 organized Torch-bearers, an affiliate of Mortar Board, national honorary for senior women.[71] In 1931, after five years of continuous service, the Torch Bearer Chapter of Mortar Board was installed at the college.

ARTIST SERIES

Outside recognition in turn encouraged greater acceptance of outside influences. Over the years, the college had frequently provided the students access to artists in various fields. Sometimes members of the faculty prevailed upon talented persons or groups to perform at the college for minimal sums when they were in the vicinity. However, that method of scheduling left much to fate. In 1921, the incoming senior class proposed that the college establish a more dependable means of securing quality entertainment. The girls estimated that $1.50 from each student, deposited in a special security fund, would guarantee enough money to entice a performer to Tallahassee, especially if he or she was already scheduled to appear in Jacksonville or Miami. The Faculty Senate presented the idea to the Board of Control, but in that inflationary time the board shied away from adding any amount, regardless of how small, to student fees.[72] In 1923, the student body petitioned the board to allocate fees so as to include the bringing of artists to the campus. Since this request came directly from the students, it received the board's approval.

Conradi appointed Dean Opperman of the School of Music chairman of a Committee on Recitals and Plays, and the Artist Series began. Among those who entertained the students and townspeople of Tallahassee during the 1920s were cellist Pablo Casals, pianist Percy Grainger, the Russian Symphonic Choir, and the Minneapolis Symphony Orchestra. Others who appeared in later years, some despite Opperman's objections, included modern dancer Martha Graham, pianists Jose Iturbi and Vladimir Horowitz, the Vienna Choir Boys, organist Marcel

Dupre, baritone Lawrence Tibbett, violinist Mischa Elman, the Barter Theater Company of Virginia, and the United States Marine Band.[73]

❧

As the decade drew to a close, the administration at FSCW faced a quandary. The students were more sophisticated in 1929 than they had been in 1919, and the college needed to liberalize its supervisory policy to acknowledge that. At the same time, as a state-supported institution, the school owed its existence to the approval of a conservative Southern public whose tax monies supported it. The problem of how to reconcile one with the other remained unresolved.

1935 *Flastacowo*

Investiture was held early in the school year. Each senior in her academic gown, accompanied by her white-clad sophomore sister carrying the senior's mortar board, processed across the stage to be "capped" by the college president. This simple rite was an annual ceremony from 1920 through FSCW's history.

1938 *Flastacowo*

An FSCW legend held that Westcott fountain would freeze over and have icicles at least once during a student's four years. For South Florida girls, this was a big event.

1936 *Flastacowo*

Dr. Olivia N. Dorman joined the Classics faculty in 1924 and became Dean of Students in 1934. Though she relaxed existing rules in the thirties, she found the social changes wrought by World War II deeply challenging, especially to the college's protective attitude toward its students. After coeducation and the inception of FSU, she returned to the classroom in the Classics Department.

Dr. Katherine Montgomery, a 1918 alumna who joined the Normal School faculty the next term, became Director of Physical Education in 1923 and remained in that position throughout the FSCW years. She helped with the design of the new Gymnasium, which was eventually named for her. "Miss Katie" strongly supported intramural athletics such as the Odd/Even rivalry.

1937 *Flastacowo*

Louise Richardson, Head Librarian, worked with the architects to design the Library and kept secret the source of the inscription over the main entrance. She established the first library science instruction program in Florida and served into the FSU years. A tough but fair taskmaster, she made everyone follow the same set of library rules regardless of rank.

1937 *Flastacowo*

1940 *Flastacowo*

Anna May Tracy came to FSCW as dietitian in 1923 and teamed with Business Manager Kellum to keep board bills at a minimum. Under her direction the kitchens were modernized and kept up-to-date in the use of new equipment and products. She also inaugurated a graduate intern program for dietitians. World War II shortages and rationing sorely tested her, but she came through to serve into the early FSU years.

1936 Flastacowo

A chorus line tryout signaled that preparations for another elaborate student production were underway. The Odd/Even demonstrations evolved from simple skits to introduce the two teams into full-blown musicals. Junior Minstrels, though produced by the junior class, drew talent from the whole student body.

1936 Flastacowo

FSCW student shoppers were always important to Tallahassee businesses. Whenever townsfolk grumbled about the college getting special treatment, Business Manager J. G. Kellum trotted out figures on average student purchases per year.

1936 *Flastacowo*

By the mid-thirties, big events such as the Panhellenic Dance and Weekend made the no-man policy of the previous decade seem ages past.

1936 *Flastacowo*

The flow of weekend traffic between Tallahassee and Gainesville increased steadily, except for the World War II years, when there were fewer men to visit or to be visited.

1943 *Flastacowo*

ca. 1930s, Florida State Archives

1936 *Flastacowo*

Beginning in 1915, FSCW developed recreation facilities at Camp Flastacowo on Lake Bradford. Rustic cabins provided sleeping quarters for students and chaperones. A wooden dock with lifeguard towers facilitated swimming and diving. Canoeing, either in craft for three or four persons or in the big "war" canoes that held up to ten, was the most popular activity.

ca. 1930, Alumni Association

The Cathedral was the name given this arm of Lake Bradford by FSCW students. It was a popular canoeing destination, located almost directly across the lake from Camp Flastacowo. In addition to the imposing buttress-like cypress trees, the Cathedral had a wonderful echo that repeated even faint sounds.

1946, Joyce Cayce Black   1947 *Flastacowo*

Soon after the New Dining Hall was completed in 1939, the tradition of Effie the Post was begun by F Club. Effie's features, make-up, and hair were refurbished by each succeeding class of F Club goats, who were also required to see that Effie was properly dressed for the events of the day.

1942 *Flastacowo*

Dr. Doak S. Campbell (left) and Dr. Edward Conradi, president and president emeritus of FSCW, posed on Westcott steps. Campbell assumed the presidency in the fall of 1941 and served through the transition from FSCW to FSU into the mid-fifties. Campbell Stadium and the Conradi Biology Building were named for the two past presidents.

1940 *Flastacowo*

The FSCW campus, from near the present intersection of Tennessee and Woodward streets, was a handsome cluster of red brick buildings on a forested hill. The foreground pastures, grazed by FSCW's substantial dairy herd, are now filled with buildings.

1942 *Flastacowo*

The Faculty Senate of 1942 presents familiar faces for FSCW alumnae of the thirties and forties. Both President Campbell and President Emeritus Conradi are seated in the first row. Right of Campbell are Walter Cowles (music) and Herman Kurz (botany). Right of Conradi is Mark DeGraff (education).

ca. 1940, Alumni Association

Brick buttresses turned the Gymnasium into a Collegiate Gothic edifice. Constructed between 1928 and 1930, it provided adequate physical education facilities, including a large indoor swimming pool, for the first time. Active physical education classes were required for all healthy freshmen.

"Angel robes," two bath towels sewn together at the shoulders, provided skimpy coverage between the drying room, where students left their formless college-issue swimsuits, and their clothes lockers. Among requirements for a bachelor's degree from FSCW was successfully passing a swim test.

1943 *Flastacowo*

The Odd/Even volleyball game was the first contest on Thanksgiving morning. In the thirties it was played in the big gym of what is now Montgomery Gymnasium, which then had a balcony. Under rules of the time, a player could strike the ball twice.

1940 *Flastacowo*

Tipoff of the 1941 Odd/Even basketball game started that year's featured contest. Odd players wore white gym suits with red and purple trim; Evens wore green with yellow trim. Women's basketball at the time was a split-court game with three forwards and three opposing guards on each half of the court. Crossing the center line drew a penalty.

1941 *Flastacowo*

1943 *Flastacowo*

1943 *Flastacowo*

By the forties, Odd/Even rivalry reached a high plateau of creative and exuberant cheers and pep songs. Both sides had stylish cheerleaders, and the Odds even had a swing band. When the Odds sang the dirge "There passed four weary horses a-dragging a hearse along . . . ," the Evens retaliated with "dem bones gonna rise again."

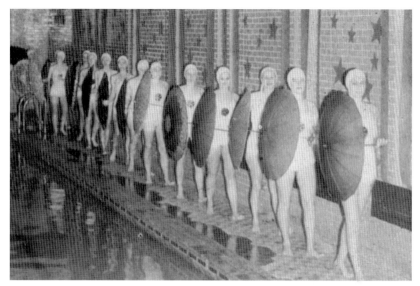

1941 *Flastacowo*

Tarpon Club members march onto the pool deck for a Thanksgiving Show. The group was a pioneer in synchronized swimming and was featured in three Grantland Rice sports films shown in movie theaters nationwide. Tarpon was unaffected by the transition to FSU and became one of the oldest activity organizations on campus.

A Thanksgiving turkey for each family-style table was one of the last dining traditions to fall during World War II. The last traditional FSCW Thanksgiving feast was held in 1945. Arrival of TBUF men in the fall of 1946 changed dining patterns forever.

1943 Flastacowo

1945 *Flastacowo*

Westcott gates and fountain were decorated each year for the Thanksgiving Homecoming and Odd/Even games. The gates, presented by the Classes of 1916 and 1918, were forever Even. The fountain, gift of the Classes of 1915 and 1917, was always Odd.

1946 *Flastacowo*

Color Rush, a series of races held just prior to Thanksgiving, decided which colors, Odd or Even, would be attached to the front doors of major campus buildings. The New Dining Hall was at stake in this dash.

Landis Hall, completed in 1939, had such luxuries as student elevators and intercom phones in each room. It housed Senior Hall, an honors program with slightly relaxed rules. Girls could sunbathe in little or no clothing on a rooftop court that student pilots discovered soon after Dale Mabry Field opened.

ca. 1940, souvenir booklet, Alumni Association

ca. 1935, FSU Special Collections

Memory's image of FSCW is brick buildings among tall pines, certainly true of the small campus that centered on Westcott. This 1935 photo of the History Building realizes that image. The building was renamed for Arthur "Pi" Williams, FSCW's first vice president, 1913–1937.

The Orchestra was open not only to instrumental music students, but also to any who successfully auditioned. Instrument faculty bolstered the ensemble and were usually first chairs. Walter R. Cowles, shown here, was a longtime conductor.

The Glee Club, under the direction of Etta Robinson, enjoyed a renown that extended well beyond FSCW's environs. The group's Christmas Vespers was a major event of the school year, and its annual spring concert drew an audience from town as well as campus.

1943 *Flastacowo*

The Marching Band made its debut on Thanksgiving Day 1941. It was truly a student creation, formed without official sanction, though cellist Owen Sellers (for whom the music amphitheater is named) bravely agreed to be director. As the band quickly won applause and approval, money was found for uniforms. It immediately became a unit capable of performing anywhere on short notice.

1943 *Flastacowo*

Glee Club members crowded into an Army truck are off to entertain the boys. Like the Marching Band, the Glee Club was highly mobile and ready to perform at nearby military bases. Both ensembles were a public relations bonanza to FSCW leaders, who could appear suitably patriotic by sending a few well-chaperoned girls "there" rather than having to welcome thousands of eager servicemen "here."

Departure for Christmas vacation, when classes for all students ceased at the same time, brought out the year's biggest fleet of special buses. It was not unusual for students to stand or lean on the armrest of an obliging schoolmate all the way from Tallahassee to Tampa or even Miami, especially during the war years.

1941 *Flastacowo*

The train station was the first view of Tallahassee for thousands of FSCW students. For many years, special trains brought the girls from all over Florida. Pullman cars that arrived after light flash were parked until the next day so the girls could sleep through the perils of late night. As travel by bus increased, special trains were no longer provided. Instead, special cars were attached to regularly scheduled trains.

1947 *Flastacowo*

1946 *Flastacowo*

Sophomore Council girls in white skirts and bright blue jackets were the incoming freshmen's best friends. They helped the bewildered newcomers through Orientation Week and serenaded them after light flash. Late in the spring semester, Sophomore Council girls tapped outstanding freshmen to repeat the cycle next year.

1942 *Flastacowo*

Chapel of the early years turned into convocation. As the quickest and easiest way to make announcements and explain administration policy, it was compulsory for most students during FSCW's 42 years. It was also one of the first traditions to fall when the ex-GIs of TBUF got to campus.

1946 Flastacowo

The Torch Bearer Chapter of Mortar Board, a national leadership, scholarship, and service honorary for senior women, was organized at FSCW in 1931. Late each spring in a hushed, twilight ceremony lighted only by their torches, graduating members solemnly tapped, one by one, the juniors chosen for the following year.

1944 Flastacowo

Mortified, long on leadership and service but short on scholarship, was a sassy spoof of Mortar Board organized in 1937. Only one of its seven members (called the Czar) could have grades of Mortar Board standards. When Mortar Board members wore their caps and gowns with silver and gold ribbons, Mortified members wore theirs with ribbons of blush pink and envy green.

In the fall of 1946, the former military buildings of Dale Mabry Field became the offices and dorms of the Tallahassee Branch of the University of Florida (TBUF). The flood of veterans using the GI Bill forced this action.

1947 Flastacowo

1945 Graduation Program

A June graduation procession wound around the fountain and into Westcott Auditorium, where the huge pipe organ thundered "Pomp and Circumstance" and raised goose bumps. Sweltering summer weather and heavy robes always led graduating seniors to talk about wearing only undergarments beneath their academic regalia. There is no record of anyone ever following through.

 Part Three

Thanks to the infusion of federal money, Florida State College for Women and the University of Florida experienced significant growth and development during the 1930s. The state's economic outlook, seriously depressed since 1927, changed for the better with the passage of New Deal legislation. Beginning in 1933, FSCW received both financial and manpower assistance through the Federal Emergency Relief Administration (FERA), the Civil Works Administration, the Public Works Administration, and the successor to FERA, the Works Progress Administration. With grants and loans from those relief agencies, the college revived its building program and expended far more realistic sums for campus construction than earlier appropriations from the state legislature had allowed.

PHYSICAL DEVELOPMENT

Over the years, J.G. Kellum's duties as business manager of the college had included general supervision of the entire physical plant. As the school grew, its daily management became more complicated, as did Kellum's responsibilities. In 1930, the Board of Control appointed H.D. Mendenhall, Kellum's brother-in-law, resident engineer for the college.[1] Mendenhall relieved Kellum of the time-consuming maintenance duties that were necessary to keep the buildings and grounds in acceptable condition and coordinated all campus construction projects. Working together, these two men continued the college building program on a surprisingly larger scale than ever before.

At the beginning of the decade, the college owned 300 acres of contiguous land. In late 1930, the Board of Control authorized Kellum to use money from the college building fund to buy 425 acres of agricultural land on Lake Bradford Road.[2] In light of the state's, and therefore the school's, precarious financial situation, this seemed a peculiar time to expend already limited resources. But college officials deemed this purchase imperative for several reasons. First, as presently situated, the farm encompassed 250 of the campus's 300 acres and comprised maintenance buildings and equipment for 125 hogs and 140 cows. The hogs, fed mostly on waste food from the kitchen, supplied all the pork served in the Dining Hall. The cows provided more than 100 gallons of milk daily for cooking and drinking. The process of milking 60 cows every day, then cooling and pasteurizing the raw milk, took place in barns and buildings on the grounds. The farm also had land under cultivation, some in grain for the hogs and cattle, and the remainder in turnips, cabbage, beets, carrots, and peas for the boarding department.[3] As of late 1930, however, dietary needs of the students far exceeded the capabilities of present farm acreage.

Second, the already insufficient agricultural space continued to decrease as the campus developed. The new athletic field already encroached on the land used for the chicken coop and yard, forcing the college to abandon that segment of its enterprise. Finally, the college agricultural property, located at the very outskirts of city limits in 1917 when the institution established the dairy, was now surrounded by incorporated land. Kellum and Conradi both agreed that the farm might become a nuisance to Tallahassee residents if it remained in its original location.[4]

Kellum probably expected a legislative appropriation in 1931 for construction of barns and other farm buildings at the new site. Instead, the state reduced the college's funding by 14 percent. Consequently, the Lake Bradford Road acreage remained idle until the winter of 1934, when the Civil Works Administration, part of Roosevelt's New Deal legislation, made available to individual states grants and loans for construction purposes. The relief agency contributed more than half of the labor and materials to erect farm buildings on the property. Revenue from the sale of agricultural products rather than state funds supplied the college's share of money for the undertaking, a detail that bore out Kellum's wisdom in maintaining the farm under difficult financial circumstances.[5]

Shortly before the entire dairy and agricultural complex moved, Kellum again used funds from the operation to purchase 330 acres adjoining the new location. Because this land had been neglected for some time, the price was less than one-third of the cost of the original acreage, but the area needed clearing before it could be used. Dairy superintendent J.P. Love finally transported the livestock to the new site in the summer of 1935. The farm and dairy complex soon became a chief attraction for visitors to the city. The state paved the road in front of the main buildings, and the college landscaped the 50-foot-deep frontage with flowers, shrubs, and oak trees.[6]

With the exception of the farm land and two minor acquisitions prior to 1932, one of 30 acres at the college camp on Lake Bradford and the other of several lots and houses on West Jefferson Street,[7] the college curtailed its land investments during the 1930s. Instead, constrained by lack of financial wherewithal, the administration focused attention on improving property already in its possession. Encouraged by Conradi's love of nature, Mendenhall created a ten-acre arboretum on one tract immediately west of the College Park Subdivision. The Botany Department set out native flora among the dense trees. Conradi planned to add walkways and benches at a later date, but that dream was never realized.[8]

The president also encouraged development of Camp

Flastacowo as a "selling point" for prospective students. He believed "the College should cultivate this phase of recreation since Florida is known the country over for its unusual facilities in water sports and outdoor life. It is one of the high class assets of the State."[9] The camp's popularity as a weekend retreat for students and faculty members increased in proportion to the severity of the Depression; the less spending money they had, the more they used the camp. Soon the single cabin at the lake site proved inadequate for recreational use. Mendenhall designed and supervised construction of a second one, similar to the original and some 250' further up the shore. With this addition, 100 students and their chaperones could spend weekends at the camp. Students slept on cots placed on upstairs sleeping porches; chaperones, often professors and their wives, slept on cots in individual rooms. When faculty members entertained guests at the lake, they had access to a small cottage originally built for and occupied by the caretaker.[10]

Some girls still hiked from campus to the lake site, some rode in automobiles owned by faculty or friends, and some paid 25¢ for a round trip on the college truck. The truck ferried groups of 12 or more to and from the lake on Friday afternoons, Saturday mornings, and Saturday afternoons. It made one run from the camp to the college on Monday morning before early classes.[11]

Improvements on the campus proper included completion of new athletic activity areas to the north, south, and west of the Physical Education Building. Mendenhall supervised the installation of 12 clay tennis courts on the west side of the Gymnasium. Tennis became so popular that college gardener Steinfuhrer predicted the removal of the garden, situated immediately south of the courts, because girls constantly trampled the flowers and vegetables while searching for tennis balls. Six basketball courts and twelve volleyball courts adjoined a combination hockey and soccer field in the area between the Gymnasium and Call Street. An archery range stretched from the south end of the Gymnasium toward West Jefferson Street. Mendenhall reserved a wide expanse of undeveloped land between the dormitories and the Physical Education Building for a park and recreation area.[12]

Until 1940, the central park area remained little more than an empty, often muddy, space transected by cypress plank walkways. It was not, however, unused. In 1932, college officials finally acknowledged that young ladies smoked cigarettes, but they still refused to allow FSCW girls to engage in so vulgar a habit in public or in the presence of men. To accommodate those students who smoked, the school designated a "girls only" smoking zone behind Jennie Murphree Hall. The students christened the area Belgium, because like that country during the First World War, it was "no man's land." By 1939, the smoking area extended from the front of the Physical Education Building to the back of Jennie Murphree, Reynolds, and Broward Halls.[13]

AUXILIARY BUILDINGS

With the exception of a new heating plant, considered an economic necessity, and an annex to the History Building, both approved and funded prior to 1930, actual construction on the campus between 1930 and 1938 consisted of essential renovation or enlargement of existing buildings. In the fall of 1929, Kellum and Conradi had presented to the Board of Control a plan to enlarge the heating plant, located at that time behind Reynolds and Jennie Murphree Halls. The board opted for an entirely new structure to be located on Woodward Avenue at the extreme western edge of college property.[14]

Even though the plant was a utility building rather than an academic or residential structure, its architectural design followed the brick collegiate style of other campus buildings.[15] Only its 175' tall radial tile tower, nicknamed *"femina perfecta"* by the students, railroad siding, and coal pits identified its function. The railroad siding, completed at the outset of the project, ran approximately three-fourths of a mile from a main Seaboard line to the new plant. The project quickly paid for itself in savings effected by eliminating the need for trucks to convey construction materials, boarding supplies, and coal from the railroad depot to the site.[16]

Within the plant two large boilers furnished hot water for all five residence halls, eliminating the need to maintain separate water heaters in each dormitory basement. The boilers also supplied hot water for kitchen, gymnasium, and laundry facilities. A six-foot-wide by six-foot-high tunnel lined with reinforced concrete extended 1,233 feet under the campus and connected the new heating plant with the old system.[17] The tunnel gave workers access to the steam pipes it contained. In later years, adventurous girls explored its "steamy, cobwebby spaces."[18] The old heating plant was converted to individual carpentry, plumbing, painting, and electrical workshops.[19]

In the spring of 1931, amid rumors of impending budget cuts, the administration initiated previously planned work on an addition to the History Building. Construction progressed rapidly during an unusually dry spring and summer. The new section contained classrooms, laboratories, conference rooms, an experimental greenhouse on the third floor for the Botany Department, and a small theater on the first floor.[20] At the request of the Spoken English Department, the college named the 415-seat theater the Augusta Conradi Little Theater in memory of president Conradi's wife, who had died in 1928.[21] The president's daughters, Elizabeth and Louisa, both earned certificates in spoken English at the college.[22]

While dry conditions were ideal for construction, the lack of rainfall exacerbated existing structural problems with two other buildings. During the drought, the pipe clay under the northwest corner of the Education Building contracted severely, causing the building to sink several inches into the ground. An inspection by the Board of Control's architects revealed large "openings" in the walls, and the college abandoned the building immediately.[23] For the next two years the Education

Building stood empty and atilt while ivy grew through cracks in its boarded windows and crumbling walls.[24] All furniture and accoutrements were removed from the condemned building and put to use in the History Building annex, thus saving the college the expense of purchasing equipment for that new wing.[25]

But thrifty reuse of materials offered little relief for the classroom situation now thrust upon the school. All mathematics, modern language, and English classes had met in the Education Building; journalism classes and the *Flambeau* offices had occupied rooms in the basement and on the first floor. Those classes and the student newspaper were relocated to the Science, History, and Administration buildings, once again putting an undue strain on academic facilities. Faculty members, many of whom had known nothing but overcrowded conditions at the college, took the inconveniences in stride. Some, like Dr. Leland Lewis of the Chemistry Department, even had some fun with the School of Education faculty members crowded into classrooms on the second floor of the Science Building. Lewis realized that a plumbing leak in a third-floor chemistry laboratory caused water to drip on the education professors' heads as they lectured, but he did nothing to remedy the situation. Eventually two of the professors asked Lewis what was dripping. Lewis assured them there was no reason for alarm, that it was "only concentrated nitric acid, allowed to drip through the floor onto their heads, because the chemistry faculty thought [education] professors were too caustic in class." His response seemed to satisfy the professors, because they returned to their classes and resumed their lectures.[26]

In 1932, Kellum approached the Board of Control with a plan to use $30,000 from dormitory rents to remodel and enlarge the kitchen and make minor renovations to the upstairs dining room. The board approved the business manager's suggestions. They ordered Rudolph Weaver to draft plans for the new facility, including specifications for a future addition to the Dining Hall.[27] As part of the project, Mendenhall converted all of the kitchen and bakery appliances to electricity or fuel oil. He installed electric freight and garbage elevators and added an incinerator to the sub-basement. The meat and vegetable storage sections were moved to the main kitchen area on the first floor, freeing four ammonia-cooled refrigerating rooms in the basement for use as freezers. The 50-foot addition to the kitchen, roofed with tile removed from the Education Building, contained automatic dishwashing facilities surrounded by a soundproof canopy. Another section of the addition included a new dressing room for the dining hall girls. In the south end of the main dining room, the campus electrician installed a large pressure fan, opposite one already in the north end, to circulate the air.[28]

INCIDENTAL IMPROVEMENTS

Kellum and Mendenhall jointly maintained the campus land, one making financial arrangements and the other supervising physical projects. Working with the State Road Department, they coordinated the paving of hard-surfaced roads in front of or around every building.[29] Mendenhall laid out concrete sidewalks along the paved roads, between buildings, and from the front entrances of Reynolds and Jennie Murphree Halls to the facing street.[30]

In 1933, the Classes of 1933 and 1935 provided funds for construction of gates at the south entrance to the campus, opposite the Sweet Shop. Brick piers, 21'4" wide and 20' high, supported a steel span with a bronze medallion in the center. The inscription on the medallion read "Memorial to the Classes of 1933–1935."[31] At the same time the college erected similar gateways (later removed) on the north side of the campus. The three new gateways and the original one at the main entrance, when closed, effectively barred automobile traffic from the campus. Night watchmen S.H. Green and John McCollum had mixed feelings about that. Open gates frequently resulted in drivers making U-turns and honking their car horns in front of Gilchrist Hall after hours; closed gates caused problems for students with special permission to return to the campus after last light flash.[32] The administration failed to devise an effective solution to the situation, and closed gates vexed all concerned for several more years.

NEW DEAL ACADEMIC BUILDINGS

In 1933, Florida had a new governor, David Sholtz, and the country had a new president, Franklin Roosevelt, but neither the state nor the nation knew when to expect economic relief. The legislature that year pessimistically reduced the operating budgets of state institutions by 25 percent. Despite the funding cuts, college officials felt it necessary to keep up appearances for public relations purposes. A neatly maintained campus and well-cared-for buildings presented an image of responsible frugality and reassured prospective students and families that their money would be well spent; unkempt grounds and listing buildings suggested questionable administration. Accordingly, it fell to Kellum, as business manager, and to Mendenhall, as construction engineer, to finance campus improvements in any way possible.

The most obvious physical need was for either repair or demolition of the Education Building. Though the 1933 Legislature reduced institutional budgets, it also authorized money for reconstruction of that building—as soon as other contributory funds became available. Kellum and Mendenhall promptly applied to the Civil Works Administration for the contributory funds requisite for repairs and alterations to the vacant building.[33] The application was approved. Work began in March 1934 with assistance from the Public Works Administration, successor to the Civil Works Administration. Laborers razed the northwest wing of the building and rebuilt it on a concrete foundation, then reinforced the remaining walls. When the crews finished the reconstruction in late summer 1935, the furniture and equipment that had been removed to the History Building four years earlier was still needed there.

The college had no money to buy new furnishings for the Education Building classrooms and laboratories.[34] The administration eventually borrowed from funds earmarked for another building to equip this one.

A situation identical to that of the Education Building arose with the foundation of the Administration Building. Conradi had warned the Board of Control in 1931 that the walls were giving way and the structure was becoming dangerous.[35] In late 1932, Mendenhall installed a set of commemorative bronze doors at the entrance to the building. Anticipating problems with the crumbling structure even then, he advised the donors, the Classes of 1925, 1927, and 1931, that the doors would "transfer to any new building if the Administration Building is replaced for any reason."[36]

The legislature characteristically ignored the questionable condition of the building as long as possible. Conradi, fearing that any publicity might adversely affect the college's reputation, chose not to force the Administration Building issue with the Board of Control. In his biennial report he merely admonished that "if these buildings had been built originally with a reinforced concrete structure these difficulties would not have arisen."[37] This mild rebuke elicited a response; the board finally sent Rudolph Weaver to examine "some dangerous looking cracks in the walls." Alarmed by what he saw, Weaver advised Mendenhall to make *daily* inspections of the section. Three months later Mendenhall and Weaver condemned the north wing of the structure. Inside the building Mendenhall closed off hallways with partitions; outside he set up barriers to warn passers-by to keep a safe distance. It was late spring 1935 and the college was unable to afford any further measures. All funds originally intended for reconstructive efforts were needed to equip and furnish the soon-to-be completed Education Building for fall classes.[38]

Once again Mendenhall and Kellum looked to New Deal relief agencies for assistance. Within a month the Business Office received word that the federal government had allocated $42,046, or 45 percent of the estimated total cost for repairs to the Administration Building.[39] The sitting Legislature, anxious to take advantage of federal funding, quickly appropriated the remainder of the estimated $92,000 needed for the project. Under Mendenhall's direction, the reconstruction incorporated as much of the building's original brick, doors, windows, terra cotta roofing tiles, and lumber as could economically be salvaged. As a crew of 80 men carefully dismantled the north wing, they came upon the cornerstone. They removed the copper box and inspected its contents. Of particular interest was a list of 196 signatures—those of students who had attended the college at the time of the building's dedication.[40]

Actual reconstruction began in the summer of 1935 and continued until the winter of 1937. By that time, four years after Conradi had first notified the board of problems in the north wing, the building's west wing and auditorium showed evidence of deterioration. Mendenhall estimated that immediate replacement of the foundations for approximately $18,000 might prevent the need for further costly reconstruction work, but the Board of Control failed to heed his advice. In mid-1940, Weaver advised the school authorities "not to use the auditorium any longer than necessary since the outside wall is not considered sufficiently strong to withstand the pressure in heavy windstorms."[41]

While the college completed arrangements for repairs to the Administration Building's north wing, President John J. Tigert of the University of Florida asked the Board of Control to allow him to change the date on the university seal from 1905 to 1853, when the East Florida Seminary opened in Ocala.[42] He "intended to correct the impression that Florida had no system of state higher education more than 25 years old."[43] Conradi was not present when Tigert presented his request, nor was his name or that of Florida State College for Women mentioned at the time.[44] The Board of Control submitted Tigert's request to Attorney General Cary D. Landis, who found it politic to confirm that the University of Florida was the direct descendent of the East Florida Seminary, and by implication that Florida State College for Women was in a direct line of descent from the West Florida Seminary.[45] Accordingly, the Board authorized the President of the Florida State College for Women to change the date on the seal of the Florida State College for Women to 1857—the date the West Florida Seminary was opened for classes on the site of the college campus.[46] Conradi silently accepted the edict, but college documents, emblems, and the seal itself never reflected the change from MCMV (1905) to 1857. However, the seal of Florida State University, implemented in 1947, shows an incorporation date of 1857.

The Attorney General's acclamation of institutional continuity incidentally validated a 1911 Supreme Court decision enforcing the terms of the will of James D. Westcott, Jr., one of the college's two benefactors.[47] Westcott, born in Tallahassee in 1839, had served as a member of the State Legislature, as State Attorney General, and as an Associate Justice of the State Supreme Court. He died in 1887, at the age of 48. According to the provisions of his will, a major portion of his estate (commercial property on the corner of Monroe and College Avenues and residential property on East College Avenue) was to be held in trust for the benefit of the West Florida Seminary, which he had attended. One-half of the money realized was designated for students of Leon County; none was to be used for buildings or improvement to the grounds.

The Westcott Estate executor had not questioned the school's change of name from West Florida Seminary to Florida State College in 1901, recognizing that only the name had changed. But when the Buckman Bill abolished the school completely and replaced it with Florida Female College, the executor claimed that the institution was no longer the one Westcott had attended or endowed. The technicality engendered a legal battle to set aside the bequest. Its resolution in

1911 in favor of Florida State College for Women allowed Kellum to administer the properties for the benefit of the college. In accordance with Westcott's will, FSCW used one-half of the income from the properties to pay the salaries of teachers who instructed Leon County students at the Demonstration School, and the remainder for other teachers' salaries.[48] The official incorporation date change to 1857 came at approximately the same time that the Administration Building reopened in 1937. The college formally acknowledged Judge Westcott's endowment, at that time estimated to be worth $129,750, by renaming the building the James D. Westcott, Jr., Memorial Building.[49]

NEW DEAL DORMITORIES

The administration continually faced the problem of too many students for the school's limited physical plant. With the completion of Gilchrist Hall in the fall of 1928, campus residence capacity had reached 1,116.[50] The college experienced a tremendous increase in enrollment during the 1930s, particularly after 1934. In 1931, with 1,676 students, FSCW ranked fourth in size among all schools for women in the United States, surpassed only by Hunter (4,614), Smith (1,986), and North Carolina State College for Women (1,704).[51]

Although FSCW boasted an admirable academic reputation, the major reason for the college's overwhelming popularity at this time was its low cost. Florida residents attended because "it was the state university and the least expensive place you could go."[52] A survey conducted in 1932 by the American Association of Colleges and Universities found that state residents' yearly expenses at Florida State College for Women ranged between $250 and $275, compared with an average cost of $308 at other Southern schools and $1,000 at Northeastern schools.[53] After 1934, the New Deal provided financial assistance for students through the Federal Emergency Relief Administration and later through the National Youth Administration. By spring of 1936, the number of students attending FSCW full-time reached 1,741. Two years later the college reported a record number of students— 1,850— and rose to second in enrollment among state schools for women, exceeded only by Texas State College for Women with 2,363 attendees.[54]

The on-campus residence capacity remained at the 1928 level of 1,116.[55] For reasons of supervision and safety, the administration preferred to have students live in dormitories, but given the constant shortage of living facilities, many girls lived off-campus, in either sorority houses or private homes. One local resident whose family lived across the street from the campus remembered that

> we [lived] on Jefferson Street, where the Delta Zeta parking lot is now. Mother had been signed up, and I can remember about four college girls that lived with us, two to a room. They paid Mother the rent, and they ate on campus. Then there was a rule that you couldn't have an unmarried male of a certain age in the family, and my brother was nine years older than I am. So when he got to a certain age, we couldn't do it anymore.[56]

An out-of-state student who lived with a family recalled that

> we were under all the [college] rules and regulations. We were not allowed to smoke in the house. The woman who owned the house acted as a housemother. She had two daughters and one of them used to always peek around to see what we were doing, so she could report to her mother that we were not behaving ourselves. I imagine there were between 15 and 20 [girls]. It was right across from the History Building, on Jefferson Street.[57]

Aware of the desperate need for additional housing facilities, Mendenhall and Kellum submitted a proposal to the Public Works Administration in early September 1935 for funds for a new dormitory, an enlargement of the college Infirmary, and an extension of the Dining Hall on the west side of the kitchens. They particularly hoped for approval of the residence hall within four months so that the desperately needed dormitory might be completed by September 1936.[58]

That date passed with no word on the new dormitory. "Dorms were full to overflowing;"[59] almost 250 students were housed in private homes near the campus. Conradi reported that "some did not come because we had no accommodations at all for them in the residence halls, some of them went to other colleges and some stayed at home."[60] By the fall of 1937, more than 700 students lived off-campus in sorority houses, in college-supervised residences, or with their families in the city. The Board of Control adjusted room rents to between $40 and $52 per year depending on the residence hall, and reserved all monies above operating expenses for use in building more dormitories.[61]

In July 1938, the Public Works Administration at last released $843,000 in grants and loans for FSCW; $428,000 of that amount was for a new dormitory. The state refused to assume such a large construction debt without a guarantee that residence space would be filled to capacity at all times,[62] so the board delayed the start of construction until it passed a resolution that made dormitory residence mandatory for all students as long as space existed.

Contractors again worked from Rudolph Weaver's architectural specifications. His plans conformed to the Tudor Gothic style, but on this building he included elaborate decorative touches: plaques of the college seal, medallions that emphasized the feminine nature of the school, and decorative trim work. The five-story, U-shaped dormitory consisted of a 200-foot-long central expanse, broken by a 12-foot-wide space through which a sidewalk passed,[63] and two flanking wings. Interior features included a men's cloakroom and sleeping quarters suitable for male guests. Student rooms each contained built-in cabinets, recessed steam radiators, and radio connections. A large reception room on the first floor featured disappearing doors, which made it possible to partition the area into smaller rooms. On the fifth floor each wing had a lounge; the main section had a clubroom with a rooftop sundeck. A three-story arcade connected the building to Gilchrist Hall, which in turn was connected to Broward Hall, and so on down the line so that dormitory residents were able to roam through six buildings without stepping outside.[64]

The new building was named Cary D. Landis Hall after the late state attorney general.[65] When Landis Hall opened in September 1939, it provided dormitory space for 371 students and brought the total residence hall capacity to 1,480, still far below the number of beds needed. As of mid-August 1939, all rooms had been reserved and 50 girls remained on a waiting list.[66] Students to whom the college assigned rooms in the new dormitory paid $68, bringing their boarding cost to more than $300 per year; others living on campus paid $52 for their dormitory room and $285 in all.[67]

New Deal Support Buildings

The second construction project included in the Public Works Administration grant of 1938 was a new Infirmary. The state architects situated this building immediately west of the medical facility already on campus. Doctors' offices, nurses' quarters, examination rooms, and an incinerator shared the ground floor; wards and private rooms on the second and third floors brought the overall patient capacity to 100. The college used the original section, remodeled and renamed the Reynolds Annex, as a residence hall for graduate and mature students; 27 students, two house directors, and two night directors moved in right away. In the event of an emergency or epidemic, the medical staff could commandeer the beds for hospital use.[68]

As soon as work on Landis Hall and the Infirmary reached a point where crews could level ground to the west of the kitchen without interfering with those projects, construction began on the third Public Works Administration building, a new dining hall. When Weaver designed the building in 1932, he placed the three-stories-high main entrance on the west side, emphasizing the inevitable campus movement away from the original cluster of buildings around the Administration Building. A bas-relief depicting the goddess of plenty complemented the entryway. Inside, three plaques on either side of the main entry doors illustrated the connection between earth producing the products and man cultivating and using them for food. Weaver also anticipated the social development of the school; he included a lobby with two cloak rooms, one for men and one for women. For easy access in inclement weather, a two-story arcade connected the building to Gilchrist Hall. In the new hall, two dining rooms downstairs each seated 400 students at tables for eight made of wheat-finished maple; two dining rooms upstairs each seated 300 students at tables made of polished oak. A mezzanine between the floors, reserved for special entertaining, could be set up to seat 75.[69]

Dietitian Anna May Tracy successfully ran the original dining rooms and kitchen because she had devised and enforced rules. She hesitated to discard long-established communal dining traditions, yet five separate dining rooms in two buildings now made some modifications necessary. She discontinued the use of tablecloths; instead students ate on bare tables for breakfast and lunch, and on mats for dinner. Working with the Dean of Students and the Director of Residences, she reordered mealtime procedures for 2,000 people in five dining rooms. Breakfast and Sunday dinner, available only in the new building, were cafeteria-style or self-service. For daily lunch and dinner, she assigned students to a dining room in the new building based on their place of residence. Freshmen continued to take their meals in the east, or original, dining room. As an impressionable newcomer to the school, Mary Ruth Weaver wrote home:

> I sit at the head of the table and serve. No one can start eating till I do, and no one can have her dessert till I do, and no one can be excused till I get up, and no one from another table can speak to someone at my table without asking me first. It's so exciting I can hardly stand it![70]

On weekends, Tracy permitted students to move to any other dining room provided they signed up in advance to do so. Neither she nor the students were happy with the plan, but Tracy knew that some system was absolutely necessary if the college was to maintain its usual mealtime standards.

Some of the carpentry, plumbing, painting, and electrical shops, installed in the old heating plant in 1931, moved to the basement of the New Dining Hall.[71] The upstairs section of the Old Dining Hall remained in use, but the college allowed State Geologist Herman Gunter to move his equipment and museum specimens to the lower space. Very soon a sign appeared at the entrance to the lower part of the Old Dining Hall—"Florida State Geological Survey Exhibit of Fossils and Minerals." A mastodon skeleton, found in Wakulla Springs in 1934, guarded the entryway; students christened the massive relic "Oscar" and visited him regularly.[72] When construction on all three buildings was finally finished, the New Dining Hall blocked access to the Infirmary. Consequently, the State Road Department cut and paved a new road that ran under the arcade connecting Gilchrist and Landis Halls, and past the west-facing New Dining Hall and Infirmary, to intersect with Call Street.[73]

While Kellum and Mendenhall had awaited federal approval and funds for the dormitory and other structures, they had filed a separate request for construction assistance on a student activity building. Faculty members and students alike felt that the campus needed some place specifically for organizations to hold meetings and for girls to participate in various activities. In 1934, Conradi had mentioned to the Board of Control that the college regularly earmarked a small portion of the student activity fees for that purpose, even though he hardly expected to garner the necessary $130,000 from that meager source. Two years later the Alumnae Association initiated a drive for dues to secure half the anticipated cost. When they reached their goal, they optimistically planned to ask the legislature for a matching grant. Meanwhile, the lounge in Broward Hall underwent a complete renovation and became the Broward Club Room, reserved for the use of student organizations.[74]

In the spring of 1938, the Works Progress Administration authorized the necessary funds and assistance for construction of the activity building. Formal ground-breaking ceremonies for the building, to be located across the street from Jennie Murphree Hall, took place on May 4. The plans, again drawn by Rudolph Weaver, called for a lounge and locker room for day students and offices for the Alumnae Association, College Government Association, YWCA, and campus publications. On the third floor were accommodations for visiting alumnae and distinguished guests.[75]

Not long after construction began, Rowena Longmire, who had founded the Alumnae Association in 1909, died at her home on College Avenue. The college and the Alumnae Association named the structure the Rowena Longmire Student Alumnae Building in honor of her contributions to the college. Thus the Longmire Building became the first structure on campus named for a faculty member.[76]

ᖇ

The Depression decade affected the physical development of Florida State College for Women in both positive and negative ways. The State Legislature, always significantly short-sighted when it came to funding educational institutions, continued to cut appropriations as state and national economic conditions deteriorated. Only the fiscal adroitness of the college business manager and the availability of federal aid made it possible for the school to manage the growth it experienced during the 1930s. Between 1930 and 1940, the college increased its non-contiguous land by more than 700 acres— yet financial constraints forced the school to reverse the rapid expansion that had previously typified Conradi's administration. The school spent more than $500,000 to build a new heating plant, History Building annex, kitchen, Dining Hall,

Infirmary, and Student Alumnae Building—yet overcrowded dining facilities, equipment shortages, and condemned classroom buildings characterized daily life on the campus. Another $500,000 financed the construction of a large and sumptuous dormitory with sleeping quarters for more than 370—yet the housing situation grew more critical each year. Various portions of Broward, Jennie Murphree, and Reynolds halls underwent almost constant remodeling and renovation—yet those older residence halls continued to show their age and the quality of their construction. By 1938, Bryan Hall, which housed 130 students, was considered unsafe for habitation.[77] The physical condition of the campus was the best it had ever been—and yet the worst.

lorida State College for Women celebrated its 25th anniversary in 1930. The institution had developed from a small educational community of fewer than 300 persons in 1905 to one that currently included approximately 2,000 students, faculty members, and administrators. In 1930, despite consistently meager appropriations and persistently low salaries, nearly one-half of the total number of faculty members at Florida State College for Women held master's degrees, and approximately one-third held doctoral degrees.[1]

FACULTY

As the decade progressed, financial considerations curtailed hiring ability to a greater than usual extent. Because of this, a majority of those who joined the faculty during the 1930s held only bachelor's or master's degrees; quite a few were graduates of FSCW. A number of the instructors new to the campus in the 1930s later took unpaid leaves of absence to pursue advanced degrees, then returned to Tallahassee and reestablished their teaching careers at the college.[2]

The few professors hired during this decade with doctorates already in hand included Julia Heinlein, Dorothy Disher, Paul W. Shankweiler, and Annie Popper. Heinlein's Ph.D. in psychology enabled her to work as an assistant professor with her husband, Dr. Paul Heinlein. In 1933, however, the

State Legislature passed a law prohibiting nepotism in state positions, and the college subsequently dismissed her. Dorothy Disher took her place the following September.[3] Shankweiler, from the University of North Carolina, became an assistant professor of sociology and worked with Raymond Bellamy and Coyle Moore.

Annie Popper came to FSCW in 1930 from the University of Chicago. As an assistant professor of history, the German-born Popper unintentionally challenged students with her thick accent and foreign pronunciation of historical names and terms. Florence Steinberg spent hours discerning the identity of "Cle-op´-it-ra" (Cleopatra); another young lady puzzled over "Guwadawalla the Turk," and the "enematack," then learned that Popper was saying "gradually the Turks" and the "enemy attacked." A third student succeeded in Popper's class by listening for a particular phrase, "Da oopsha fas," meaning "the upshot was," and then paying close attention to what followed.[4]

By 1932, the college employed 150 faculty members—27 men (25 of whom were married) and 123 women (116 of whom were unmarried).[5] A marked decrease in enrollment in 1933 resulted in a layoff of instructors. Those faculty members who remained faced considerable reductions in salaries that were already "perceptibly below that of first class institutions." Conradi cautioned the Board of Control that highly trained teachers who possessed the characteristics and personalities desired by the college "usually cannot be found at the bargain counters," but his remarks concerning salaries were to no avail.[6]

Despite limited financial remuneration, Conradi and Dodd were able to hire Marion Irish, a candidate for her doctorate in political science from Yale University,[7] to replace Dr. Bessie Randolph, who assumed the presidency of Hollins College in Roanoke, Virginia. For the remainder of the decade, the college hired as few teachers as possible, usually replacements for those faculty members whose resignation, retirement, or death left a vacancy in an essential position. Consequently, the number of faculty members increased by only 20—to a total of 170. Two of that number became important to the School of Music: cellist Owen Sellers, who joined the faculty in 1931 to teach orchestral instruments and direct the Demonstration School orchestra, and Karl Ahrendt, an associate professor of violin. Both had studied at the Cincinnati Conservatory of Music.[8]

Many senior administrators and faculty members at FSCW had been hired before 1909 by A. A. Murphree, or by Conradi shortly after he came to Tallahassee. After 20 or more years at the college, these older faculty members remained dedicated to their profession, but their degree of commitment and ability to inspire students diminished as their ages increased. History professor Arthur "Pi" Williams, 73 years old in 1931, taught classes in Biblical history and Biblical literature until 1937 while students sat in the back of the classroom and caught up on letter-writing, reading, knitting, or sleeping.[9] The perceptible aging of Williams as well as several others, including Conradi, heralded an inevitable change.

Shortly after the death of Classics professor J.B. Game in 1935, the Board of Control established a "special status" category for faculty members. Three teachers who had come to the school at least 20 years earlier—Williams (1901), Lanas Barber (1909), and Maud Schwalmeyer (1912)—elected special status assignments to begin in the fall of 1937. Only Barber lived long enough to experience the arrangement for an appreciable length of time. Williams, then 79 years old, died in July 1937. Schwalmeyer, Director of the Model School and later head of the Demonstration School's primary division, died that December at the age of 72. The Board insisted that Dean Nathaniel Salley relinquish his post as Dean of the School of Education and accept special status, but in his case the term was a euphemism for medical leave.[10]

In 1939, the Legislature established a retirement system specifically for public school teachers (including college and university faculty) that permitted elective retirement after age 60 and specified compulsory retirement after age 70.[11] Conradi celebrated his seventieth birthday in February 1939 but made no move to retire. With his voice faded to little more than a husky whisper, he continued to address the girls at his beloved convocations, encouraging them to aspire to high ideals. Sara Krentzman recalled that "he made little speeches—little sermons. For four years he talked about the finer things of life, with variations." Rhea Miller reminisced that "there was a favorite phrase of Dr. Conradi's that was often repeated, and sometimes a little laughed at, but really it was taken seriously, 'the finer things of life'." He no longer taught classes, so most girls knew him only from convocations and from his frequent rambles, when he "would follow us all over campus and stop and talk to us." They described him as "gentle," "kind," and "compassionate."[12]

Just as Conradi depended on Kellum and Mendenhall, particularly during the 1930s, to manage the business and physical aspects of the college, he relied heavily on Dean William G. Dodd, described as "Prime Minister of the Deans,"[13] to maintain the school's academic direction. By mid-decade, however, a nationwide dissatisfaction with college and university curricula occasioned criticism that FSCW was "not fitting students for life." Dodd turned his attention to modifying the college's liberal arts agenda. Under his direction, the College of Arts and Sciences became one of the first in America to offer majors in the fields of art and speech, thus eliminating the last of the two-year courses of study for which the institution granted certificates rather than diplomas.[14]

Overall, Dodd's efforts resulted in the inauguration of a program of "integrated courses," four general courses that taught the significance of a large field of knowledge rather than specific techniques. Beginning in the fall of 1936, all freshmen and sophomores (except those who passed exemption examinations) took a five-hour course in biological science, physical science, humanities, or social studies as part of their program each semester.[15] The object of the integrated system was to emphasize that

> no matter what vocation or profession a student may engage in after leaving college, she serves society in her chosen activity all the better for being the improved 'person' she may be through the pursuit of liberal knowledge.[16]

In 1938, at the age of 64, Dodd cited ill health and asked Conradi to relieve him of some of his numerous campus duties. He told the president, "people in the college lean on me, and even try to shift their own responsibilities to me. I am sure I should not any longer have to carry this." He asked "to take [his] place on the faculty as a teacher, free from all administrative duties."[17] Conradi appointed Guy Diffenbaugh as Assistant Dean of Arts and Sciences, but Dodd continued to supervise the daily liberal arts life of the college until his retirement six years later.

Younger faculty that replaced the venerable elder generation possessed teaching qualifications that equaled, if not surpassed, those of their older colleagues.[18] Unfortunately, as the size of the student body increased, the professor-student relationship necessarily became more impersonal; in the 1930s and 1940s, a student often spent four years on the campus and never took a class from a given professor. By the same token, unless a professor taught a student, he or she possibly did not know that particular young lady existed among more than 1,800 girls. Consequently, with the exception of Dr. Olivia Dorman of the Classics Department, few of those extremely competent younger teachers ever attained the college-wide recognition of their predecessors, even though they determined to a great extent the future of FSCW.

CHANGING OF THE GUARD

By 1930, much of the behavior that adults had considered outrageous ten years earlier was no longer thought improper.

While at home, girls generally dated, danced, and not only rode in automobiles but also drove them. Many smoked, often with their parents' knowledge and permission.[19] The administration, however, continued to view dating, dancing, smoking, and riding in automobiles with males as unseemly and even indecent conduct. Consequently, many girls who thought they were behaving appropriately found themselves restricted or suspended. Complaints about overly restrictive regulations, heard in the 1920s, continued into the 1930s, particularly from parents of girls who were judged in the wrong.[20]

In the summer of 1932, Dr. Alban Stewart, professor of botany and bacteriology, visited 17 colleges and universities in the Northeast, including Smith, Simmons, Wellesley, Mt. Holyoke, Radcliff, and Goucher. Only Smith exceeded FSCW in enrollment, but Simmons and Wellesley closely approached the number at the Florida school. At each institution, he spoke with personnel or assistant deans about that school's regulations for students. He found that out of a combined enrollment of 7,994, these six institutions had dismissed only eight students for misconduct during the 1931–1932 school year. FSCW, with 1,776 students, had dismissed 18, fifteen for infractions that involved riding with men. According to Stewart, "none of the six . . . dismiss girls for riding with men. They all permit it with certain liberal restrictions." One administrator with whom Stewart spoke expressed the opinion that "the girls were breaking neither civil nor moral law by so doing, and were only doing what they had been accustomed to do at home and thought nothing about it." Stewart suggested that "in regard to girls riding with men, we have considered this to be a major offense so long that we have finally established it as such in our own minds."[21]

His investigations also indicated to him that FSCW fell decidedly behind the times with regard to young ladies dancing and smoking cigarettes. All of the schools he visited permitted dancing with men not only on their campuses, but also in approved places in town and in surrounding towns.

They allowed their students to smoke (not in college buildings at some institutions because of the fire risk), and, moreover, they provided students with "an opportunity to smoke under pleasant surroundings."[22] At FSCW, students typically received four-to-six weeks of restrictions for smoking anywhere but in isolation behind Jennie Murphree Hall.[23]

Stewart proposed that FSCW allow dancing in sorority houses, sponsor college dances in the Gymnasium, permit smoking in "more pleasant places than are at present provided," and modify the rules for riding with men. He capped his presentation with a reminder that political interference with college management was entirely possible:

> We have already made some enemies, by sending girls home, that we can ill afford to have, and it is possible that this indignation might become so great that outside influence might be brought to bear upon us that would force us to change our policies. It would, indeed, be very unfortunate to be told that we do not know how to run our job.[24]

He astutely predicted that, if the college continued its present policies, "our troubles have just begun."

Stewart's account justly criticized social restrictions formulated by Tissie Cawthon in and for a more conservative era. Unfortunately, neither Mina Kerr, Cawthon's immediate successor, nor Charlotte Beckham, who assumed the Dean of Women's post in 1927, possessed appropriate skills to reconcile changing social mores with the particularly conservative attitudes of FSCW's administrators.

In fact, by 1932 students and faculty members complained frequently to Conradi about Beckham. They felt she was "seriously careless" in her everyday dress, that she talked too much about her personal problems "so that there [is] a sacrifice of dignity and poise," and that she overemphasized her social contacts in the community to the neglect of her campus duties. Students especially resented her autocratic manner, and claimed that even when she was available for counseling, she handled their problems in a hasty and tactless fashion.[25] Unfortunately, salary cuts and faculty layoffs made it impractical, if not impossible, to replace her just then.

The complaints continued over the next two years. Finally, Conradi appointed Dr. Olivia Dorman as Acting Dean of Students. A favorite with students as a teacher, Dorman also enjoyed the respect of all who worked with her. She assumed the deanship full-time in September of 1934 and promptly initiated changes in the student social code "to allow the college to grow up and reach the maturity level at other schools in the country."[26]

During the last half of the decade, changes in college government regulations, those rules that the administration established to protect not only students but the good name of the institution, reflected Dorman's influence. In 1935, the "lights out at 10:35" rule, disparaged by upperclassmen as "too suggestive of kindergarten days," changed to 11:30. For the first time ever the administration permitted students to dance with men at campus-sponsored entertainments on Friday nights and at sorority houses on Saturdays.[27] The problem became one of where to find enough young men with whom to dance; at weekly dances in the Gymnasium, the females always outnumbered the males.[28]

Each dormitory and sorority house provided a smoking room for its residents. While the administration continued to prohibit students from smoking in public, it now approved smoking "in residence lounges, in private homes, in the private dining rooms of hotels or tea rooms, in dressing rooms of theaters or stores, booths of beauty parlors, in private cars when riding outside the business section of Tallahassee."[29]

Restrictions on riding engagements, though relaxed, still remained closely supervised and presupposed that the student's parents or guardian had filed a general riding permit with the college. Groups of two or more freshmen or sophomores were allowed to ride in the daytime, juniors were permitted to ride without another student during the day but not at night, and seniors could ride without another student at any time, day or night.[30] If a girl specified a particular destination when she signed out, and then went anywhere else, the administration exacted punishment for the transgression if it was discovered:

> One evening when I signed up to go riding, my boyfriend suggested that we drive to Monticello to visit my parents. When we returned to campus, the house mother said I had left Tallahassee without permission. I was campused for two weeks for going to see my parents![31]

Dating rules remained complicated. Unofficially, any conversation with a male that lasted longer than ten minutes was considered a date. Only seniors had unlimited dating privileges; the school dictated the number of engagements for members of other classes. Approved off-campus destinations included the movie theater, a local tearoom for lunch or dinner, and church. Escorts met their dates in the residence hall parlors and were introduced to the house director or chaperone. The college still maintained a blacklist with names of men considered unsuitable companions.[32]

Ostensibly, FSCW relaxed its objections to smoking, dating, and dancing after 1935. But college officials remained fearful of parental and/or political repercussions for being either too strict or too permissive about those activities. In light of that paradox, regulations somehow reverted to pre-1935 status on the occasion of any college-sponsored public event. For instance, in 1937 the Junior-Senior prom lasted from 8:00 P.M. until midnight with no intermission because authorities were afraid to allow the girls outside and out of sight of the chaperones. To enjoy a cigarette, a student's escort was forced to step outside while his date waited inside. University of Florida students who attended the event suggested that FSCW's administration "stop worrying about the small number of Victorian parents and critics remaining and instead consider the post-college days of its students."[33]

After that the administration relented; for the 1938 prom, girls and their dates were permitted to leave the dance at will for as long as 30 minutes at a time. By 1939, FSCW sponsored monthly dances to which the Dean of Women invited the entire student body of the University of Florida. When 576 men and only 300 women attended the first dance of the year, murmurs of "just like a coed college" were heard around the ballroom.[34] Cotillion Club held weekly dance classes for the girls to keep them abreast of the contemporary steps. The appearance of males on the campus pleased the young ladies but taxed the already crowded dining rooms when girls brought their dates to dinner.[35]

Under Dean Dorman's guidance, administrative control of social life on campus gradually became more realistic. Academic regulations were another matter entirely. The point of contention with the greatest longevity during these years was class absences or cuts, under discussion in the 1920s and still unresolved to student satisfaction in the 1930s. In 1936, the administration finally revised the system to make grades the determining factor in the number of cuts allowed. Students with an A or B average began each quarter with 16 cuts; those with a C average or below were granted eight cuts. If a girl exceeded her cut allowance, the college placed her on academic probation and deducted the excess number of cuts from those allowed her in the next quarter. Continued and indiscriminate cuts resulted in expulsion.

The administration made no provisions in its cut policy for illness, as the Infirmary staff felt that many girls faked sickness to cut classes, especially on Mondays. As a result, college officials faced a quandary of their own making: in trying to preclude misuse of the Infirmary, they made it impossible for students to get medical treatment. Since Infirmary doctors prescribed hospital stays even for colds, students stayed away from the medical facility and spread viruses in classes. Common sense eventually prevailed after students suggested that absences due to illness be excused at the discretion of the

Infirmary staff, retroactive to the first of the school year.[36]

Medical personnel were not officials, though, and the administration's Cut Committee, whose members remained suspicious of Infirmary-approved cuts, reviewed all medical excuses. The committee questioned the absence of one student who elected to go home for a tonsillectomy rather than have the surgery on campus; they were willing to excuse her absence only if the college physician had specifically ordered her to have the operation. The school medical staff was permitted to give day students (those girls who lived at home in Tallahassee with their parents) excuses for missed classes only if the young ladies presented written statements from their attending physicians or parents on the very day they returned to classes.[37] Despite the numerous "if" clauses attached to the new cut policy, the *Flambeau* looked at the bright side and commented, "At least death will not go down in the Registrar's office as a cut."[38]

TRADITIONS

As the number of students and faculty members increased, the closeness of the campus community diminished. Convocation, the only traditional gathering of students that remained compulsory during the 1930s, was held just once a week after 1935. Most seniors still objected to the required attendance, and students in general considered the programs of little value. In 1939, a letter to the editor of the *Flambeau* expressed a popular opinion regarding convocation: "girls do not come because they are made to want to, they are made to come because they do not want to."[39] But like it or not, mandatory attendance at weekly convocations remained part of campus life.

The content of other traditional ceremonies, established to create a bond among the students, varied from year to year. Each successive Dean of Students and pageant chairman altered the particular elements just enough so that original meanings fell victim to innovation. As the Depression dragged on, objections arose to squandering money on "mean-ingless" activities. Still, the college maintained a calendar of traditional events that began in October when seniors received their caps and gowns at Investiture.[40] The speakers changed from year to year, the number of seniors increased consis-tently, but this ceremony remained patently the same.[41] After Investiture, tradition required seniors to wear their caps and gowns to weekly convocation.

In 1936, even that tradition came under fire. While the garb added dignity to the occasion, many upperclassmen felt that wearing the apparel every Tuesday detracted from its significance at Investiture and Commencement. Others found it extremely impractical, if not impossible, to return to their living quarters after their 10:30 A.M. class on Tuesday morn-ings, don their caps and gowns, rush back to the auditorium for convocation at 11:00 A.M., then carry or wear their gowns to the Dining Hall for lunch because they lacked the time to make another trip to their rooms.[42] The problem remained unresolved.

In the fall calendar, Torch Night (now written as two words) came shortly after Investiture. In 1930, Dean Beckham incor-porated a motif she referred to as Lampadedronia, which she described as a torch race held by the Greeks in honor of Prometheus. According to Beckham, runners posted at inter-vals handed off a torch kindled from an altar flame at the shrine of Prometheus. "It was the duty of each to keep the torch burning brightly and to return it undimmed to the altar whence it came," she told the girls. To adapt the image to FSCW, she substituted for Prometheus the deity Alma Mater, in whose honor the festival was held. *Vires, Artes,* and *Mores* became the personifications of Apollo (strength), Pallas Athena (arts and crafts), and Aphrodite (beauty of person and char-acter). The deities were attended by nine muses who sym-bolized various activities of the college.[43]

In 1933, the student pageant director, probably unaware of the original symbolism, further corrupted the Torch Night ceremony with a torchbearer's race. Relay runners from each class carried flaming torches to four altars set up in the Gilchrist Hall courtyard. Seventy-five freshmen ran behind the torchbearers and received their own small torches at the end of the relays.[44]

The spectacle grew like Topsy. In 1936, a group of 100 freshmen marched from one end of the athletic field to a stage erected at the other end. When they arrived at the podium, they pledged their loyalty to Alma Mater. The next year saw a return to the original script of 1927, at which each freshman accepted a flaming torch from a member of the sophomore class and promised to uphold the ideals it represented. In 1939, Torch Night was not held at all. The chairman of the pageant reported that unsettled weather, delayed plans, and conflicts with other student productions caused the cancelation, and promised that the event would be held next fall, early in the school year.[45]

Next on the calendar of traditional events came Fealty, Mina Kerr's revision of the Freshman-Junior Wedding. Between 1930 and 1933, a new script each year confused the relationship between the freshmen and juniors. By 1935, a disillusioned junior class agreed to discontinue its part in Fealty, since freshmen now pledged allegiance to the entire school instead of that class. Over the next two years the college attempted to adapt the traditional ceremony to a modern plot and setting. In a new script, totally alien to the original intent of the Freshman-Junior Wedding or Fealty, a sculptor carved a frieze representing FSCW and dedicated to the women of Florida. When the sculptor fell asleep, he dreamt that the figures he had carved came to life and pledged loyalty to the central character, Alma Mater (*Femina Perfecta*).[46]

Students used that theme for two years, then returned to the original medieval pageant of earlier years, with updated elements. The junior class, once again considered an integral part of the ceremony, chose a "King" who handed down the traditions of the realm to his successor, "Prince Charming" of the freshman class. The ceremony took place in the Court of Saint Westcott, under the watchful eyes of the Duke of Academia (Conradi) and the Duchess of Students (Dorman). This scenario involving faculty members harkened back to the original wedding ceremony performed by the president. The following year it changed again; Prince Freshman was crowned as the ruler of FSCW and guardian of its traditions.[47]

After ten years of "traditional" Torch Night and Fealty ceremonies that changed each year, the student senate recommended that the two be merged and that the Fealty script be retained. The *Flambeau*, which over the previous ten years had vacillated between keeping the school's several traditions and abandoning them, proposed that the college retain Torch Night. According to the editor of the paper, the validity of the torch theme endured while that of Fealty had changed so much that it bore little resemblance to the original purpose.[48] The administration phased out the Fealty ceremony over the next year.

Odd/Even rivalries endured practically unaltered throughout the 1930s; the only changes were enhancements in the creation of honorary organizations. On Friday night, October 24, 1924, a group of Odds met in a downtown cafe and created an honorary society that they called Spirogira. They selected a skull and crossbones for their emblem and black and white for their colors; members were chosen from Odd classes for their outstanding leadership, loyalty, and service. Six years later, Evens followed suit with an honorary society they called Esteren. Founded on December 14, 1930, the organization stated as its purpose "the perpetuation of Even traditions, class loyalty and friendship." Its symbol was a large cauldron over an outdoor fire. The faculty approved both organizations and enjoyed membership in them.[49]

The highlight of the fall athletic season, Odd/Even basketball and volleyball games on Thanksgiving Day, survived attempted modifications. In 1933, Katherine Montgomery, head of Physical Education, tried to replace the traditional basketball and volleyball with hockey and soccer. Students objected, and the holiday games remained unchanged.[50]

The winter and spring calendar of events included annual college-wide birthday accolades on February 20 for President Conradi, quasi-traditional events such as the Junior-Senior prom, and various class productions such as Freshman Carnival and Junior Minstrels. An addition to the spring events came in 1936, when the College Government Association and the YWCA combined the Freshman Commission and Freshman Cabinet to create the Sophomore Council, with tapping of new members in the spring. May Day celebrations remained unchanged except in 1937, when heavy rains caused the postponement of the celebration. The identities of the queen and members of her court, always a closely-kept secret until the pageant, had already been given to state newspapers for publication. A message to kill the announcement, frantically sent over the Associated Press wires, reached the various newspapers too late. The queen's name was well known by the time of her coronation two weeks later.[51]

Changes in the Sophomore-Senior breakfast, held in conjunction with the May Day celebration, occurred because of the elective nature of participation in such ceremonies. Without an established freshman-junior connection, formed through the erstwhile wedding or Fealty ceremony, seniors no longer automatically had sophomore sisters. Those in the older class who wished to join in the early morning festivities placed their names on a list for pairing with the younger girls. Participants still dressed all in white and enjoyed a traditional Southern breakfast of fried chicken, grits and gravy, biscuits, and strawberries.[52]

ORGANIZATIONS

Organizations formed on campus during the 1930s ranged in purpose from seriously academic (Phi Beta Kappa), to skillfully entertaining (Tarpon Club), to satirically quasi-academic (Mortified). Installation at the college of the Alpha of Florida

Chapter of Phi Beta Kappa still holds special significance for Florida State College for Women and its successor, Florida State University, in that it came a full three years before the honorary granted permission to the University of Florida for installation of the Beta Chapter. FSCW's eight-year quest for this academic recognition began in January 1926, when ten members of Phi Beta Kappa then on the faculty created the Phi Beta Kappa Association of Tallahassee to consider the means of establishing a chapter of the fraternity at the college. Apparently the University of Florida had either already approached or was in the process of approaching the national headquarters of the organization with regard to a chapter at Gainesville. When the national secretary visited FSCW, he indicated that joint consideration with the university might be in order.[53] Conradi and the local association deemed that feasible and awaited word from the University of Florida.

No further official action took place until February 1929, at which time a game of one-upmanship ensued between the two institutions. Representatives from FSCW met with the new president of the University of Florida, John J. Tigert,[54] and two of the seven or eight Phi Beta Kappa members on the faculty at UF. At that time, Tigert seemed little interested in the proposal. Subsequently, the Gainesville members indicated that they preferred to present their case independently, "upon its own merits." FSCW organizers replied that "since the Phi Beta Kappa Association of Tallahassee, 16 of whose 20 members are on the College Faculty, felt that the Florida State College for Women merited the recognition of Phi Beta Kappa, we decided to proceed with our own case."[55] University interests responded that they had received information indirectly indicating they would receive their chapter in the very near future.[56] Their application was subsequently turned down, however, ostensibly because the university did not offer classes in Greek.[57]

Over the next three years, the college and Phi Beta Kappa exchanged requests for information and data. In September 1934, FSCW and Connecticut College for Women at New London became the first women's colleges in the United States to be granted independent chapters of Phi Beta Kappa. The honorary organization installed the Alpha Chapter of Florida at Florida State College for Women on March 4 and 5, 1935.[58]

Some six months later the Gainesville Phi Beta Kappa Association suggested that the Alpha Chapter petition the national organization for a bilateral section of the chapter to be extended to the University of Florida, thereby obtaining membership for the university as soon as possible. Members of the Alpha Chapter were reluctant to interfere with national procedure so soon after inception, but they did notify the national secretary that they had no objections to such an arrangement. The national society determined that the university should await a separate charter.[59]

The Tarpon Club, a synchronized swimming team, created a new entertainment tradition on campus when it came into existence in 1936. The Life Saving Club, whose members taught swimming and supervised water activities at both the Gymnasium pool and Camp Flastacowo, sponsored the group. Once organized, the swimmers lost no time in becoming well known both statewide and nationwide. With an eye to positive publicity, Dean Dorman and President Conradi granted permission to Fox Movietone News to film one of the club's first water pageants, presented in the Gymnasium pool during the 1937 Thanksgiving festivities; problems with camera positions and lighting arrangements caused the plans to fall through. In 1939, Grantland Rice Movie Sportlights arranged to film 25 Tarpon Club swimmers in a staged performance at Wakulla Springs for a movie short feature.[60] This presented such a good opportunity to advertise FSCW that the administration even allowed club members who had used up their class cuts to participate with no penalties.[61]

The third organization to appear on the campus during the decade was Mortified, founded on April 27, 1937, between dinner and that evening's Mortar Board induction. Mortified's purpose was "to recognize leadership and service and to counsel its members to strive for scholarship during the remainder of their college years." It offered alternative recognition for girls who contributed their time and efforts to the campus but didn't exactly maintain a superior grade point average, one of Mortar Board's requirements. Each year at the close of the very dignified Mortar Board tapping assembly, members of Mortified leaped noisily from their seats in the auditorium wings, vaulted over the modesty railing, and dragged their newest members to the stage for a brief but raucous ceremony. Those girls who belonged to Mortified proudly wore their organization's emblem, a safety pin nestled on a bed of blush pink and envy green ribbons. The guiding spirit of the group was Jimmy Durante, selected in recognition of his famous lines, "Am I mortified? Am I mortified? Hahhhhhhh!!!"[62]

THE DEPRESSION

The Depression affected enrollment at the college only marginally prior to 1935, and never in a negative sense unless one takes into consideration the extremely overcrowded conditions resulting from increased attendance. It did affect how girls paid for their education. Dr. Elizabeth Gordon Andrews, Director of Personnel, recorded a striking increase in the number of students who inquired about financial aid. In 1930–1931, she interviewed 55 girls regarding assistance; in 1931–1932, she met with 406. That same year she also received 309 applications for the 96 dining room scholarships available.[63]

In 1934, the federal government, acting through the Federal Emergency Relief Administration, granted the college a monthly stipend of $1,700 with which to employ approximately 180 students in part-time clerical and other assorted positions at 30¢ per hour. The personnel office selected the students on the basis of need, character, and ability to do college work. Later the National Youth Administration provided jobs to keep students in school and sponsored a variety of educational work activities. On campus, the NYA provided funding for 185 student jobs. The students carried out necessary duties, particularly in the library, where they did "work long needed to be done."[64]

Clerical skills came in handy. Loretta Ellias performed secretarial duties for Dr. Herman Kurz, head of the Botany Department, to help pay for her education. "I was only supposed to work about 15 hours per week, but he was writing manuscripts and working in research. He would dictate to me and I'd take it down in shorthand."[65] Marian Conn worked for Katherine Montgomery in the Physical Education Department, typing and doing "what ever else had to be done." By 1937, Dean Andrews reported that there were at least three applicants for every student employment position on campus.[66]

Outside of building and maintenance costs, the single most expensive element in the college budget was the food service.[67] There the school economized in various ways. Full breakfasts became a thing of the past. In 1932, a typical morning meal consisted of grapefruit, muffins and butter, bacon, scrambled eggs, and coffee. Four years later students were served grapefruit, bacon, cereal or biscuits, and coffee. "One day you'd have bacon and biscuits or toast and the next day you'd have an egg and biscuits or toast. You didn't have bacon and eggs on the same day."[68] When campus milk consumption outstripped the supply available from the college dairy, hot cocoa was discontinued as a breakfast beverage in order to conserve milk. To avoid wasting food at other times, three tables in the dining room served only soup, crackers, and milk for girls who from time to time did not feel like eating a full meal; occasionally girls on weight-loss diets dined there.[69]

Anna May Tracy never sacrificed nutrition in her efforts to conserve, but sometimes she struggled for variety. Occasionally the boarding department purchased produce directly from the parents of students, allowing the exchange to apply to the cost of room and board. For a while thereafter that particular fruit or vegetable became a menu staple.[70] In the spring of 1934, Katherine Blood's family traded three truckloads of oranges from their grove in Winter Haven for the semester's expenses, and for quite a while after that oranges appeared on the menu regularly.[71] Another student recalled:

> There [were] always at least two vegetables and always a salad and always a dessert, and all the milk you could ever drink, all the bread you could eat and butter. The meals were nutritional and well balanced, but there was always one or two things we hated, like creamed eggs.[72]

One meal, Thanksgiving dinner, remained as lavish as ever:

> We'd all be in the [Old Dining Hall], and everybody'd come in, nicely dressed, and then we'd sing the blessing. Then, out of the kitchen would file the student servers. Each one would have a platter with this great big turkey on it, one for each table. Eight girls massacred a turkey. I think we made turkey sandwiches for that night also. It was gentility, kind of homey-like and everybody just went 'ahhhhhh' to see those turkeys.[73]

The search for revenue sources occasionally meant relaxation of unnecessarily rigid standards. In 1932 and 1933, the Executive Council, composed of the deans and college officers, voted against the *Flambeau*'s request to accept cigarette advertising, a relatively new but very lucrative possible source of income for the paper.[74] By 1935, however, advertisements for both Lucky Strike and Chesterfield cigarettes appeared in the publication. The school's capitulation was complete when the Phillip Morris bellboy, on a promotional tour of the South, dined on campus as a guest of the students; after dinner he climbed up on a table in the Dining Hall and gave his popular radio call, "Call for Phil-lip 'Mor-a-ess'."[75]

ᨀ

The uncertainty of the Depression years and the increasing number of persons attending or employed by the college caused some friction between city and school officials. Citizens in danger of losing their homes resented the fact that

FSCW paid no municipal taxes on its property, valued at more than $3 million by 1936. Nor were they happy to find that as crime rates rose in relation to hard times, the college received police protection free of charge. Kellum not only supervised campus development during the 1930s, but he also presented fiscal facts to city residents to lessen opportunities for conflict. He spent many hours speaking in behalf of the school, stressing that the institution paid for and provided services to the town. As its largest customer, the school paid the city-owned utility system more than $20,000 annually for its electricity, water, and gas. Faculty members had between $150,000 and $200,000 invested in personal homes or residential rental property in or near the city, and of course they paid property taxes. The Demonstration School, financed entirely by the college but open to the community, saved the county approximately $40,000 in buildings and teachers' salaries.[76] Moreover, the student body of more than 2,000 spent an average of $200 per person each year, mostly in Tallahassee.

Chapter X
Changes in the Air: 1940-1946

n the early 1940s, the administration of Florida State
College for Women, reacting to situations beyond
its control, unintentionally ushered the school and
students into the modern age. Wartime, the presence of soldiers, an unprecedented increase in enrollment, a change of
leadership, and finally, a long overdue change in outlook
anticipated the inevitable conversion from women's college
to coeducational liberal arts university.

A NEW PRESIDENT

President Edward Conradi celebrated his 71st birthday in
February 1940. A year earlier, on reaching the age of 70, he
had informed the Board of Control that he believed himself
to be in good health and did not choose to resign. Despite
the legislative policy that mandated retirement at age 70, the
board had reappointed Conradi as head of FSCW that spring
and did so again in March 1940.[1] Then a series of perplexing
circumstances ensued. In July 1940, the *Florida Times Union*
reported that Conradi's retirement was imminent.[2] The president, who at that time had no intention of resigning, discussed the issue with board members at their July meeting
and apparently left under the impression that the announcement had been a mistake. Shortly thereafter the board met
with J.W. Matherly, Dean of the College of Business Administration at the University of Florida, and discussed the possi-

bility of his appointment as president of FSCW. Matherly told the board that its salary offer of $6,000 per year was inadequate since he currently received $6,250 at the university. The board subsequently arranged to provide housing for him in Tallahassee, then elected him president of the college, to assume his duties when the school session began in September 1940.[3]

Conradi, unaware that he was expected to step down, was vacationing in Montreat, North Carolina, when Florida newspapers again carried notice of his retirement. He learned of the matter through a letter from the president of Rollins College.[4] Understandably upset, Conradi wrote to Henry P. Adair, Chairman of the Board of Control, and advised him of the apparent misunderstanding; he repeated that he had no desire to retire. Meanwhile, Matherly sent a telegram to Adair saying, "I have decided to withdraw entirely. Please act accordingly. I think this is the best way out for all concerned."[5]

The timing of the newspaper report and the wording of Matherly's communication suggested that some predetermined plan of action had gone awry, as did the embarrassed retraction of a notice that had appeared in the *Alligator* announcing Conradi's retirement.[6] Adair telephoned Conradi and "suggested" that he tender his resignation in March 1941, the time when appointments were usually made for the upcoming year, to be effective in June To ensure Conradi's commitment to this agreement, Board Secretary J.T. Diamond released a notice to the Associated Press stating: "The Board of Control is pleased to announce that Dr. Edward Conradi will continue as president of Florida State College for Women during the coming college term ending June 30, 1941."[7] Students celebrated Conradi's birthday in February 1941 with particular sentiment. "A special group sang two special songs and we all shed a tear."[8]

Meanwhile, the Board of Control continued its search for a new president for FSCW. The members finally settled on

Doak Campbell, Ph.D., Professor of Education and Director of the Division of Surveys and Field Studies at George Peabody College for Teachers in Nashville, Tennessee. Campbell's scholarly interest in women's colleges and the problems they faced, and his familiarity with the Tallahassee institution through recent inquiries and reports, placed him in an ideal position to assume the presidency in October 1941 with little disruption of student and faculty life.[9]

On Monday night, October 6, a severe storm hit Tallahassee with 65-mile-per-hour winds that stripped and uprooted pines, toppled three large sycamores near the Music Annex, and littered the grounds with debris.[10] Because some electric wires on campus blew down, the administration insisted that the girls remain inside for much of the next day. With the wires repaired, the campus reopened in time for the regular weekly convocation, and the new president addressed the student body for the first time. He began his introductory speech with the quip: "I hope in future years when you remember the big blow, you will be referring to the storm."[11]

According to Mart Pierson, president of the College Government Association, the campus accepted Campbell at that moment. He quickly impressed both students and state residents with his contemporary attitude. When asked his views of such things as young ladies smoking, Campbell stated, "I don't like it, but I do not feel that it is up to me to dictate to others that they should not do on the campus what they are permitted to do at home." An editorial in a central Florida newspaper agreed with him, noting that keeping girls from smoking cigarettes was not a major function of a college, and that the smoking of cigarettes by girls was no longer considered among the major sins.[12]

Though Campbell clearly brought an active leadership style to the presidency, promising a tenure significantly different from that of his predecessor, he and Conradi maintained a polite friendship. The Board of Control elected Conradi President Emeritus; he retained an office in Westcott until his unexpected death on December 1, 1944.[13]

FACULTY AND ADMINISTRATION

The exodus of the mid-1930s continued into the 1940s as the remaining "original" faculty members reached retirement age. Elmer Smith, a member of the faculty since 1903, turned 71 in December 1941 and retired the following June.[14] An overworked, tired, and barely active William G. Dodd retired on July 1, 1944. Dr. Guy Diffenbaugh, named Dodd's assistant in 1938, replaced him. Diffenbaugh quickly learned what his predecessor had known all along, that dual roles as dean and professor were extremely difficult to juggle. Within a few months, he abandoned his teaching duties; the following year the college hired Dr. Claude Flory to teach Diffenbaugh's courses.[15]

Shortly after Dodd took his leave, Ella Scoble Opperman, Dean of the School of Music, stepped down. Campbell named Karl O. Kuersteiner acting dean in her place. The final member of Conradi's entourage to quit daily campus life was John G. Kellum, who retired on March 31, 1945. His career had included 16 years as Assistant Chief Clerk of the Florida House of Representatives (1901–1917), 12 years as the secretary to the Board of Control (1905–1917), and 38 years as business manager of FSCW (1907–1945). During his time at the college he established a campus book store, the farm and dairy, the on-campus laundry, Camp Flastacowo at Lake Bradford, funding for student publications, the college post office, and the campus bank.[16] His shrewd financial management over the years enabled the school to survive on the paltry sums meted out by the State Legislature.

PHYSICAL PLANT

Campbell, like Conradi 32 years before, inherited an overcrowded and underfunded campus. Immediately upon assuming the presidency, he initiated a study of plant and equipment utilization and determined that housing was "taxed considerably beyond its capacity." Moreover, he found classroom, laboratory, auditorium, and office facilities "much below minimum standards for the present student body."[17] Conradi had reported to the Board of Control in 1940 that, despite the opening of Landis Hall a year earlier, all dormitories and other residential sites such as sorority houses, the dietitian's cottage, approved houses near campus, and living quarters in the Infirmary were filled to capacity.[18] The situation as Campbell saw it in 1941 remained unchanged.

The physical condition of Bryan Hall (now reserved exclusively for freshmen, along with Reynolds and Jennie Murphree halls), with its too-small, dark, badly ventilated rooms, cracked walls, worn floors, and shabby furniture added to the housing problem.[19] Leaks over the upper Atrium and three second-floor bedrooms made it necessary for residents to have buckets available at all times to catch rain water. Several parents who inspected campus housing facilities over the summer of 1941 withdrew their daughters from school rather than allow them to spend their freshman year in Bryan Hall. Attorney Wilbur Whitehurst of Wauchula advised the business office that he had canceled payment on the check for his daughter's housing, saying:

> Mary Elizabeth did not register at the college due to the fact that when she arrived the place was so thoroughly and completely crowded and overfilled that there was no place for her to stay. The place assigned to her in the basement of Bryan Hall is no place to live.[20]

Fourteen girls simply refused assignment to rooms there, and several more moved into the dormitory under protest. With the country's entry into World War II in December 1941, a government ban on nonessential construction work and a correlated shortage of building materials curtailed plans to renovate the hall. Instead, the college painstakingly arranged alternative housing for as many girls as possible.[21]

Bryan Hall was not the only dormitory in poor condition in 1941. The October wind-and-rain storm that greeted the new president did enough damage to two-year-old, $500,000 Landis Hall that a janitor opined, "That ain't no building—just a show and mighty shabby put together!"[22] The college charged girls $16 more per year to live in the newest and most luxurious residence hall on the campus, yet already pipes leaked, flooding all the rooms on the fourth and fifth floors, and rainwater seeped into rooms through ceilings and walls. Still worse, sewage pipes leading to West Jefferson Street frequently backed up and overflowed into the basement.[23]

Gilchrist Hall, completed in 1928, fared little better in students' eyes. A resident described her room as

> a delightful little rat-hole in the basement, with windows so arranged that we have to stand on a chair to see out. Also, bushes outside keep out the sunshine and light. It is next door to the smoker, so we shall enjoy daily the aroma of stale tobacco smoke.[24]

Not only was the room in the basement, but it was also infested with flies and ants, the latter of which had "thrown up an earthworks under our radiator and set up housekeeping." Throughout the rest of the dormitory, 46 students lived in rooms intended for half that number, and those assigned to the fifth floor had only small dormer windows for ventilation. Double occupancy of single rooms was also common in Reynolds Hall.[25]

The situation deteriorated steadily. In 1943, the first year that FSCW's freshman class enrollment exceeded one thousand, the housing office abandoned attempts to evacuate Bryan Hall. Once more girls were assigned to its dilapidated main section; the college even set up cots in the old dormitory's leaky tower rooms. That year numerous freshmen spent their first semester at FSCW living in kitchens, smokers, and recre-

ation rooms. By spring of 1944, advance registration promised a student population approaching 2,400. The registrar
restricted enrollment to state residents and those out-of-state
students who had attended during the previous (1943–44)
session.[26]

The War Production Board granted FSCW emergency permission to construct a temporary dormitory with living space
for 154 girls. The school also purchased and renovated six
houses for 110 more students.[27] When heavy rains in August
and September slowed completion of the projects, the administration asked upperclassmen to delay their arrival at the
college until there were accommodations for them on campus. Sixty-six girls arrived in mid-October, but the situation
had not improved. Housing officers went room to room in
the residence halls asking roommates if they would accept a
third person for a week or so; those who agreed found their
tiny quarters even more cramped by the addition of an army
cot and mattress roll for their "guest." The situation concerned
Campbell enough that he asked Governor Spessard Holland
to assure parents that renovations on the three residences
and completion of the new dormitory were imminent and
would significantly ease the overcrowding.[28]

Plans for the emergency dormitory originally specified
wood construction. But constraints on building materials
caused the contractors to use concrete block instead, making
the structure more permanent and the most nearly fireproof
building on campus. The single-story white structure, situated immediately south of the Physical Education Building,[29]
looked completely at odds with the surrounding architecture.
At first called New Hall and later Magnolia Hall, it offered
residents the same or more amenities as the other halls. Rooms
had separate closets with luggage compartments for each
occupant, separate dressers, and fluorescent lamps for each
desk. Central lavatories and baths with glass brick partitions,
a basement laundry and kitchen, and a large lounge with an
open fireplace added to the residents' comfort.[30] This "tem-

porary" dormitory remained part of the campus landscape for more than 30 years.[31]

Of the six houses purchased by the college, three stood adjacent to the campus on West Jefferson Street: Parkside, Hillside, and Campusside, a college-approved boarding house already in use as a freshman dormitory. The three residences were remodeled but met only minimal housing standards; Hillside had so many fire scares over the next year that its residents nicknamed it Hellside. In addition to those three domiciles, Campbell purchased the Cockrell, Van Brunt, and Lang houses, which were located downtown on the site of a proposed extension of the Capitol. When unexpected delays arose in finding new homes for the families currently in those houses, girls assigned to live in The Village, as the group of three houses was later known, were guests in faculty homes and the Home Management House while they awaited the completion of their quarters.[32]

Eventually movers transported the Lang house to the west side of campus and positioned it facing the tennis courts. Over the next several weeks 32 freshmen took up residence there.[33] The Van Brunt house was moved piece by piece to its new foundation at the same locale. Finally the Cockrell house arrived *in toto*, and 17 girls moved into it in January 1945. In the interim, students became accustomed to seeing half a house resting on the archery range.[34]

As Allied Forces moved closer to victory in Europe, Campbell reiterated earlier demands for physical improvements on the campus. Citing historically consistent inadequacies in both student housing and educational facilities, he called for more than $3 million in funding for new buildings. His priorities included "at least one additional housing unit for approximately 240 students," an extension of the History Building, construction of the already-planned north wing of the Physical Education Building, a new auditorium capable of seating at least 3,500 persons, and most particularly a modern music building for what he described as "the most poorly housed recognized music school in the country." His demands yielded approval for the addition of 16 classrooms and a number of offices for the History Building,[35] but delays in getting materials slowed work on the structure so much that students and teachers preempted the first-floor rooms even before the addition was completed late in 1946. An enrollment of more than 2,400 in 1945 necessitated the addition of housing for 75 more students. The school converted storage space on the top floor of Reynolds Hall into rooms and leased two large residences near the campus—Hutchinson House on the corner of Jefferson and Copeland Streets and Fisher House at the corner of Macomb and Pensacola streets.[36]

WORLD WAR II

World War II affected every minute of life on the campus, from the threat of American involvement during the 1940–41 session to VE Day on May 8, 1945, and throughout the 1945–46 academic year. Early in 1940, First Lady Eleanor Roosevelt, as a guest of the Alumnae Association, spoke to college and state officials, students, and citizens. Students jammed the side aisles, the balcony aisles, and the back of the room as she addressed the largest crowd ever assembled in Westcott Auditorium. Mrs. Roosevelt's presence proclaimed American strength and security to the girls in particular, for most of them were extremely concerned about and frightened by world events. When she finished speaking, the applause was thunderous.[37]

During the summer of 1940, Tallahassee citizens formed a Committee for the Defense of America and elected physics professor Harold Richards its general chairman. President Conradi, Registrar Simeon Doyle, resident engineer H.D. Mendenhall, and numerous professors served actively in the organization. In the fall, students arrived on campus interested in aiding the European war effort. An active "Bundles for Britain" drive was under way in a room on the fourth floor of the barely completed Longmire Building. Chairman

Dr. Marion Hay supervised the collection of money, reconditioning of clothing, and knitting of new articles to send to British soldiers and families besieged by the German Luftwaffe's nightly bombing raids.[38] One freshman described the effort as follows:

> Everybody up here is knitting. Ever since the Bundles for Britain drive started, the girls have been knitting socks, caps, sweaters, helmets, gloves, and wristlets for Britain's boys. I'm in with the bunch who are mending old clothes to send to the women and children. They [volunteers] are out of needles. Dr. Hay had to send to Jacksonville and Gainesville for more.[39]

Indirect involvement in the war was one thing, but when the consequences of war came closer to home, commitment at first wavered. In the fall of 1940, the *Flambeau* stridently opposed the adoption of the Burke-Wadsworth Act, the country's first peacetime conscription plan, for what it admitted were purely selfish reasons.[40] On a campus that had until recently rigorously regulated all contact between males and females, the newspaper felt it was unfair to force the girls to spend both their weekdays and their weekends "minus young men and dates and dances and corsages." The "image of the road to Tallahassee [from Gainesville] devoid of orange rat caps, thumbs pointing north, convertibles adorned with gator stickers" appalled them.[41] But that attitude soon changed.

At the first Artist Series program of the 1940–41 session, the U. S. Marine Corps Band and Glee Club performed for a standing-room-only crowd in Westcott Auditorium. The uniformed members of the Glee Club, singing to the impressionable students, "grinned, and put their hands over their hearts, and winked." Students described the campus as "swarming with soldiers looking for dates. Very exciting." On weekends girls hung out their residence windows "to see who was riding by because there were just boys everywhere. It was just wonderful."[42]

The administration considered the prospect of soldiers

swarming over the campus more threatening than "exciting" or "wonderful." Granted, since 1935 the college had relaxed dating restrictions to a considerable extent, but both Conradi and Dorman remained uncomfortable with the concept of too many boys in proximity to the campus. Dorman wanted outdoor lights installed in the open-air theater and at the west side of the campus near the heating plant to prevent students from "involving themselves in undesirable and dangerous conduct with young men at night." She also insisted that police service extend to the entire campus rather than just the dormitory and building areas "for the moral welfare of the students and the reputation of the institution."[43]

With more than 2,000 members of the Army Air Corps expected to arrive at Dale Mabry Field, less than three miles from the campus, the college instituted an emergency ruling forbidding students to leave the grounds after 6:30 P.M. in groups of fewer than four, regardless of class standing. Apparently the new regulation met strong opposition, for in convocation the following week Conradi implied that the administration had taken the action not on its own initiative but at the suggestion of Dale Mabry Field authorities. That being the case, College Government Association officers and members of the editorial staff of the *Flambeau* invited the base commander to come to campus and discuss the situation with them. The commander did so, and told the young ladies that the base authorities had made no such suggestion as to changing campus rules and regulations, nor would they presume to do so in the future. He added that in his opinion the army base posed no threat to the daily life of the college, and both the officers and enlisted men "would be delighted to attend any sort of dance or reception which the college saw fit to give."[44]

Despite military assurances, the regulation remained,[45] along with an added edict that future interviews with persons not connected to the campus be cleared through the college publicity office. Conradi and Dorman attempted to stem student complaints with a well-chaperoned social gathering. In April, nearly 1,500 students attended an "informal but highly dignified" reception in Landis Hall for 200 enlisted men who had been carefully selected by the base chaplains for the invitation-only event.[46]

With the exception of Conradi's retirement and Doak Campbell's arrival, college life continued on a fairly normal course during the fall of 1941. That ended on Sunday afternoon, December 7, when news of the Japanese attack on Pearl Harbor reached the campus. Then "a kind of chill" settled on everyone. Maryanne Cannon and several of her sorority sisters had spent the weekend in Gainesville at the Kappa Alpha's Antebellum Ball. On Sunday the girls returned to Tallahassee and found "the whole school was in a bedlam. News of Pearl Harbor had reached the campus while we were enroute."[47] Loretta Ellias was in the Bacteriology Department preparing materials for her Monday class when she learned of the attack:

> I heard this knocking on the door of the laboratory and I heard someone calling to me almost hysterically. It was my roommate come to tell me that Pearl Harbor was bombed. Many of the students went to their religious student houses, gathered there, and others gathered in the living rooms of the dormitories or they went to their sorority houses. People wanted to congregate.[48]

On Tuesday at convocation Campbell cautioned students not to panic or pass on rumors.[49] To assure parents of their daughters' safety and prevent a mass withdrawal from school, the Board of Control authorized the president to have military police placed on the campus "at any time in his judgement it is necessary to provide proper protection for the students," and to have the campus placed "out of military bounds" if he felt it necessary or desirable to do so.[50] The girls were torn between consideration of their "responsibility to men in the armed forces" and cooperation with the administration in its attempts to protect them from "unfortunate situations." The *Flambeau* suggested that college officials sponsor socially approved meetings between "college girls and soldier boys,"[51] but Dorman took no immediate action.

As head of the Tallahassee Defense Committee, Dr. Richards attended a special defense preparation program at the University of Florida. He reported that the federal government regarded every place within 300 miles of any coast as a target area; therefore, residents of the campus and the city must assume that Germany would bomb Tallahassee. Girls were instructed to turn out the lights every time they left their rooms, even if for only a minute, "because it is said that one lighted window can reveal an entire community." It was a Judiciary offense to forget the rule.[52] The possibility of attack suddenly became more real to students when the school received two air-raid sirens to be synchronized with those in the city. The sirens were placed on the roofs of Landis Hall and Westcott and were audible far beyond the Sigma Kappa house on West Park Avenue at Macomb. Girls were assigned to various shelters established in the basements of the Library and the History Building, the first floor of Westcott, the first and second floors of Gilchrist and Landis Halls, or the basement and first floor of the Longmire Building.[53]

Students considered air-raid drills, like fire drills, necessary evils and grumbled, "Even if it's a real air raid this time, I cannot go down to the basement shelter in Gilchrist Hall and back up those five flights of stairs another time this week."[54] Nevertheless, they cooperated. Once girls reached their assigned shelter, many spent the prescribed seven minutes' waiting period in the dark, rolling their hair or cleaning their faces. When the "all clear" sounded, the lights revealed creamed faces, complexion masks, and pincurls. On one occasion, a student declared fervently that she hoped "Gainesville never ever paid a surprise visit during an air raid drill!"[55]

As the sky over the campus resounded with airplanes swooping low, their motors wide open,[56] numerous members of the campus community and more than 400 students and graduates enlisted in the armed services or left to do voluntary war work. Lt. Marion Clark Phillips, FSCW 1932, a member of the Army Nurses' Corps serving in Europe, was the only alumna to lose her life in the line of duty.[57] To those who remained on campus, Katherine Montgomery of the Physical Education Department declared it was the faculty's patriotic duty to be fit. She proposed that they all meet daily on the open recreational area north of Landis Hall to run for one hour; the suggestion received little support.[58]

A campus defense council chaired by Lucy Lester, associate professor of French, quickly enrolled faculty and students in Red Cross first aid classes. Beginning in the fall of 1942, the council added "unfamiliar courses with masculine names" such as "Defense Mechanics" and "Radio Code Practice" to the curriculum. FSCW was the first school in the South to offer a course in military mapmaking, which trained students to read, interpret, and compile cartographic war materials in preparation for employment in wartime agencies. Every one of the 27 students who completed the first course found a job with the federal government in Washington, D.C., most with the Cartographic Drafting Department of the Army Map Service.[59]

The Botany Department offered credit for a defense gardening course and furnished seeds for tomatoes, turnips, radishes, beets, carrots, potatoes, lettuce, spinach, and peas. Because of the wartime labor shortage on campus, the girls even plowed their own plots. The produce harvested belonged to the girls, who made arrangements to have it canned, gave it to their families or to friends in town, or sold it.[60]

The food service coped with the problems of wartime in several ways. At first, Anna May Tracy initiated her own rationing system to forestall raising boarding costs. The dietitian declared that neither the quantity nor the quality of the food had suffered or was going to suffer because of national defense,[61] but, as it did for all Americans, the food situation got worse before it got better. Tracy, always practical and in command, asked students to "forget their likes and dislikes for the duration."[62] Of course, some students complained about any inconvenience:

> The starving Greeks would get a lot to eat if they should come to our dining hall. At every meal someone wishes for them. If someone leaves a half of a bun, or a smidge of butter, or a string bean on her plate, she is reminded of the starving Greeks.[63]

By early 1943, the boarding department no longer planned menus and then purchased the required foodstuffs; on the contrary, Tracy waited until the available food arrived, then created her menus. The fact that large quantities of spinach appeared on dinner plates each time the ground's crew cut the ivy around Bryan Hall was considered purely coincidental. When national sugar rationing went into effect, the dining hall collected coupons from each student, served more fruits, sweetened bakery products with honey or cane syrup, and served unfrosted cakes cut into 80 pieces instead of the usual 60. Hot chocolate, once a victim of the Depression, now became the victim of cocoa rationing. A temporary freeze on butter meant FSCW served butterless toast and rolls for a week. To everyone who asked why the college had a shortage of butter when it had its own dairy, Tracy explained that all of the milk was used for drinking and cooking and that they were lucky to get that. When the Dining Hall experienced difficulty obtaining meat, the kitchen staff compensated. Sometimes they served eggs three times a day. One of the less popular meatless meals consisted of large baked potatoes covered with gravy reconstituted from a powdered mix.[64]

PRESENCE OF MILITARY PERSONNEL

By September 1942, faced not only with the existence of Dale Mabry Field but the recently established Camp Gordon Johnston (whose personnel the local newspaper described as "husky, alert lads with a look of determination in their eyes"), both Campbell and Dorman accepted the inevitability of encounters between students and servicemen. Rather than try to eliminate all contact, school officials determined to control the nature of those contacts. They formulated plans for weekly picnics, dances, at-homes, and Sunday music hours, to which girls invited groups of soldiers. The college insisted that the ratio of females to males at these functions be at least two to one. Once each month the administration sponsored a formal dance in the Longmire Building for approximately 200 couples.[65] Delighted students and nervous administrators looked forward to the entertainments for the soldiers:

> As a part of the new social plans there is to be a soldier party this Saturday night. Miss Dorman has it planned to the minutest detail. One hundred soldiers have been invited and two hundred girls. There will be a party each Saturday night. Miss Dorman will have nervous prostrations if it's a flop.[66]

Students cooperated with the security restrictions for the most part, but many still felt that FSCW fell far behind the rest of the city in recognizing its wartime responsibilities, particularly with regard to social situations. Once again the *Flambeau* took a provocative position, citing Stetson University and North Carolina State College for Women as examples of schools that allowed their female students to attend USO Officers' Club dances. George Anderson, editor of the *Sunday News-Democrat*, agreed that FSCW should allow its students to attend social affairs at the local USO and Servicemen's Club, as did the director of the club and Secretary of State R. A. Gray. Regardless of local opinions, FSCW's administration had no intention of allowing its charges to associate with just anyone who might wear a uniform. They did respond to the criticism, however, and permitted student organizations such as the Glee Club and the Band to participate in functions at nearby military bases.[67]

Little did the administration realize that students provided entertainment for some military personnel from Dale Mabry

Field even while confined to campus. Girls sunbathing on the rooftop sun deck of Landis Hall, often with their halter tops removed, waved cheerily or scrambled for towels when planes on training flights dipped and swooped lower than necessary over the building. Rumor had it that many of those planes contained nose-mounted cameras.[68]

In mid-March 1944, the campus suffered an annoying and potentially dangerous outbreak of bacillary dysentery. Dr. June Fletcher, in charge of the Infirmary, became alarmed when more than the "normal" number of students reported intestinal disturbances within a few hours' time. Because the military bases in the area feared the contamination might spread to their personnel, Dr. Paul Coughlin, acting Director of the Leon County Health Unit, spoke to students in a hastily-called convocation and explained the situation. The girls voluntarily agreed to a quarantine of the campus. After first trying to minimize the seriousness of the situation, Coughlin finally advised the local community that 350 students had been treated for a "mild but contagious" disease that was now under control. At the peak of the outbreak the Infirmary was filled to capacity for several days, and quantities of the prescribed medication, sulfa-guanidine, were airlifted to the campus.[69]

Though the ailment seemed to be under control within two weeks, local doctors needed approval from the State Board of Health laboratory in Jacksonville to lift the quarantine. When a third week passed with no word from Jacksonville, students were desperate for outside entertainment. The administration made arrangements with the Florida Theater on North Monroe Street for a private screening of its current feature, *Madame Curie*, starring Greer Garson and Walter Pidgeon. Two columns of girls, 1,200 in all, halted traffic as they marched to and from the movie house. When the state finally lifted the quarantine at the end of three weeks, the college gave students a five-day holiday. To celebrate the girls' return to the world outside the gates, Dale Mabry personnel put on an air

show, a party, and a tea for the campus community and dis-
patched army trucks to bring them to the base.[70]

As the eventual outcome of fighting in Europe became
more certain in late 1944, the college discontinued its use of
the Westminster chimes in the Westcott tower. In November,
Campbell announced to students and faculty that the next
time the chimes sounded, they would play the national anthem
to proclaim an Allied victory in Europe. Throughout the long
spring of 1945, everyone on campus eagerly awaited the sound
of the chimes. Finally, on May 8, heads turned and tears flowed
as the "Star Spangled Banner" reverberated from the tower.[71]
Dorothy Binger always remembered the sight of Anna May
Tracy on that day:

> [She] had struggled all through the war to feed us, and did a
> marvelous job. I was working near a window in the Registrar's
> office, and it was on the second floor. It looked out over the back
> of the campus. The bells started ringing, and the first thing I saw
> was Anna May Tracy jumping hedges to get to the Dining Hall.
> She was probably one of the happiest people on campus.[72]

Classes were dismissed for one hour, and everyone gathered
behind the building for prayers and song.[73]

Thousands of servicemen, whose presence had complicated and enlivened the lives of FSCW girls for four years,
soon left the area. Over that summer, the War Department
designated Dale Mabry Field and Camp Gordon Johnston as
separation centers, but the commanders of both bases asked
FSCW to continue its entertainment program for the 9,000 to
10,000 men awaiting discharges, and the campus responded.

Meanwhile, student attention returned to such mundane
concerns as the elimination of light regulations and the fact
that most girls found compulsory convocations a waste of
time. The Spic and Span, a combination corner-store and soda
shop located across Copeland Avenue from the main gates,
attracted attention for a while when its new owner held a
contest to rename the establishment. The judges, six students

who did not participate in the contest, selected "The Mecca" as the winning entry.[74]

<h2 style="text-align:center">TRADITIONS</h2>

Traditions ideally serve as a constant in lives beset by turmoil. At FSCW that held true for the most part during the tumultuous war years. The college even established a new organization that became a tradition—a marching band. In 1938, several students had started a cadet drill corps called the Tally Troopers. Dressed in white twill military trousers, garnet socks and shirts, white skull caps, sweaters, and oxfords, the corps of 39 girls debuted at the Odd/Even games held on Thanksgiving morning.[75] The corps hoped to present marching demonstrations throughout the year. Instead, the organization lasted only a few months, for Dean Opperman of the School of Music believed parading to be an unladylike activity and insisted that they disband.[76]

In March 1940, Charlotte Cooper, Jean Hitchcolk, and Alice Ludlum, students who had played in marching bands in their high schools, sidestepped Dean Opperman and "went around to every dormitory room and asked the girls in the dormitory if they could play an instrument." With a list of those who responded in the affirmative, the three went to cellist Owen Sellers and asked him to direct them; he agreed. The School of Music declined to recognize the band at the time, but that technicality did not stop the girls from holding regular tryouts and practice sessions in Westcott Auditorium.[77]

On Thanksgiving Day 1941, band members dressed in garnet jerkins, white silk shirts, and white skirts led Color Rush and proudly presented exhibition drills after the athletic contests. Student and faculty enthusiasm for the group ran so high that Business Manager Kellum solicited and received permission from the Board of Control to purchase 30 band uniforms. Opperman grudgingly accepted the inevitable; she devoted two sentences to the organization in her biennial report to the president, noting that "Band members initiated their Garnet and Gold regalia at the Inauguration of President Doak S. Campbell."[78]

More than anything else, though, America's entry into World War II ensured the acceptance of the band:

> All the military camps wanted entertainment, and this was the only group that could really perform that function because its music was different and it would be glad to play outdoors or indoors. Also the fact that everybody in the group was female didn't hurt any, either, for the military bases. So after a while the music faculty, including Dean Opperman, began to accept it because it had received so much appreciation.[79]

Sellers remained the band's director until he enlisted in the Army Air Corps in early 1943, at which time the college hired Frank Sykora as his replacement. Sykora, the son of a Russian military band leader, jumped into the directorship with a vengeance. By 1944, several musicians threatened to walk out because of his unreasonable demands and verbal abuse. But despite some discontent with the temporary director, band concerts quickly became traditional at FSCW.[80]

Between Conradi's retirement in 1941 and his death in 1944, the college continued to celebrate the president emeritus's birthday. Beginning in November 1941, students recognized Doak Campbell's birthday in similar fashion. College Government Association officers invited the new president and his wife to dine with them in the Landis Dining Room on November 11, three days before his actual birthday, to allay any suspicions he might have. Anna May Tracy brought two cakes to the table for dessert, but still his dinner companions said nothing. Finally, several hundred students met him on the Dining Hall steps and sang happy birthday as he exited the building, then presented him with an electric clock for his office desk. The next year, CGA officers reprised their roles, and seniors in caps and gowns who took a birthday cake to his home later that evening were invited in to share the confection.[81]

The Thanksgiving holiday with its accompanying Odd/ Even demonstrations, sports events, Color Rush, and dance, underwent disruptive alterations during the early 1940s as a result of the war, President Conradi's death, and continuing attempts by the Physical Education Department to replace the traditional basketball and volleyball games with soccer and hockey. A record number of girls—210—turned out in the fall of 1940 to practice for Odd/Even games. As the holiday approached, spirits were high; the Even Demonstration was titled "Dr. Jeven and Mr. Hodd," and the Odds produced "Odds A'Poppin'." The Evens won Color Rush as well as both the basketball and volleyball games. The Tarpon Club showed its world-famous aquatic style, and the dance on Saturday night was a grand success.[82]

By Thanksgiving 1942, holiday traditions were changing. Because of travel restrictions during wartime, the college expected fewer out-of-town alumnae to return for homecoming festivities and also quietly discouraged local citizens from attending the events. Odds and Evens vied not only on the courts but for honors in selling war stamps. The Thanksgiving dinner menu remained the same, but due to rationing the college had only enough coffee for each person to have one cup at breakfast, so the social committee canceled the traditional after-dinner coffees in the residence halls. Because of further rationing and food shortages in early 1943, the 600 sophomores and seniors who attended the traditional May Day breakfast ate shredded wheat and hot biscuits with strawberry preserves rather than the fried chicken and fresh strawberries served in the past. Thanksgiving dinner that year consisted of creamed turkey, potatoes, beets, and cranberry sauce.[83]

Traditional Thanksgiving ceremonies reached a nadir in 1944, not because of the food situation but because of the unexpected death of President Emeritus Conradi on Thanksgiving night. In keeping with his love of the Thanksgiving traditions, his family requested that Odd/Even sports events and the holiday dance, scheduled for Saturday, be held as usual. Campbell acquiesced with regard to the games, but he canceled the dance.[84]

∞

FSCW's boarding department recovered sufficiently from the deprivations of wartime shortages by November 1945 to serve a sumptuous repast on Thanksgiving Day. No one asked how Miss Tracy was able to offer 2,000 pounds of turkey accompanied by sweet potatoes, lima beans, corn, cabbage, celery, rolls and butter, and pecans for dinner, followed by 75 gallons of ice cream and 246 dozen cookies for dessert.[85] The campus community enjoyed the feast, unaware that the end of worldwide hostilities meant the end of Florida State College for Women.

Chapter XI
The End of the Beginning: 1946~1947

ducation for women in Florida came full circle on May 15, 1947, when the state abolished its first and only state-supported college for women. Forty-two years after the Buckman Bill established the Florida Female College, Governor Millard Caldwell signed a legislative act that redefined the state system of higher education for whites. Henceforth, it would consist of one university located at Gainesville, to be known as the University of Florida, and one university located at Tallahassee, to be known as Florida State University. The designated institutions were to admit both white male and white female students respective of adequate housing and other facilities.[1]

COEDUCATION IN FLORIDA

When the Buckman Bill established a state-supported university for men and a state-supported college for women in 1905, one undeniable intention on the part of the politicians who crafted and supported the legislation was the justification of unequal facilities for men and women. Except for an ill-conceived and ultimately unsuccessful attempt in 1906 to move the Normal Department of the Florida Female College to the Gainesville campus and merge it with that of the University of the State of Florida,[2] the lawmakers of the state showed no interest in combining the facilities of the two institutions except in instances that would benefit the university. In 1925, the legislature enacted a law that allowed women to attend the University of Florida if they met certain conditions:

> Women who are at least 21 years of age and who have received credit from a reputable educational institution in at least sixty semester hours of academic college work shall be eligible to enroll as students in the University of Florida in such subjects and courses as they are unable to obtain in any other institution under the supervision of the Board of Control.[3]

The statute resulted in misunderstandings between faculties at the two institutions concerning the interpretation of the phrase "unable to obtain." Under the auspices of a 1929 Educational Survey Commission study that had been intended to clarify the situation, the presidents of the two institutions recommended that the university be open to women "for professional and advanced academic courses in education." Conradi fumed ineffectively over a decision, based on the same study, to fully develop the graduate capabilities of the university, "offering advanced (Ph.D.) degrees, fostering research and public service, and maintaining a great library," but to maintain the women's college as "primarily an undergraduate teaching institution limiting its advanced degrees to the Master of Arts and Master of Science." The same report recommended that special funding for the two schools be apportioned at 60 percent to the university and 26 percent to the college, leaving 14 percent to be divided between the Institute for the Blind, Deaf, and Dumb and the Normal and Industrial College for Negroes.[4]

From time to time between 1929 and 1944, the question of coeducation at one or the other collegiate institution for white students attracted interest. The legislature, still meeting in odd-numbered years, regularly entertained such measures in committees or on the floor beginning in 1937. While many students at FSCW professed contentment in their female world and believed that the absence of males enhanced their scholarly opportunities, the idea of coeducation tantalized. At every opportunity staff members of the *Flambeau* commented on the issue. In 1937, the paper published a remarkably prophetic article regarding the presence of men on the campus. According to the author:

> The gymnasium would have a companion stadium, the dining room system would not work, Odd/Even competition would be overshadowed by intercollegiate sports, girls' athletics would be subordinated to masculine talent, enrollment would increase but grades would decrease.[5]

Most persons connected with higher education in the state, however, remained reluctant to violate the provisions of the Buckman Bill.[6]

During the 1939 legislative session, Representative Wilbur Whitehurst of Highlands County introduced a bill that provided for coeducation at both the University of Florida and Florida State College for Women. His bill also changed the name of the latter back to Florida State College. FSCW students favoring the measure invited legislators to a campus meeting to speak for and against the proposal. Conradi, however, believed such actions to be against college policies (which forbade students to interfere in politics) and demanded that the girls rescind their invitations. Subsequently, college officials ordered students not to contact their legislative representatives or make their support of the bill known in any way. The bill died, and student activism concerning the issue subsided until the Legislature reconvened in 1941, at which time editorials in support of coeducation reappeared in the *Flambeau*.[7]

In 1943, representative Ira J. Carter of Alachua County, cognizant of the drastically low enrollment at the Gainesville campus since the United States' entry into World War II, introduced a bill to make the University of Florida coeducational for the duration of the war and for two years thereafter.[8] Carter's action reflected his concerns about reduced revenues among his constituents, but Board of Control members felt that to support such a move would set the stage for severe over-crowding in the future, when ex-GIs and other students returned in force to the Gainesville campus. Consequently, the board advised the Committee on Education that "such legislation at this time [was] most untimely and ill advised."[9] The committee heeded the board's advice and never brought the bill to the floor.

Lack of official support failed to deter the commercial sector in Gainesville, which tried a new tactic in early September 1943. The community pressured the Board of Control to open the University of Florida's College of Education to females, ostensibly to alleviate some of the obvious over-crowding at FSCW. However, completion of Magnolia Hall and refurbishing of six recently purchased houses on the FSCW campus provided adequate residential facilities for the coming academic year and eliminated the possibility of expansion to the Gainesville campus.[10]

Tallahassee residents in the meantime assured the college community of their support. The Junior Chamber of Commerce launched a campaign to protect the interests of FSCW (and those of the economic community, of course) when the question of coeducation arose once again. Chamber members had no objections to coeducation at the University of Florida, so long as FSCW received the same consideration and various scholastic divisions were equitably distributed between the two schools. They especially felt that the law college belonged in their city, the seat of state government.[11]

During the winter of 1945, considerable attention again focused on the coming legislative session and the expected reappearance of the coeducation issue. The *Flambeau* noted that Florida was the only state that did not have a state-supported coeducational college or university, and it discussed the pros and cons of the idea. A sample poll of FSCW students showed that more than 90 percent of them favored coeducation for the college, but less than half of the student body participated in the poll. The *Alligator* sponsored its own straw vote on the Tallahassee campus: 477 of those who responded favored coeducation at both institutions, 347 favored it only at the university, 15 wanted it only at FSCW, and 58 opposed any change.[12]

As the *Flambeau* editors saw it, the Legislature had three viable alternatives: it could leave things as they were; it could make the University of Florida coeducational on a temporary basis until the war ended and its enrollment increased substantially; or it could make both schools coeducational, an option the editors feared meant duplication of facilities and costly competition between the two institutions. They considered untenable a fourth option[13]—that of permanently making the university coeducational and leaving the college as it was. Studies of enrollment at state-supported women's colleges in Alabama, Mississippi, Georgia, North Carolina, South Carolina, Oklahoma, Virginia, and Texas all showed that when any correlated colleges or universities in the respective states became coeducational, the women's institutions ceased to grow, and in all cases their enrollments decreased by 16 to 25 percent.[14]

In the 1945 legislative session, Senator Wallace E. Sturgis of Ocala introduced the expected bill to make only the University of Florida coeducational. Board of Control Chairman Henry P. Adair reiterated his belief that the university would be unable to accommodate all the male applicants at the end of the war, so every girl admitted would be taking a place from a serviceman.[15] Beth Walton Moor, Secretary of the FSCW Alumnae Association, supported a proposal for an impartial citizens committee to study the situation and report back to the 1947 Legislature. Governor Millard Caldwell, who had earlier declared that coeducation in the state's schools should be determined by the needs of education, not the desires of a community to profit by it, also favored a careful study. Sturgis withdrew his bill. The legislative body then passed a bill that permitted husbands and wives of veterans who were attending either institution to attend the same one, regardless of gender.[16]

Name-calling and finger-pointing began almost immediately. Before and during the legislative session of 1945, the interest in coeducation exhibited by residents of both Tallahassee and Gainesville had stemmed more from possible political advantage and financial remuneration than from a concern for the welfare of Florida's students in higher education. The *Gainesville Sun* claimed that "joint political maneuvering inspired principally by the Tallahassee interests has dropped the cause of coeducation in the 1945 legislature." The Tallahassee *Daily Democrat* responded that coeducation without careful planning "might reduce the national recognition now accorded the college for women."[17] In the midst of the clamor, the Florida Citizens Committee on Education began to formulate a plan for the future development of the state's system of higher education.

Over the 1945–46 academic year, while the committee considered the futures of Florida State College for Women and the University of Florida, the federally-enacted Servicemen's Readjustment Act of 1944 (informally called the GI Bill of Rights) created unexpected pressures at both schools. Along with many other veterans' benefits, the GI Bill of Rights granted stipends that covered tuition and living expenses while ex-servicemen attended college. That in itself posed no threat to FSCW other than the possibility of further overcrowding, a situation Campbell planned to remedy shortly. In March 1946, the Board of Control opened bids for a new dormitory with a capacity of 280, to be located north of the Infirmary and behind Jennie Murphree Hall. Campbell and the Beers Construction Company of Atlanta optimistically predicted completion of the $733,745 building by September 1947.[18]

Like Landis Hall, the five-story brick dormitory would consist of two wings and a central courtyard, complete with stone trim and reliefs. Unlike Landis, its two sections were separate, divided by a fire wall. It would be the last FSCW edifice on campus to conform to the original (and expensive) Gothic style and the first to have a blower system for heating and air conditioning. The contractor followed original specifications that called for a stone relief of "FSCW" to be placed at one entrance, even though the building was not completed until 1948.[19] The administration named the new residence hall for the first Dean of the College Home, Sarah Landrum (Tissie) Cawthon.

In the meantime, enrollment applications reached 2,544 by mid-July 1946—two hundred more than at the same time in 1945. Campbell acquired the officers' quarters at recently decommissioned Dale Mabry Field for use as temporary housing for students. The barracks offered sufficient living space for approximately 300 girls "and the necessary number of social directors" until the new dormitory was habitable. The new business manager, Rod K. Shaw, purchased a bus to make an estimated 37 round trips per day from the base to the campus.[20]

TALLAHASSEE BRANCH, UNIVERSITY OF FLORIDA

For the University of Florida, the GI Bill caused considerable problems. At the end of World War II, the university made provisions for 6,000 students; by the summer of 1946, more than 8,200 men had applied for admission.[21] Rumors abounded concerning the possibility of sending some of the applicants to Tallahassee to attend FSCW. Milton Carothers, the college registrar, expressed the confusion of faculty members in a memorandum to Campbell in mid-August: "I do not know how seriously to take the talk about admitting men in September."[22]

Veterans living in Tallahassee or nearby presented a petition to Campbell asking that they be allowed to attend FSCW because there was insufficient room for them at the school in Gainesville. The Tallahassee *Daily Democrat* reported that, at the request of Governor Caldwell, President Campbell and President Tigert were working out details for approximately 1,000 male students to attend FSCW. Florida's Attorney General, Thomas J. Watson, declared it illegal for any men other than husbands of veterans to attend the college. Secretary of State R. A. Gray believed that any legal question could be circumvented by having the men attend under the name and direction of the University of Florida, as if a branch campus existed in Tallahassee.[23]

At a joint meeting of the Boards of Education and Control on September 2, 1946, the governor and others present created the Tallahassee Branch of the University of Florida (TBUF) for the benefit of between 500 and 1,000 male students. FSCW proposed to house the men at Dale Mabry Field, in 30 temporary buildings recently obtained by the city housing authority from the War Assets Administration and donated to the campus for the emergency. Campbell appointed Milton Carothers as Director of TBUF, Coyle Moore as Registrar, and Otis McBride, recently hired associate professor of English, as Dean of Men.[24]

While the male administrators of FSCW concerned themselves with housing and curriculum for the TBUF students, Dean Dorman turned her attention to necessary changes in social regulations for women. Since she expected the men at TBUF to own or have access to automobiles, she asked the Board of Control to rescind the 15-year-old rule forbidding girls to have cars while enrolled at FSCW. The administration, however, placed stringent constraints on the girls' possession and use of the vehicles. Female students who wished to keep and/or use cars in Tallahassee needed written permission from their parents, who also had to agree in writing to relieve the college of all responsibility for accidents on or off campus; liability insurance on the car was essential. Before the car owner could take another student for a ride, the college required that the rider have formal permission from her parents. Campbell noted that only "half a dozen students [met] the restrictions." The *Flambeau* did report a major parking problem developing on campus, but the administration declined to create a special parking lot.[25]

The administration's tolerant attitude toward men on the

campus astounded the female students. Of major interest to the girls were changes in the Student Handbook, called the Gold Book. For years, the women had railed unsuccessfully against weekly convocations, yet with the arrival of male students, college officials converted the sessions to monthly College Government Association (CGA) assemblies. Unlimited dating privileges suddenly extended to all but freshmen. The annoying rule that declared any conversation with a male of longer than ten minutes' duration to constitute a date vanished. No longer did the college consider activities that took place in the Sweet Shop, Mecca, Longmire Building, residence hall parlors, or any other place on or near campus to be dates. Since the men smoked anywhere they pleased, eventually Dorman designated the sidewalk between the History and Science Buildings, the east door of the Education Building, and the grassy area south of Magnolia Hall as smoking areas.[26]

Girls who purchased tickets for the Sophomore Hop or the Junior-Senior prom received a total of three—one for themselves and two to give to unescorted men. The presence of men revived an emphasis on clothes; class dress "shifted to clothes that flatter the figure and gain the most valuable impression." Some proposed changes were less appreciated than others, such as the suggestion that the name of the college annual, *Flastacowo*, be changed, perhaps to *Flastaco-ed*. Otis McBride, acting Dean of Men, humorously suggested *Flastaco-woo!*, but he knew "the alumnae wouldn't like that."[27]

The most profound change of all came at Thanksgiving, when results of a CGA canvas revealed that more than two-thirds of the 2,300 FSCW students favored canceling the traditional Thanksgiving activities (with the understanding that activities of a similar nature would be provided later in the year), and all but 34 supported cancelation of classes on the Friday and Saturday following the holiday. Odd and Even nights out, demonstrations, and sports contests were moved to the weekend before Thanksgiving. Color Rush was eliminated altogether; the Athletic Association minutes contained the telling comment,"we will have it first quarter next year if we have it at all."[28] A *Flambeau* editorial noted the passing of a tradition:

> When the time comes that the past is no longer adaptable to the present, then the past must give way. That does not mean that the past should be forgotten. So it is with our Thanksgiving Day activities, our Odd/Even rivalry.[29]

Campbell saw the quasi-coeducational situation that existed on the Tallahassee campus as an opportunity to negotiate for equality within the state educational system. It was obvious to him that the uniform treatment promised to Edward Conradi in 1909 had been lacking for most of the past 40 years.[30] Bolstered by FSCW's successful six-month administration of both the main campus and the TBUF campus, when the time arrived to present biennial budgets, Campbell insisted that the financial estimates be prepared on the same basis for both schools. He notified the Board of Education that he expected salaries at both institutions to be on a par from then on.[31]

In January 1947, the Citizens Committee on Education reported in favor of coeducation for both the University of Florida and Florida State College for Women.[32] Students at FSCW overwhelmingly favored the change. Members of the YWCA went so far as to hand out postcards to FSCW and TBUF students to use in asking their parents to make sure legislators were aware of their support of the committee report.[33] The committee noted that

> Florida has been the slowest of any of the state universities to admit women due primarily to the fact that there were pressures from many sources to keep either the University or the Florida State College for Women from engaging in useless competition or to prevent either from gaining an advantage over the other.[34]

Campbell accepted the prospect of coeducation as a foregone conclusion and asked Dean Dorman to set up a joint committee of men and women students to plan student government under coeducation. The FSCW Alumnae Association, once opposed to the idea of coeducation, now endorsed the committee's recommendations for coeducation at both schools.[35]

Not everyone saw the presence of male students as desirable or beneficial. After living through five months of constant turmoil and change in social standards, Dean Dorman decided to resume her position as head of the Classics Department on a full-time basis; she resigned effective June 30, 1947. In accepting her resignation from the post of Dean of Students, Campbell recognized that during her 13-year-tenure

> many substantial developments have taken place which are reflected in the social, personal, and professional standards of the college. CGA was reorganized and enlarged, the housing program was systematized, the social program in the residence halls has been developed and made a special function, and a program of student counseling under professionally trained personnel has been instituted on a full time basis.[36]

Dorman's protégé, Assistant Dean Katherine Warren, eventually filled the new post of Dean of Women.

Anna May Tracy and her staff had their problems with male students on campus as well. The *Flambeau*'s new column written by TBUF students, "Male Eye View," chronicled the mealtime situation on both the main campus and at Dale Mabry. The writer recounted the pleasure with which the men looked forward to the opening of a cafeteria at the old base, since until then TBUF students had been eating "girl-sized meals" in the campus Dining Hall. "Men need more for breakfast than a lukewarm cup of coffee and a tired slice of half toasted bread," he stated. But when the base cafeteria finally opened, they found more to complain about—lunch. "One day it was two thin cheese sandwiches, a bowl of rabbit food, and little fruit." The author patiently explained that most men needed three times as much to eat.[37] Obviously, some alterations in menu-planning would be necessary in the near future. The final resolution: Tracy and Campbell renamed the Old Dining Hall the Suwannee Room and transformed it into a cafeteria.[38]

PASSING THE TORCH

When the Legislature met in 1947, it immediately took up the question of coeducation at the state institutions. Opposition came from the editor of the *Gainesville Sun*, who claimed that coeducation for both the college and the university was a "trumped up plot by the Tallahassee Chamber of Commerce to destroy the University of Florida." Both the incoming and outgoing student body presidents from UF appeared on the floor of the state House of Representatives, touted the glory of their university, and claimed that coeducation at FSCW would "sacrifice one of the country's great women's colleges for a second rate University of Florida at Tallahassee." Despite these speeches, a compromise bill passed the Legislature, changing the name of Florida State College for Women to Florida State University and making the newly named institution coeducational along with the University of Florida.[39] In recognition of the latter's fears of the loss of superiority in the state educational system, a provision stated: "No college, school, department or division now existing at either of said universities shall be moved to the other university and all unreasonable duplications shall be avoided."[40]

On the morning of May 15, 1947, Governor Caldwell signed his name to the legislation. Though Florida State College for Women at that moment passed the torch to a new entity, its well-established, nationally recognized liberal arts program formed the institutional core of the new university. Later in the day, the Board of Control authorized Doak Campbell to have a new seal made for FSU.[41] Campbell wisely retained the three torches and the motto *Vires, Artes, Mores* for the FSU seal and replaced the original incorporation date of MCMV (1905) with 1857. For obvious reasons, he eliminated the words *Femina Perfecta*. Many of FSCW's traditions lost their meaning for future classes, and others took new forms that obscured

their old identities. As an example, when the new coeducational university established the honor societies of Gold Key
for men and Garnet Key for women, the latter considered
Esteren and Spirogira members its alumnae.[42]

FSCW diplomas had already been ordered for the June
graduating class, and it was doubtful whether new sheep-
skins bearing the name Florida State University would arrive
in time for Commencement. The problem was solved when
the printer was able to use the original diplomas imprinted
with the name of Florida State College for Women by adding
the phrase "issued by Florida State University." On June 9,
1947, Charles E. McAllister, Dean of the Cathedral of St. John
the Evangelist in Spokane, Washington, delivered FSU's first
Commencement address to 431 female and 12 male graduates.[43] The Class of 1947, the last graduating class of Florida
State College for Women, became the first graduating class of
Florida State University.

*"What we call the beginning is
often the end, and to make an end is
to make a beginning. The end is where
we start from."*

T. S. Eliot

The editors of the 1935 Flastacowo *used this photo
to symbolize the closing of the school year.
It is used here to symbolize the closing of an era.*

Appendix A—Memorabilia

Often while interviewing individuals or reviewing scrapbooks and other memorabilia, the author uncovered interesting facts, events, and details that she did not consider germane to the main narrative flow of the book. The publishers felt that a sampling of this unused, incidental material would further convey the color and character of FSCW. A selection is included in this Appendix.

Faculty Tales

Dr. William G. Dodd, who taught English literature and also served as Dean of Arts and Sciences, was late to class one day. After waiting ten minutes, his students left. When the class next met, he asked where they had been. They explained, and he asked, "Didn't you see my hat on the desk? That meant I was here." When Dodd arrived for the next class meeting, he found no students, but each chair had a hat on its seat.

∞

President A. A. Murphree was so determined that Florida's women's college would be more than a normal school for teacher training that he set extremely high entrance standards. In fact, President Andrew Sledd of the men's school in Gainesville complained to Murphree that they were *higher than those of the university*. The women's college required one year of Greek or modern language, which the men's school did not, and more history and more Latin.

Faculty wives who participated in campus life often became endeared to students, and none more so than Hazel Richards, wife of physics professor Harold Richards. Mrs. Richards, known for her sense of humor, high spirits, and marvelous laughter, was for many years a sponsor for Mortar Board, as well as a frequent subject in her husband's lectures. His classes were often memorable for the comic and dramatic presentation of subject matter. To demonstrate the principles of X-rays, Dr. Richards examined one of "my wife Hazel's" pocketbooks. To everyone's amusement, the outline of a pistol showed up on the screen—this in an era when "Pistol Packing Mama" was at the top of the charts.

∽

RECEIPT

FLORIDA STATE COLLEGE FOR WOMEN
TALLAHASSEE, FLORIDA

First Semester

Sept. 18 19 44

Received of *Jean J. Lewis*

For *Self*

DINING HALL	100	00
RESIDENCE HALL	28	00
INFIRMARY FEE	7	00
PHYSICAL EDUCATION FEE	4	00
STUDENT ACTIVITY FEE	9	00
LAUNDRY FEE	10	00
POST OFFICE FEE		65
REGISTRATION FEE	10	00
NON-STATE TUITION		
PIANO PRACTICE		
ORGAN PRACTICE		
VOICE HARMONY		
WIND INSTS. STRING INSTS.		
SPEECH DIPLOMA		
CASH DEPOSIT (Student Bank)	11	35
TOTAL	180	00

180 00 paid

H2- 7050 J. G. KELLUM, Treasurer

By

THANKS. THIS IS YOUR RECEIPT.

REDIFORM—SOUTHERN BUSINESS SYSTEMS, INC., ORLANDO, FLA.

When Odd and Even spirits were high near Thanksgiving, Dr. Ralph Bellamy could often be seen tipping his fedora, revealing his red, white, and purple Odd cap. Traditionally, Dr. Bellamy was the official starter for the Color Rush for Westcott. Instead of using a whistle to start the race, he used his shotgun with an, "On your mark, get set." BOOM!

∞

Dr. Paul Heinlein, psychology professor, was easily recognized on campus by the oversized amplifier for his hearing aid that he carried around and placed on his desk during classes. On occasion, when he tired of lecturing, he would tell students to read their assignments and do their work. He would then remove his hearing aid and sit quietly undisturbed at the front of the class. While calling the roll one day, he became alarmed, fearing that something had gone wrong with his hearing apparatus. Each girl had responded by silently mouthing "here" or "present" when her name was called.

∞

For many years, accounting teacher Luella Richey was the sole woman Certified Public Accountant in Florida. At FSCW, which was at that time the only woman's college in the United States to offer a four-year accounting program, she taught all aspects of the subject. Graduates of the Richey program were allowed to sit for the CPA exam after just one year of public accounting practice, while all others were required first to practice for three years.

∞

Attendance was known to double in Dr. Sarah Parker White's freshman hygiene class when handsome Tallahassee physician Edward Annis (later president of the American Medical Association) was invited to be guest lecturer on the subject "The Wedding Night."

Modern dance instructor Nellie-Bond Dickinson, an early student of Martha Graham, repeatedly asked Dean Opperman, Chairman of the Artist Series Committee, to book Miss Graham. Finally, Dean Opperman asked skeptically if Miss Graham would "come in on the stage and just roll around?" Miss Dickinson replied, "Dean Opperman, I can assure you I have never yet seen her come in on the stage and 'just roll around.'" Martha Graham was booked to appear at FSCW in Westcott Auditorium. The house lights went down, and the curtain went up. Miss Graham made her solo entrance, walked very, very slowly to center stage, sank down to the floor, and rolled over.

✿

FLORIDA STATE COLLEGE FOR WOMEN

Tallahassee

The following information will aid you in entering and enrolling:

1st: When you arrive at college, present your room certificate and secure your room.

2nd: Take your trunk check to Business Office and get transfer check for delivery of your trunk from depot to your room.

3rd: Go to Bryan Hall office and get enrollment card and group number.

4th: Fill out enrollment card and take it to Main Business Office in Administration Building and pay board and all regular fees, and get receipt and classification card.

5th: All new students go to Registrar and secure credits.

6th: Take classification card, receipt and credits to registration committee and be enrolled.

7th: Take enrollment slip you get from the Committee, to the Business Office, pay all special fees required for the course for which you have enrolled, and get card for admittance to class.

8th: Take receipt with enrollment slip to class and present to teacher.

9th: The College will not be responsible for money or valuables kept in students' rooms. The College maintains a College Bank for the safe keeping of all money or valuables.

ca. 1915

Diminutive professor of philosophy Anna Forbes Liddell was the first woman to receive a Ph.D. from the University of North Carolina. At the age of 81, and in a wheelchair, Dr. Liddell appeared before the Florida Legislature to testify in support of the Equal Rights Amendment. "The opposition is wrong to assume that every woman has a sweet, wonderful, protective husband. I'm an old maid—and I've never had a husband—not mine nor anyone else's. In every position I've held, I was preceded by a man, and I was followed by a man . . . so I guess you can say I do a man's work."

❧

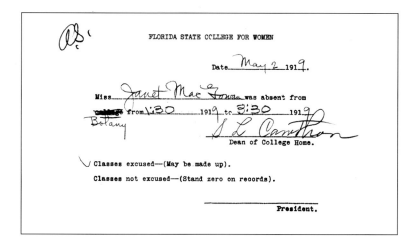

CAMPUS RULES

In 1914, two students who were caught smoking claimed they had only smoked three times and had only taken two or three puffs each time. All privileges, nevertheless, were revoked for six weeks.

❧

During the legislative session of 1915, students were forbidden to dine out in local hotels unless accompanied by their father—or a "settled" brother.

> Because you _Dolores Dunphy, failed to_
> _sign off the books in the office after the_
> _holiday weekend._
>
> **you are receiving a formal warning from Lower Court of College Government Association. If another offence is made, you will automatically be penalized.**
>
> _Jean_ Chairman of Lower Court
>
> _Lillian Lowrie_

ca. 1940

❧

One student was disciplined for not staying at the bus station in Tallahassee after arriving in the middle of the night from a classmate's wedding. Aware of the potential danger of hanging around a bus station all night, she chose to return to campus, never dreaming she would be punished for her prudence.

❧

In 1927, two students who had received permission to travel by train to Orlando decided instead to go by "aeroplane." When the administration learned of this daring venture, the girls were asked to withdraw for the remainder of the semester.

❧

The first student to request permission to fly had her parents' approval but also needed that of her dormitory director, who referred her to the Dean of Students, who in turn sent her to the college president. No one, it seems, in the 1930s, wanted to take responsibility for giving a student permission to fly.

❧

In 1935 the administration relaxed its rules for some summer school students. Married students were allowed to have dates with their spouses without special permission from their dormitory directors.

⧠

Many students recall being offered a ride to town by a considerate gentleman. After the students informed the driver that students were not allowed to accept rides from anyone, and especially not from a man, he in turn told them that it was okay—he was President Conradi.

THE DINING HALL

Students who received scholarships for working in the dining room were not allowed to join sororities. Instead they formed their own—Delta Rho Gamma (Dining Room Girls)—with their own little safety pins and ribbons. Sorority girls, however, were allowed to work at the Three Torches, the Dutch Kitchen, and the Florida Grill, local tearooms where during the 1940s they earned 35¢ an hour plus meals.

⧠

To the Students:

    Until established custom approves of bare legs as being in good taste for all occasions, I must ask that you do not come into the Dining Room without stockings on.

Anna M. Tracy

ca. 1925

One dining room girl recalled a day when the soup was unusually good and she was asked to serve seconds. As she pulled the ladle from the big metal pitcher, much to everyone's surprise a bar of Octagon soap fell out.

∞

As Dietitian Anna May Tracy struggled during World War II with food shortages and rationing, some of her efforts made lasting memories. One was a prune whip dessert that seemed to be made of whipped egg whites instead of whipped cream. It strenuously resisted being swallowed and is still the butt of humorous remarks from alumnae of that era.

MISCELLANY

Early in World War II, a squadron of Chinese student pilots was sent to Tallahassee's Dale Mabry Field for fighter training. Among the rigorous requirements for these elite Chinese cadets was the ability to speak English. Mart Pierson, student body president, was asked to preside over a table of cadets at a formal dinner, during which she remarked to the cadet on her right that FSCW was the nation's "third largest college purely for women." She was amazed to hear him tell the cadet next to him that FSCW was the nation's "third largest college for pure women."

∞

In the mid-forties, several unathletic students launched a friendly spoof of F Club. Their organization was called the So Sissy Sad Sacks, or S Club. Each member had a club name such as Feebly or Weakly. The club pin was an S-prin (aspirin) to be swallowed instead of worn. Provisional members were "sheep" as opposed to F Club's "goats," and were assigned to tend and clothe Essie, the fire hydrant just south of Effie, the lamppost tended by F Club goats. While Effie was usually attired for some activity, Essie was garbed in pajamas or another outfit suitable for inactivity. At initiation, if ever held, a sheep would be required to "turn a little pale (pail) and kick the bucket."

Opening of the school year in September brought a sea of trunks to the Tallahassee railroad depot, each to be delivered to a particular student's room. All the college's male work crews—janitors, gardeners, groundskeepers, general laborers, and special hires—tackled the awesome job. In older buildings without freight elevators, it was exceptionally brutal work. Then, once emptied, each trunk had to be removed to storage, usually in the basement or attic of the student's dorm. At the end of the year, the whole process was reversed.

ஊ

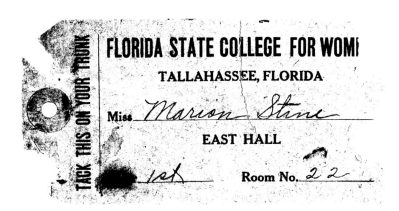

ஊ

The Umbrella Man was a familiar figure along the sidewalks near classroom buildings and the Library. This gentle, rumpled eccentric would give a blossom or two from his flower garden to whomever stopped to exchange greetings and a few words. Besides his flowers, his distinguishing trademarks were mismatched coat and trousers, battered felt hat that he tipped politely, and, always, a black umbrella. Considering Tallahassee weather, his ever-present umbrella may not have been so eccentric.

ஊ

Not only did a steady supply of fresh vegetables flow from the college gardens, but also beauty. With a slat-house for ferns, a greenhouse for potted palms and tender plants, and rows of hardy annuals outside, the gardens were up to almost any campus event—stage greenery for concerts, recitals, academic ceremonies, or special occasions, and bouquets of flowers for dormitory parlors, administrative offices, teas, receptions, and other socials. Sometimes gardenias and rose buds were spread out under the pines behind the auditorium for students to tuck into their hair.

ಬಿ

Early on the morning after freshman elections, losing candidates were traditionally awakened to be tapped for the Defeated Candidates Club (DCC). The surprise and hilarity of being tapped with the black and blue ribbons of DCC (symbols of the bruises of defeat) helped take away disappointment and provided the happy illusion that losing was even more fun than winning.

Some Memorable Graduates

Irita Bradford (1908), editor of *The Talisman* while at FSCW, was later editor of the "Books" section of the *New York Herald Tribune*. After receiving a master's degree from FSCW in 1909, she left for New York City to pursue a doctorate at Columbia University, where she met and married noted biographer and literary critic Carl Van Doren. As editor of "Books" she sponsored a series of book and author luncheons. Among speakers selected for these occasions were many emerging literary lions of the day (Edna Ferber, Carl Sandburg, John Gunther, and Dorothy Thompson, to name but a few), whose careers were enhanced by her nurturing and friendship.

ಬಿ

Mary Mahon (1912) was the first woman appointed an officer in the Federal Reserve Bank system.

In 1934, John Boynton of Havana, Florida, became the first male to be graduated from FSCW. He attended summer schools and pursued directed-reading programs to become certified in selected high school subjects, eventually earning sufficient credits for a bachelor of education degree. He later earned a master of education degree from FSU and a doctorate from Duke University. His daughter and three nieces attended FSCW, and three sons attended FSU.

∞

					ENGAGEMENTS IN TALLAHASSEE		
Name_____ Classification_____							
Room number_____ On Academic Probation_____							
Sorority_____							
Date	Begins (Time)	Destination	Time of Expected Return	Ends (Time)	Others in Party	Full Name of Young Man Caller	Approved

∞

Almost from its beginnings, outstanding graduates of FSCW returned to join its faculty. In the earliest years, these young women had only their brand new bachelor's degrees, but soon the returnees held advanced degrees, usually from other institutions. Among the alumnae with distinguished teaching careers at FSCW during its last decades were Dr. Katherine Montgomery (1918) and Dr. Grace Fox (1928), physical education; Elizabeth Thomson (1927), speech; Dr. Lynette Thompson (1942), Classics; Katherine Blood Hoffman (1936), chemistry; Ruth Schornherst Breen (1926), botany; Sara Krentzman Srygley (1936), library science; and Dr. Daisy Parker Flory (1937), political science. All these stayed on as faculty of FSU and were joined by many other FSCW alumnae. Dr. Flory also served FSU as Dean of Faculties (1973–1984).

Nancy Culp (1943) achieved success as a character player in movies and television. Classmates at FSCW who remembered her comic antics in Odd Demonstrations were not surprised. TV viewers will know her as Miss Hathaway, the banker's spinster secretary in "The Beverly Hillbillies," seen today in reruns.

೧೮

Isabel Rogers (1945), after teaching theology and ethics at the Presbyterian School of Christian Education in Richmond, Virginia, for twenty-five years, was elected Moderator of the General Assembly, the highest elective office in the Presbyterian Church in the United States. Isabel was president of College Government Association at FSCW, a member of Phi Beta Kappa, a founding member of the "S" Club, and the daughter of English professor and noted Browning scholar W. Hudson Rogers.

—MLN and SLM

೧೮

FLORIDA STATE COLLEGE FOR WOMEN Form 225
Office of Dean of Students
WITHDRAWAL CARD

Date January 22, 1941

Miss Bessie Rumph

Withdrew from College on January 22, 1941

Reason To get married.

_____ M. Norman
Dean of Students

೧೮

Appendix B—Maps

The following maps of the FSCW campus in 1905, 1920, 1930, and 1947 are composites from several sources and drawn at various scales. They are not presented or intended as professional scientific renderings but as aids in locating sites.

1905

1. Gymnasium
2. College Hall
3. East Hall
4. West Hall

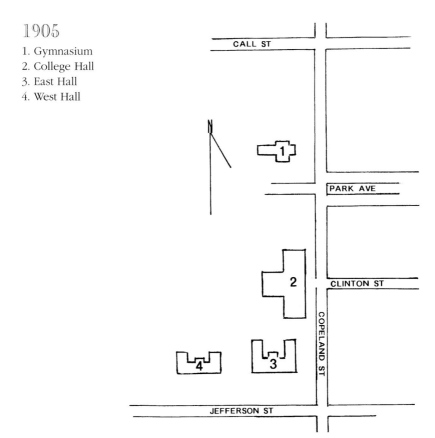

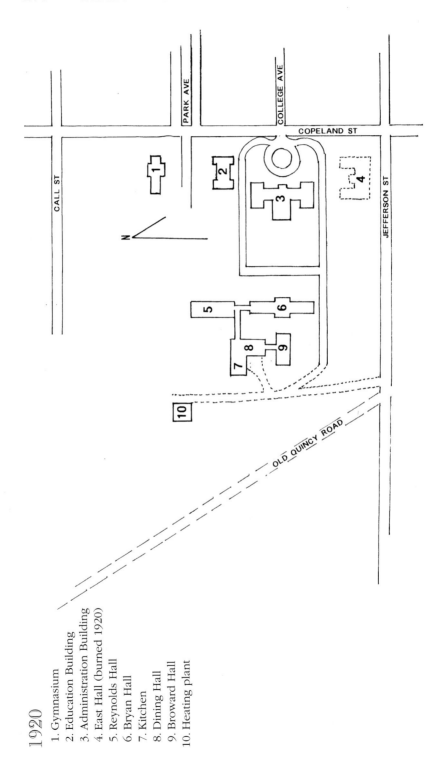

1920

1. Gymnasium
2. Education Building
3. Administration Building
4. East Hall (burned 1920)
5. Reynolds Hall
6. Bryan Hall
7. Kitchen
8. Dining Hall
9. Broward Hall
10. Heating plant

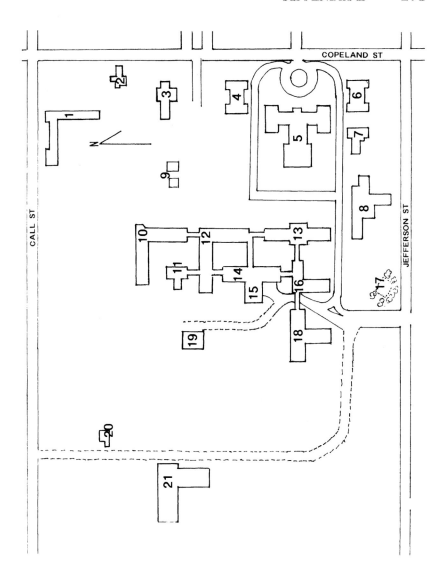

1930

1. Demonstration School
2. Home Management House
3. Music Annex
4. Education Building
5. Administration Building
6. Science Hall
7. History Building
8. Library
9. Dietitians' Cottages
10. Jennie Murphree Hall
11. Infirmary
12. Reynolds Hall
13. Bryan Hall
14. Dining Hall
15. Kitchen
16. Broward Hall
17. Outdoor Theater
18. Gilchrist Hall
19. Heating plant
20. Farm manager's house
21. Gymnasium

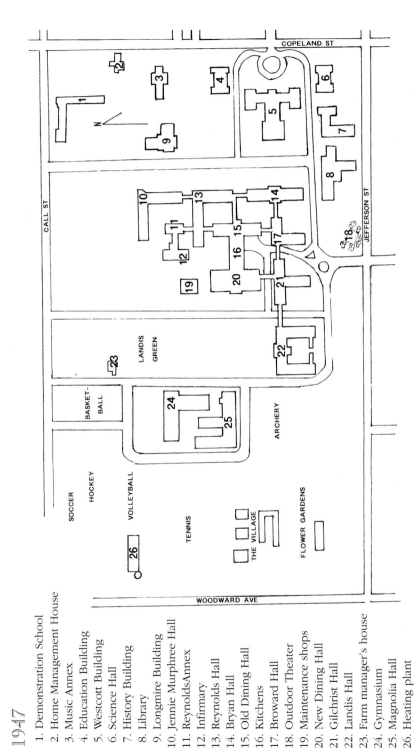

1947

1. Demonstration School
2. Home Management House
3. Music Annex
4. Education Building
5. Westcott Building
6. Science Hall
7. History Building
8. Library
9. Longmire Building
10. Jennie Murphree Hall
11. ReynoldsAnnex
12. Infirmary
13. Reynolds Hall
14. Bryan Hall
15. Old Dining Hall
16. Kitchens
17. Broward Hall
18. Outdoor Theater
19. Maintenance shops
20. New Dining Hall
21. Gilchrist Hall
22. Landis Hall
23. Farm manager's house
24. Gymnasium
25. Magnolia Hall
26. Heating plant

Appendix C—Membership

FSCW/FSU CLASS OF 1947
GIFT COMMITTEE

Virginia Ailstock Rankin
Marjorie Austin*
Eugenia Avant McJunkin **
Ruth Blair Crider
Juanita Bowles Haynes
Laura Cason Morrison*
Rachel Chambers Peacock
Mary Cooney Crum**
Mary Celia Diamond Findley
Ruth Ervin Davis
Sonya Heyman Morris
Robin Hill Murphy
Mary Groover Holland Lewis
Kathleen Johnson Sledge
Margaret Johnson Poppell
Harriet Kirk Crago*
Flora Kurz Ayala
Frances Ledbetter
Ouida Martin Croker
Betty McRae Hamrick
Kay Moore Morse **

Frannie Myers Burgisser
Nita Nord Little
Ann Parker Emerson*
Louise Peeples Jackson
Mary Perfect
Betty E. Redd
Bobbi Rees**
Ruby Richbourg Hutchins
Shirley Rodgers Tellander*
Virginia Sapp Keel
Aileen Sayers Warford
Betty Schwartz Peterson*
Betty Anne Shiver Staton
Phyllis Singer Fleet
B. J. Singleton Triplett*
Frances Taylor Mathis
Pat Thomas Meginniss
Frances Traxler Greiff
Cora Lea Wells **
Ina Jo Wrench McKenzie

* Book Select Committee
** Heritage Tower Design Select Committee

Notes

ABBREVIATIONS

AAM Corres.   A. A. Murphree Correspondence, P. K. Yonge Library of Florida History, University of Florida, Gainesville, Florida.

BOC   Board of Control Minutes, Florida State Archives, Tallahassee, Florida.

Colman Letters   Marian Colman (FSCW 1918) to her parents. James P. Jones Collection, Tallahassee, Florida.

DD   Tallahassee *Daily Democrat.*

DC Corres.   Doak Campbell Correspondence, RG450, S1360, Florida State Archives, Tallahassee, Florida.

EC Corres.   Edward Conradi Correspondence, RG450, S1361, Florida State Archives, Tallahassee, Florida.

EC Papers   Edward Conradi Papers, Special Collections, Strozier Library, Florida State University.

FF   *Florida Flambeau.*

FSU OHC   Florida State University Oral History Collection, History Department, FSU, Tallahassee, Florida.

Kellum Scrapbook   John G. Kellum Scrapbooks, Special Collections, Strozier Library, Florida State University.

"Lassie"   "Tallahassee Lassie 1940–1944." Letters from Mary Ruth Weaver to her family in Kissimmee, Florida.

Letterbooks   A. A. Murphree Letterbooks, Special Collections, Strozier Library, Florida State University.

Memoirs   *Memoirs of Edward Conradi, President of FSCW 1909-1941.* (Tallahassee, Florida: Florida State College for Women, 1945). Special Collections, Strozier Library, Florida State University.

Memory Book   Kathlyn Monroe (FSCW 1918) Memory Book, James P. Jones Collection, Tallahassee, Florida.

NOTES TO CHAPTER I (PAGES 1–17)

1. Charlton W. Tebeau, *A History of Florida* (Miami: University of Miami Press, 1971), 134, cited hereafter as Tebeau, *Florida History*.

2. The federal census for 1850 indicated that Santa Rosa County had slightly over 200 white residents between the ages of five and eighteen, and Dade County had only sixteen.

3. *Florida Senate Journal*, 1850–51, 209–212.

4. *Laws of Florida*, 1852–53, 87.

5. William G. Dodd, *History of the West Florida Seminary* (Tallahassee: The Florida State University, 1952), 6, cited hereafter as Dodd, *West Florida*.

6. Ibid., 5–7.

7. Groene, Bertram H., *Ante Bellum Tallahassee* (Tallahassee: Florida Heritage Foundation, 1971), 97.

8. L. M. Bristol, *Three Focal Points in the Development of Florida's State System of Higher Education: Lectures Given at the College of Education, University of Florida* (Gainesville: University of Florida Press, 1952), 11, cited hereafter as Bristol, *Focal Points*.

9. Francis A. Rhodes, "The Legal Development of State Supported Higher Education in Florida." (Ph.D. diss., University of Florida, 1948), 23, cited hereafter as Rhodes, "Legal Development."

10. Dodd, *West Florida*, 8.

11. Ibid.

12. Caroline Mays Brevard, *A History of Florida* (New York: American Book Company, 1904), 116–119.

13. Dodd, *West Florida*, 27.

14. Ibid.

15. Rhodes, "Legal Development," 38; George Gary Bush, *History of Education in Florida* Bureau of Education Circular of Information No. 7, 1888 (Washington, DC: Government Printing Office, 1889), 33.

16. *Florida Senate Journal*, 1881, Appendix, 185; Dodd, *West Florida*, 57–59.

17. *Biennial Report of the Superintendent of Public Instruction of the State of Florida*, 1894, 37, cited hereafter as *Biennial Report*.

18. *Laws of Florida*, 1870, 45; *Florida Senate Journal*, 1889, Appendix, 354.

19. Alfred Hugh Adams, "A History of Public Education in Florida" (Ph.D. diss., Florida State University, 1962), 134, cited hereafter as Adams, "Public Education." This request was probably a reaction to West Florida Seminary's 1901 name change to Florida State College.

20. University of Florida Catalogue, 1904–1905, 107; Dodd, *West Florida*, 104.

21. Rhodes, "Legal Development," 165; *Florida Times Union*, 27 April 1905, 4; Bristol, *Focal Points*, 22.

22. *Biennial Report*, 1894, 37; *Laws of Florida*, 1905, 53.

23. Samuel Proctor, "The University of Florida: Its Early Years, 1853–1906" (Ph.D. diss., University of Florida, 1958), 485–86.

24. Milton Lee Orr, *The State-supported Colleges for Women* (Nashville, Tenn: George Peabody College for Teachers, 1930), ch. 1–6 passim.

25. Adams, "Public Education," 142.

26. Florida Female College Catalogue, 1905–1906, 13, cited hereafter as FFC Catalogue; William G. Dodd, "Florida State College for Women: Notes on the Formative Years," 1958–59, 10, cited hereafter as Dodd, "Formative Years;" Edward Conradi, *Memoirs*, 7.

27. Tallahassee *Weekly True Democrat*, 5 July 1905; Orland Kay Armstrong, *The Life and Work of Dr. A. A. Murphree*, (Gainesville: Orland Kay Armstrong, 1928), 25.

28. Orland Kay Armstrong, 37.

29. A. A. Murphree to J. H. Fellows, 15 July 1905, Letterbooks.

30. BOC, vol. 1, 50.

31. A. A. Murphree to C. G. Puleston, 13 July 1905, to J. A. Forsythe, Jr., 13 July 1905, to Edward P. Watson, 15 July 1905, Letterbooks.

32. A. A. Murphree to J. A. Forsythe, Jr., 13 July 1905, to Orville Brewer, 11 July 1905, to Captain A. Bryan, 13 July 1905, Letterbooks.

33. BOC, vol. 1, 12; FFC Catalogue 1905–1906, 21–22. The Buckman Bill mandated completion of the 10th grade for admission to Florida Female College and of the 12th grade for admission to the University of Florida. The Board of Control equalized these requirements.

34. BOC, vol. 1, 50–51.

35. FFC Catalogue, 1905–1906, 10–11.

36. Ibid., 71.

37. Ibid.; A. A. Murphree to Marion E. Jones, 27 July 1905, to Robert Ranson, 29 July 1905, Letterbooks; BOC, vol. 1, 11.

38. A. A. Murphree to Alma Jackson, 16 August 1905, to Essie M. Bessent, 21 August 1905, to Miss Anesta Abernathy, 29 September 1905, Letterbooks.

39. FFC Catalogue, 1905–1906, 23–29.

40. A. A. Murphree to Mrs. W. P. Corbett, 1 August 1905, Letterbooks.

41. FFC Catalogue, 1905–1906, 110–111.

42. A. A. Murphree to Inez Abernethy, 1 August 1905, to L. C. Povell, 29 August 1905, to Bertha Gatch, 2 August 1905, Letterbooks.

43. A. A. Murphree to Miss Nellie [no last name], 21 August 1905; to Mrs. L. Webe, 16 August 1905, Letterbooks. The correspondence to Miss

Nellie is handwritten; Murphree asked her to keep this offer confidential outside her immediate family.

44. A. A. Murphree to Miss Jean Patterson, 29 September 1905, to Professor E. R. Smith, 14 September 1905, Letterbooks.

NOTES TO CHAPTER II (PAGES 18–32)

1. Edward Conradi, Preliminary notes for *Memoirs of Edward Conradi*, 7, 20, EC Papers, cited hereafter as Conradi, Preliminary notes. William G. Dodd, "Early Education in Tallahassee and the West Florida Seminary, Now Florida State University, Part I," *Florida Historical Quarterly*, vol. 27 (July, 1948): 22. This is the present site of the Westcott Fountain.

2. Dodd, *West Florida*, 98.

3. A. A. Murphree to Helen Hunt, 10 April 1907, Letterbooks. Each room was 13' x 15'.

4. BOC, vol. 1, 16. The pool was 18' wide x 34' long; depths ranged from 3.5' to 5.5'.

5. A. A. Murphree to Fred W. Kettle (his secretary), 22 July 1905, Letterbooks.

6. A. A. Murphree to Miss A. J. Groves, 13 December 1905, Letterbooks. The house at 60 West Clinton Street belonged to Mrs. Arthur Maxwell.

7. Fenton Davis Avant, *My Tallahassee* (Tallahassee, Florida: L'Avant Studios, 1983), 6.

8. BOC, vol. 1, 236–7. The fire occurred on 22 December 1906.

9. Ibid; Tallahassee *Weekly True Democrat*, 28 December 1906; President's Report to the Board of Control, 15 February 1907, Letterbooks, cited hereafter as President's Report. The leased cottages were on Clinton Street and were owned by the Langston, Hartt, Bassett, DeMilly, and Hines families.

10. Tallahassee *Weekly True Democrat*, 28 December 1906.

11. Tallahassee *Morning Sun*, 20 April 1907.

12. Tallahassee *Weekly True Democrat*, 20 September 1907; BOC, vol. 1, 269. The property was purchased from Robert H. Mickler on 31 August 1907 for $2,000.

13. BOC, vol. 1, 270–71, 304. The original bids came in between $82,000 and $90,000; the Legislature had appropriated $40,000. Final cost was $46,566.07.

14. Tallahassee *Weekly True Democrat*, 29 November 1907, 11 September 1908.

15. FFC Catalogue, 1908–1909, 13; Tallahassee *Weekly True Democrat*, 28 August 1908; *The Talisman*, vol. 6, no. 1, 31; *FF*, 30 May 1930. Bed-

rooms were 14' x 8.5'; studies were 12' x 14'.

16. Tallahassee *Weekly True Democrat*, 24 December 1909, 20 February 1914, 16 January 1914; *The Talisman*, vol. 7, no. 2, 47; *FF*, 15 January 1916.

17. A. A. Murphree to B. C. Bondurant, 19 July 1905, Letterbooks; BOC, vol. 1, 15.

18. A. A. Murphree to Orville Brewer, J. W. Blair, A. W. Mill, H. S. Kellogg, Anna M. Thurston, 11 July 1905, Letterbooks.

19. Interview with Edna Rees Williams by James P. Jones, 28 March 1977; *FF*, 6 December 1929; BOC, vol. 1, 53, 164.

20. *The Talisman*, vol. 2, no. 2, 30, vol. 3 no. 3, 44; Fenton Davis Avant, *The Davis-Wood Family of Gadsden County and Their Forebears* (Easley, South Carolina: Southern Historical Press, 1979), 110.

21. FFC Catalogue, 1905–1906 71.

22. A. A. Murphree to Dr. Edward Conradi, 22 July 1907, Letterbooks; to Dr. L. W. Buchholz, 11 March 1909, AAM Corres.

23. Florida State College for Women, Illustrated Bulletin, vol. 9, no. 3, (July 1916):1. Enrollment for 1905–1909: 1905–1906=205; 1906–1907=220; 1907–1908=240; 1908–1909=257.

24. FFC Catalogue, 1905–1906, 107–108.

25. *FF*, 30 May 1930.

26. *The Talisman*, vol. 1, no. 1, 36.

27. Faculty Senate Minutes, 1905–1906, vol. 1, 1–2.

28. Perhaps because Murphree had supported the athletic program at Florida State College with so much enthusiasm.

29. *The Talisman*, vol. 2, no. 3, 34, 45.

30. Faculty Senate Minutes, vol. 1, 37; Tallahassee *Weekly True Democrat*, 6 March 1908; A. A. Murphree to Helen Hunt, 10 April 1907, Letterbooks. After the game, a Stetson linesman admitted that she had called several fouls "for spite."

31. *The Talisman*, vol. 3, no. 3, 44.

32. Faculty Senate Minutes, vol. 1, 54; Louise Bryant (FSCW 1933), "History of the Odds and Evens," *Flastacowo* 1933, np.

33. *The Talisman,* vol. 1, no. 1, 26.

34. Pat Thomas Meginniss, interview by author, 17 April 1993.

35. *The Talisman*, vol. 4, no. 4, 36, 47.

36. Tallahassee *Weekly True Democrat*, 4 August 1905; *The Talisman*, vol. 2, no. 1, 31; Board of Control, *Report of the Board of Control of the State Educational Institutions of Florida*, 1908–1909, 7.

37. BOC, vol. 1, 326–336; Rowena Diamond, "History of Florida State College for Women," unpublished manuscript, 19; Dodd, "Formative

Years," 30. Yonge specifically requested that the *current* presidents do this before they moved on to their new positions.

38. Hallijeanne Chalker to author, 16 November 1993.

39. Dodd, "Formative Years," 30; *FF*, 21 April 1923; Louise Bryant (FSCW 1933), "History of the Odds and Evens," *Flastacowo* 1933, np.

40. BOC, vol. 2, 45.

41. A. A. Murphree to Dr. J. F. McKinistry, Jr., 20 April 1909, AAM Corres. According to Dodd, "Formative Years," 26, Murphree wanted to stay in Tallahassee but responded "to the call of duty" and "passed out of the life and history of the FSCW." Documents discovered by the author do not support Dodd's sentiments.

42. BOC, vol. 1, 344.

NOTES TO CHAPTER III (PAGES 33–55)

1. *Memoirs,* 20.

2. Ibid., 21, 22.

3. BOC, vol. 1, 334.

4. *Memoirs,* 27–8.

5. Tallahassee *Weekly True Democrat*, 4 June 1909; BOC, vol. 1, 373–4.

6. Tallahassee *Weekly True Democrat*, 17 September 1909, 19 September 1909; BOC, vol. 1, 394. The contract was for $85,169.

7. Edward Conradi to A. A. Murphree, 12 March 1910, AAM Corres; Tallahassee *Weekly True Democrat*, 11 March 1910.

8. Edward Conradi to A. A. Murphree, 12 March 1910, AAM Corres.

9. It is difficult to say which catalogue this was, for the original one published in March of 1909 by the Florida Female College did not reflect the changes that occurred after that date. Once Conradi took over, the college did not issue a catalogue until May 1911.

10. Tallahassee *Weekly True Democrat*, 11 March 1910, 28 October 1960.

11. Kellum Scrapbook. 195 [551] West College Avenue is now a parking lot.

12. Ella Scoble Opperman, *Annals of the School of Music, 1905 to 1947*, 18–19. The dimensions were 90' x 56' x 25' high. The auditorium seated 826 persons in opera chairs and had room for 174 extra chairs.

13. President's Report, 5 January 1911, 94, 1 November 1912, 107.

14. Tebeau, *Florida History*, 337.

15. A contract in the amount of $48,680 was eventually awarded to J. A. Anderson of Atlanta.

16. Tallahassee *Semi-Weekly True Democrat*, 2 July 1912.

17. Colman Letters, 1 November 1914; Tallahassee *Semi-Weekly True Democrat*, 7 February 1913.

18. Florida State College for Women Catalogue, 1914–1915, 14, cited here-

after as FSCW Catalogue; BOC, vol 2, 175; *FF,* 20 October 1919. The dining room was 116' by 52'; the kitchen wing was 59.5' by 42.5'. The contract was for $25,640.

19. President's Report, 10 October 1914, 30; Tallahassee *Weekly True Democrat,* 27 August 1909. The Johnston Building, built in 1939 for use as a dining hall, stands on this site today.

20. Kellum Scrapbook. Montgomery Gym, Strozier Library, the Conradi Building, the Business Buildings, and the University Union now stand on the original dairy acreage.

21. BOC, vol. 2, 197; President's Report, 1 September 1914, 14, 1 September 1916, 228.

22. President's Report, 1 September 1914, 4; BOC, vol. 2, 429.

23. Illustrated Bulletin, vol. 9, no. 3 (July 1916): 1; BOC, vol. 3, 105. Enrollment for 1912–1916: 1912–13 = 413; 1913–14 = 477; 1914–15 = 636; 1915–16 = 818.

24. *Florida Times Union,* 14 August 1917; *FF,* 12 January 1918.

25. President's Report, 10 October 1918, 210.

26. *FF,* 12 October 1918.

27. Ibid., 22 February 1919.

28. Florida Master Site File, Survey #3004, State Bureau of Historic Preservation, Tallahassee, Florida, cited hereafter as Survey #3004; *FF,* 30 May 1930, 23 October 1915. Board of Control architect William Edwards designed the fountain and piers. Child Brothers of Tallahassee built the fountain; O. C. Parker built the gateway arch. In 1988 Florida State University replaced the original fountain with an exact replica.

29. Marion Colman, "The Gates."

30. BOC, vol. 3, 167.

31. Tallahassee *Weekly True Democrat,* 11 June 1909, 18 June 1909, 27 August 1909.

32. Ibid.

33. Angeline Yent Ashbrook (FSCW 1910–1912), interview by Dr. James P. Jones, 28 December 1976. Game's home was on the present site of the Jeffwood and Penwood Apartments, on the southwest corner of Jefferson Street and Woodward Avenue. Woodward Avenue did not follow its current route at that time.

34. BOC, vol. 2, 437; Tallahassee *Weekly True Democrat,* 26 August 1910. The Kappa Delta sorority house occupies the site now.

35. Tallahassee *Semi-Weekly True Democrat,* 25 October 1912.

36. Angeline Yent Ashbrook (FSCW 1910–1912), interview by Dr. James P. Jones, 28 December 1976; Colman Letters, 17 January 1915; Alberta Lee Davis Scrapbook, 27 October 1918.

37. *The Talisman,* vol. 4, no. 1, 55, 29.

38. *Flastacowo* 1911, 168.

39. Caddabelle Farr Beeson (FSCW 1911), Alumni Files, Florida State University; *The Talisman,* vol. 6, no. 4, 51.

40. Tallahassee *Weekly True Democrat,* 2 June 1911; Tampa *Morning Tribune,* 21 August 1911.

41. A. W. Calhoun to Edward Conradi, 15 September 1911, EC Papers.

42. Tallahassee *Weekly True Democrat,* 30 October 1911.

43. A. W. Calhoun to Edward Conradi, 16 February 1939, EC Corres.

44. Bly Pickett Garnand (FSCW 1911) to Alumni Association, 19 January 1961. Alumni Files, Florida State University.

45. BOC, vol. 1, 652; Dodd, "Formative Years," 39; Colman Letters, 5 December 1916; *FF, 9* December 1916.

46. Dodd, "Formative Years," 39.

47. Colman Letters, 15 April 1917, 29 April 1917; BOC, vol. 2, 463.

48. Alban Stewart, Jr., interview by author, 27 April 1993; Lucy Lang (FSCW 1926), interview by author, 5 April 1993.

49. Colman Letters, 7 March 1915, 28 January 1915, 14 February 1915; Faculty Senate Minutes, vol. 1, 175; *FF,* 1 February 1919.

50. Colman Letters, 5 November 1916.

51. President's Report, 10 October 1918, 206.

52. FSCW Catalogue 1943, 150–51; President's Report, 10 October 1918, 205–6; *DD,* 15 May 1919.

53. BOC, vol. 3, 355.

54. *FF,* 12 May 1917; BOC, vol. 3, 51, 55; Colman Letters, 1 December 1918. The dye was supposedly extracted and sold; the proceeds were then used to help Belgian children.

55. Betty and Guyte McCord, Jr., interview by author, 10 January 1994.

56. RG402, S249, Florida State Archives, Tallahassee, Florida.

57. *FF,* 16 February 1918, 4 March 1922.

58. BOC, vol. 3, 79–80.

59. Joe Earman to Lt. C. A. Muller, 1 April 1918, to William Sheats, 1 May 1918, RG402, S249, Florida State Archives, Tallahassee, Florida.

60. Edward Conradi, "1917," EC Papers.

61. J. B. Hodges to Edward Conradi, 3 January 1921, EC Papers.

62. *FF,* 7 April 1917.

63. Ibid., 28 April 1917.

64. Sue Pope and Ruby Leach to Edward Conradi, 30 April 1917, EC Papers. The letter is written on Miami *Daily Metropolis* letterhead.

65. Ibid.

66. *FF,* 6 October 1917.

67. Grace Dupree to Sue Pope, 2 April 1918, EC Papers.
68. Sue Pope and Ruby Leach to Grace Dupree, 11 April 1918, EC Papers.
69. Between 1911 and 1933, Helen Hunt used her position at the *Florida Times-Union* and her implied friendship with Governor Sidney J. Catts to pressure the Board of Control, A. A. Murphree, and particularly Edward Conradi, to confer upon her a bachelor's degree from FSCW, even though all professors involved agreed that she had not completed the required course work. She finally received her diploma from FSCW, predated to 1908, in 1933.
70. Sue Pope to Grace Dupree, 16 April 1918, EC Papers.
71. Faculty Senate Minutes, vol. 1, 172.
72. Edward Conradi to Mrs. Kate C. Havens, 24 April 1918; Faculty Senate Minutes, vol. 1, 172.
73. *FF,* 27 April 1918.
74. Sue Pope to Grace Dupree, 16 April 1918, EC Papers.

Notes to Chapter IV (pages 56–80)

1. FSCW Catalogue 1924–25, 36.
2. Tallahassee *Weekly True Democrat,* 3 December 1909.
3. Hampton Dunn, *Yesterday's Tallahassee,* (Miami, Florida: E. A. Seemann, 1974), 97; *FF,* 22 May 1915. Today City Hall stands on the site.
4. BOC, vol. 1, 513; William Meigs to Mary Lou Norwood, 20 March 1995.
5. Customs and Regulations Book, 1918, 4, EC Papers.
6. Colman Letters, 13 March 1915.
7. Monroe Memory Book, 30 November 1914, 16 November 1914, 7 November 1914; Tallahassee *Weekly True Democrat,* 24 April 1914.
8. YWCA Student Handbook, 1911–1912, 7.
9. *FF,* 23 November 1918.
10. Ibid., 9 October 1920, 23 January 1915; Tallahassee *Weekly True Democrat,* 5 November 1915.
11. Angeline Yent Ashbrook (FSCW 1910–1912), interview by James P. Jones, 28 December 1976; *FF,* 27 February 1915.
12. Martha Vicinus, "Distance and Desire: English Boarding-School Friendships," *Signs: Journal of Women in Culture and Society,* 9 (Winter 1984): 601–622, cited hereafter as Vicinus, "Distance and Desire."
13. "Crushes," *FF,* Spring 1915, Monroe Memory Book.
14. Ruby Leach to Kathlyn Monroe, Monroe Memory Book, no date.
15. Vicinus, "Distance and Desire," 617.
16. Angeline Yent Ashbrook (FSCW 1910–1912), interview by James P. Jones, 28 December 1976; *FF,* 15 May 1915.
17. Rovanna Duparc (FSCW 1944), interview by author, 11 May 1993;

Mary Rimbey Christian (FSCW 1920) to author, questionnaire response; Mary Reed Bridges (FSCW 1939) to author, 25 January 1994; Ella Taylor Slemons Bisbee (FSCW 1919) and Theresa Yaeger Palmer (FSCW 1919), interview by James P. Jones, 24 March 1977.

18. *FF*, 29 April 1916.
19. Suggestions Concerning Table Manners, 3 August 1925, EC Papers.
20. *FF*, 22 February 1919.
21. A. A. Murphree to Miss Mabelle Williams, 27 August 1907, Letterbooks.
22. Liva Baker, *I'm Radcliffe! Fly Me!* (New York: Macmillan Publishing Co. Inc., 1976), 84.
23. Thomas Woody, *A History of Women's Education in the United States* (New York: The Science Press, 2 vols., 1929), 2:199–200, cited hereafter as Woody, *Women's Education*.
24. FSCW Catalogue, 1912–13, 19.
25. Mrs. S. L. Cawthon to Edward Conradi, no date, EC Papers.
26. Ibid.
27. Tallahassee *Semi-Weekly True Democrat*, 17 October 1913.
28. Customs and Regulations 1918, 7–9, EC Papers; Tallahassee *Weekly True Democrat*, 22 October 1915.
29. Faculty Senate Minutes, vol. 1, 161–2.
30. YWCA Student Handbook, 1911–12, 9.
31. Faculty Senate Minutes, vol. 1, 117; College Government Association Secretary's Book, vol. 1, 13, cited hereafter as CGA Book.
32. CGA Book, 32–3.
33. Ibid., 36.
34. Ibid., 34–5, 43, 50–1, 54–5, 57, 224.
35. Ibid., 220, 239.
36. Customs and Regulations 1918, 6, EC Papers.
37. CGA Book, vol. 1, 253.
38. Ibid., vol. 2, 11, 28–9; vol. 1, 293; vol. 2, 21.
39. Faculty Senate Minutes, vol. 1, 78, 80; *The Talisman*, vol. 6, no. 3, 27–8.
40. *The Talisman*, vol. 8, no. 4, 31; Tallahassee *Semi-Weekly True Democrat*, 11 April 1913.
41. *The Talisman*, vol. 9, no. 4, 119; Tallahassee *Semi-Weekly True Democrat*, 11 April 1913.
42. *FF*, 13 March 1915, 27 March 1915.
43. YWCA Student Handbook 1918–19, 22; *FF*, 27 March 1920.
44. Tallahassee *Semi-Weekly True Democrat*, 10 December 1912.
45. Colman Letters, 15 November 1914, 29 November 1914.
46. *Flastacowo* 1915, 165, 156; Tallahassee *Weekly True Democrat*, 19 November 1915; *FF*, 13 November 1915; *FF*, 20 November 1915,

4 December 1915.

47. *FF*, 19 November 1916, 31 March 1917, 23 November 1918, 22 November 1919.

48. Ibid., 26 October 1918, 2 November 1918.

49. Ibid., 22 November 1919.

50. Ibid., 7 February 1920, 27 March 1920.

51. Tallahassee *Democrat,* 3 February 1993; *FF*, 19 January 1918; Colman Letters, 4 February 1917.

52. *FF*, 13 October 1917*,* 20 October 1917.

53. Colman Letters, 4 November 1917; *FF*, 10 November 1917.

54. *FF*, 13 January 1917; Colman Letters, 9 April 1917; *FF,* 31 March 1917, 14 April 1917, 21 April 1917.

55. *FF*, 12 May 1917, 13 October 1917, 16 February 1918, 23 February 1918.

56. Ibid., 12 October 1918, 26 October 1918, 17 November 1917.

57. Ibid., 27 October 1917, 6 April 1918, 11 May 1918.

58. Ibid., 16 March 1918, 16 November 1918.

59. Ibid., 22 November 1919.

60. Ibid., 25 May 1918; Ella Scoble Opperman Scrapbook, 107.

61. *FF,* 6 October 1933.

62. Ibid., 23 October 1915.

63. Ibid., 30 May 1930; Dodd, "Formative Years," 64. Miss Freeman later became Mrs. L. A. Yates of Tallahassee.

64. *FF,* 30 January 1915,

65. Ibid., 28 October 1916, 14 February 1920.

Notes to Chapter V (pages 105–126)

1. Henry B. Plant's railway system merged with the Atlantic Coast Line Railroad in 1902 and established a Richmond-Tampa route.

2. Completed in 1924 and 1928 respectively.

3. *DD*, 19 November 1921.

4. Edward Conradi, Calendar of College Improvements and Events, 4–5, cited hereafter as Calendar, EC Papers.

5. BOC, vol. 4, 353. Calendar, 6; Agreement between Lewis State Bank and FSCW, EC Papers; *Memoirs,* 30. Leon County Deed Book Number 10, 333. The signers were: L. C. Yaeger, William Child, Guyte P. McCord, Dr. Henry E. Palmer, Dr. F. Clifton Moor, Dr. William E. Van Brunt, Dr. Ephraim Brevard, Rutledge Alford, Dr. J. B. Game, and Dr. Edward Conradi. Total purchase price, including interest and attorney's fees, was $10,501.34.

6. *FF*, 20 February 1915; President's Report, 1 September 1916, 232–3.

7. President's Report, 1 November 1920, 234.

8. Sue Love Liske (FSCW 1942), FSU OHC; President's Report, 28 September 1926, 11.

9. *The Talisman*, vol. 6, no. 4, 40; President's Report, 1 September 1916, 233.

10. Louisa Conradi Ekermeyer (FSCW 1928), interview by author, 17 November 1992.

11. *FF*, 4 May 1918, 18 May 1918; BOC, vol. 3, 364.

12. *FF*, 30 October 1920; CGA Book, vol. 1, 37; *FF*, 23 October 1920; *Flastacowo* was also the name given to the college annual, published from 1910 to 1914, and from 1921 to 1947.

13. *FF*, 9 April 1921, 21 May 1921, 18 March 1922.

14. Ibid., 6 May 1922, 26 April 1924, 17 May 1924.

15. Alumni Bulletin, vol. 47, no. 5, 14; Athletic Association Minutes, 6 May 1926, np; BOC, vol. 6, 46, 376; *FF*, 28 February 1930. The value of the camp house, boat house, and boats was estimated at $5000.

16. *DD*, 11 August 1922.

17. Ibid., 18 September 1920.

18. The Science Building later occupied that site; the Diffenbaugh Building stands there currently. Colman Letters, 10 December 1916; *FF*, 15 February 1919, 22 November 1919; BOC, vol. 3, 330-331, 338; CGA Book, vol. 2, 18.

19. Jeanne Compton Stone (FSCW 1928), FSU OHC.

20. *FF*, 6 November 1920, 10 November 1933.

21. Ibid., 6 November 1920; *DD*, 1 November 1920.

22. Jeanne Compton Stone, "It's Old East Hall A-Burning in the Mornin!" Personal papers and scrapbooks of Jeanne Compton Stone, used by permission of Mode Lee Stone, Jr.

23. Ann Onn, "L'Envoi." Personal papers and scrapbooks of Jeanne Compton Stone.

24. "We had some trouble with this, but got with Van Swearington and we prepared a milk and mush opinion that put us by." J. B. Hodges to Bryan Mack, 22 November 1920, Stetson University Archives, Deland, Florida.

25. *DD*, 5 November 1920, 11 November 1920; *FF*, 19 February 1921, 26 October 1928.

26. President's Report, 5 October 1922, 232–3; *FF*, 14 May 1921, 30 April 1921.

27. *DD*, 18 June 1921, 9 May 1922; *FF*, 2 April 1921; Tallahassee *Democrat*, 21 September 1952. Martha Murphree Troxler (FSCW 1924) later lived in Coral Gables, Florida. Her daughter, Jennie Henderson Wallace, lived in Jennie Murphree Hall during her freshman year at FSU (1952).

28. *DD*, 11 September 1922, 13 September 1922; President's Report, 5

October 1922, 233; *DD*, 12 December 1922.

29. *DD*, 9 April 1923, 10 April 1923, 13 June 1923.

30. Ibid., 13 June 1923, 29 September 1923. H. H. Brown of Dothan, Alabama started work in November 1923.

31. Frederick Lewis Allen, *Only Yesterday* (New York Perennial Library, Harper & Row, 1964), 228. Merrick insisted that all buildings conform to what he called "modified Mediterranean" architecture which incorporated Spanish tile roofs.

32. President's Report, 25 September 1924, 3, 28 September 1926, 3.

33. Ibid., 5 October 1922, 236; *DD*, 11 November 1925; Mary Logan McCullough (FSCW 1928) to author, questionnaire response; FF, 1 March 1924. The standard fire drill routine called for closing all windows before leaving the room.

34. Faculty Senate Minutes, vol. 2, 57; BOC, vol. 4, 479. Between 1921 and 1925 enrollment rose 82 percent, from 645 to 1183.

35. *FF,* 4 October 1924, 17 October 1925.

36. *DD,* 23 November 1925, 24 November 1925.

37. Ibid., 6 September 1928.

38. BOC, vol. 5, 124, 170; *DD*, 19 March 1926.

39. BOC, 300–01; President's Report, 28 September 1926, 9.

40. President's Report, 28 September 1926, 11. According to Mary Lou Norwood (FSCW 1947), the college insisted that a mature married woman be in residence at all times and that the household include no unmarried males over sixteen years of age.

41. BOC, vol. 5, 379.

42. *FF,* 10 January 1930, 3 December 1927; BOC, vol. 5, 203, 70, vol. 6, 31. This section was built by Leo Alsheimer of Deland, Florida.

43. President's Report, 28 September 1926, 8–9, 11 October 1928, 12, 10 November 1930, 87.

44. Faculty Senate Minutes, vol. 1, 176–7; President's Report, 5 October 1922, 232.

45. Tallahassee *Democrat and Weekly Record*, 15 February 1924.

46. Ibid.

47. Faculty Senate Minutes, vol. 2, 57; *DD,* 4 October 1928.

48. *FF,* 10 January 1925, 14 December 1928.

49. *DD,* 20 December 1928; *FF,* 11 January 1929.

50. President's Report, 5 October 1922, 232–5; FSCW Catalogue 1924–25, 20.

51. *FF,* 4 November 1922; Faculty Senate Minutes, vol. 2, 49; Conradi, Calendar, 7.

52. President's Report, 1 November 1920, 231; BOC, vol. 4, 10; *FF,* 12 November 1921.

53. *DD,* 9 October 1923; President's Report, 25 September 1924, 3. The contractor was C. A. Fulghum of Pensacola.
54. FSCW Catalogue, 1926–1927, 22.
55. President's Report, 28 September 1926, 6–7, 25 September 1924, 8–9.
56. *FF,* 28 April 1928, 29 September 1929; Survey #3004. Berg-Marshall Contractors of Lakeland did the work; estimated cost was $163,000.
57. Lucille Higgs (Assistant Director, University Library, 1949–1985), FSU OHC.
58. *FF,* 8 October 1923.
59. BOC, vol. 3, 249, 314, 410.
60. Ibid., vol. 4, 4.
61. *DD,* 12 December 1923.
62. BOC, vol. 5, 11.
63. President's Report, 28 September 1926, 3; *FF,* 4 March 1922, 17 October 1925; President's Report, 5 October 1922, 239.
64. BOC, vol. 5, 290. E. D. Thomas and Son of Jacksonville submitted a low bid of $90,000.
65. *FF,* 16 April 1927; BOC, vol. 5, 425; President's Report, 11 October 1928, 3.
66. President's Report, 11 October 1928, 3; BOC, vol. 3, 365.
67. *DD,* 8 October 1923; *Florida Education Association Journal,* 1, no. 4 (December 1923): 21.
68. *FF,* 3 March 1928.
69. President's Report, 28 September 1926, 6; *FF,* 4 March 1922; Sue Love Liske (FSCW 1942), FSU OHC; President's Report, 25 September 1924, 11.
70. *FF,* 25 November 1932.
71. Dr. Grace Fox (FSCW 1928), interview by author, 17 April 1991.
72. *DD,* 24 October 1928, 4 April 1929.
73. BOC, vol. 6, 385.
74. Mary Lou Norwood (FSCW 1947), FSU OHC; *FF,* 21 September 1928; Faculty Senate Minutes, vol. 2, 138.

NOTES TO CHAPTER VI (PAGES 127–150)

1. BOC, vol. 4, 442; Faculty Senate Minutes, 55.
2. FSCW Catalogue, 1920–21, 28.
3. Faculty Senate Minutes, vol. 2, 2; BOC, vol. 3, 410.
4. FSCW Catalogue, 1920–21, 108, 1922–23, 43.
5. Lylah Scarborough Barber (FSCW 1929), FSU OHC; FSCW Catalogue, 1922–23, 88. Lylah Barber graduated from this program and found employment at the University of Florida infirmary, where she met her future husband, Walter "Red" Barber.

6. *DD*, 19 September 1924.
7. *Flastacowo* 1923, 84.
8. Bulletin of the State College for Women, vol. 1, no. 1, 16.
9. Mary Dorothy Bulloch (FSCW 1927), FSU OHC.
10. Ibid.
11. Bulletin of the Florida State College for Women, vol. 18, no. 3, 67, and vol. 1, no. 1, 16; President's Report, 25 September 1924, 42.
12. Marion Phillips Burnett (FSCW 1933), questionnaire response.
13. Dodd, "Formative Years," 36.
14. President's Report, 25 September 1924, 6–7; Raymond Bellamy to Class of 1921, 30 May 1923. Alumni Files.
15. President's Report, 28 September 1926, 5.
16. FSCW Catalogue, 1923–24, 45, 1924–25, 33, 1925–26, 35. This represented a 500 percent increase.
17. President's Report, 25 September 1924, 21, 37–8; *DD*, 19 March 1926.
18. *FF*, 16 October 1926, 26 October 1928. Based on enrollment: Hunter College; College of Industrial Arts, (Denton, Texas); Smith; Winthrop; North Carolina College for Women; Wellesley; Florida State College for Women; Mississippi State College for Women; Baylor College for Women; Vassar; Radcliffe; Goucher; Georgia State College for Women.
19. *DD*, 20 December 1928, 23 September 1929.
20. FSCW Catalogue, 1920–21, 7–11. Edward Conradi, William Dodd, J. B. Game, E. A. Hayden, Alban Stewart, Raymond Bellamy, and Horatio Hughes had doctorates; Arthur Williams, Elmer Smith, Lanas Barber, Edmund Gage, Rowena Longmire (honorary), and several others held master's degrees.
21. Joe Earman to Edward Conradi, 30 March 1918; Joe Earman to Governor Sidney J. Catts, 22 April 1918. Board of Regents Correspondence, Florida State Archives, Tallahassee, Florida.
22. BOC, vol. 3, 373.
23. President's Report, 25 September 1924, 6. Hazel Lois Bowman (FSCW 1937) to FSU Alumni Affairs, 6 May 1964. Bowman derived her information from a study of salaries made by the Gainesville chapter of the American Association of University Professors, no date.
24. Williams, Game, Salley, Stewart to Edward Conradi, 8 July 1926; President's Report, 28 September 1926, 4–5; BOC, vol. 5, 261–2; President's Report, 11 October 1928, 36.
25. *DD*, 29 October 1921, 18 March 1922.
26. Katherine Montgomery (Physical Education), 1918–1956; Olivia Dorman (Classics), 1924–1956; Ralph Eyman (Education), 1928–1956; Paul Finner (Psychology), 1922–1954; Herman Kurz (Botany),1922–

1956; Harold Richards (Physics), 1925–1956; Hazel Stevenson (English), 1920–1956; Anna May Tracy (Dietitian), 1922–1956.

27. Until 1923, the Department of Physical Education was known as the School of Physical Culture and Expression. Its director was Dubose Elder. This department was the forerunner not only of Physical Education but of the Speech and Drama Department at FSCW. Bernice Conklin Coleman (FSCW 1929), questionnaire response.

28. Montgomery earned a master's degree from Teachers College, Columbia University, and a doctorate from New York University. Dr. Grace Fox (FSCW 1928), interview by author, 17 April 1991.

29. Alumni Bulletin, vol. 52, no. 2: 12.

30. "History of the Library," typed manuscript, no author cited; Ruth Woolman was Librarian between 1920 and 1922.

31. Lucille Higgs (Assistant Director, University Library, 1949–1985), FSU OHC.

32. BOC, vol. 4, 77. *Flastacowo* 1921, 8; 1923, 23.

33. Edward Conradi to W. R. O'Neal, 2 April 1917, Rollins College Archives, Winter Park, Florida; BOC, vol. 3, 191.

34. *FF*, 1 February 1919, 10 December 1921; FSCW Catalogue, 1919, 11.

35. Anna May Tracy, interview by Dr. James P. Jones, 29 December 1976.

36. Nancy Stewart Boots (FSCW 1938) to author, 11 June 1994.

37. Mary Logan McCullough (FSCW 1928) to author, 22 November 1993.

38. *FF*, 22 April 1922, 11 November 1922.

39. Lucy Lang (FSCW 1926), interview by author, 5 April 1993.

40. *FF*, 25 September 1926, 26 March 1927.

41. Alumni Bulletin, vol. 47, no. 9: 8. She earned her M.S. at Cornell. In 1916 she marched for women's rights on Fifth Avenue in New York. In 1979, confined to a wheelchair, she paraded at a rally before the Florida House of Representatives to protest the legislature's failure to ratify the Equal Rights Amendment.

42. Mary Dorothy Bulloch (FSCW 1927), FSU OHC.

43. Raymond Bellamy, "History of the Department of Sociology at FSU," unpublished manuscript, no date, 11, cited hereafter as Bellamy, "Sociology."

44. Tallahassee *Daily Democrat*, 10 February 1921, 18 February 1921.

45. *Miami Metropolis*, 25 February 1921.

46. Faculty Senate Minutes, vol. 2, 7–9.

47. Ibid.

48. *FF*, 5 March 1921.

49. Bellamy, "Sociology," 34.

50. President's Report, 10 October 1918, 207.

51. Notes in Edward Conradi's handwriting, EC Papers.
52. Walter Scott McNutt to P. K. Yonge, 31 March 1926, EC Papers.
53. William G. Dodd to Edward Conradi, no date, EC Papers.
54. Ibid.
55. Boob McNutt was the central and extremely gullible character in a popular Sunday newspaper comic strip drawn by Rube Goldberg.
56. Edward Conradi, "Purity League," no date, EC Papers.
57. Bryan, the cousin of ex-governor William S. Jennings (1901–1905), first bought property in South Florida in 1912. In 1923 George Merrick, developer of Coral Gables, hired Bryan to sit on a raft in the middle of Venetian Pool and lecture to prospective buyers on the beauties and advantages of owning property in southeast Florida.
58. *Laws of Florida*, 1923, I, 506.
59. Tallahassee *Democrat and Weekly Record,* 25 January 1924.
60. Mary Duncan France, "A Year of Monkey War: The Anti-Evolution Campaign and the Florida Legislature," *Florida Historical Quarterly* 54, no. 2 (October 1975): 156–177. Clearwater *Evening Sun,* 21 November 1925, 28 December 1925. The friend was George F. Washburn, a Clearwater realtor.
61. Tampa *Morning Tribune,* 24 April 1926.
62. This was Harry Chase, later president of the University of North Carolina at Chapel Hill.
63. L. A. Tatum, copy of presentation before Board of Control, 17 May 1926, EC Papers.
64. Edward Conradi to P. K. Yonge, 17 May 1926, EC Papers.
65. A. A. Murphree to Fred H. Davis, Attorney General of Florida, 20 August 1927, to Senator Edgar Waybright (Jacksonville), 25 April 1927, AAM Corres.; Warren Kuehl, *Hamilton Holt: Internationalist, Journalist, Educator* (Gainesville: University of Florida Press, 1960), 223–25.
66. Mary Duncan France, 156–177; Laws of Florida, 1927, I, 1623–24; *Florida State News,* 2 June 1927.
67. Bellamy, "Sociology," 29.
68. A. A. Murphree to Fred H. Davis, 20 August 1927. Murphree Correspondence.
69. A. Pichard, L. A. Tatum, "Psychoanalysis of Filthy Dreamers, and Other Insidious Teaching Under the Guise of Science in Tax Supported Institutions of Learning." Bulletin No. 1, Tallahassee, Florida, 27 September 1927, 2, EC Papers.
70. A. A. Murphree to L. A. Tatum and A. Pichard, 28 October 1927, EC Papers; Carl Van Ness, University of Florida Archivist, to author, 30 July 1993.

71. J. B. Game to Edward Conradi, 10 October 1927, EC Papers.

72. Ibid.

73. Louise Richardson to Edward Conradi, 27 October 1927, EC Papers.

74. *FF*, 29 October 1927.

75. Guyte P. McCord to Edward Conradi, 1 November 1927, EC Papers.

76. Student Resolution, 22 November 1927, EC Papers.

77. *DD*, 3 July 1928. Signed by the Tallahassee Chamber of Commerce Board of Directors: Frank D. Moor, R. H. Gibson, G. E. Lewis, W. A. Bass, O. C. Collins, W. Theo Proctor, L. A. McCants.

78. Friedreich von Falkenberg to Edward Conradi, no date, EC Papers.

79. FSCW Catalogue, 1928–29.

80. *Chapel Hill Weekly*, 16 September 1932.

Notes to Chapter VII (pages 151–174)

1. Pearl Walsh Jones (FSCW 1923), questionnaire response.

2. *FF*, 6 September 1924, 13 December 1924.

3. Ibid., 13 December 1924, 29 May 1926; *DD*, 7 September 1928.

4. Elaine Kendall, *"Peculiar Institutions:" An Informal History of the Seven Sister Colleges* (New York: Putnam, 1976), 168.

5. *FF*, 18 November 1923.

6. Elizabeth Robinton (FSCW 1927–29). Memory Book, Alumni Association, Florida State University.

7. Mary Weedon Keen (FSCW 1926). Talk given 16 April 1986 at 75th anniversary of Gamma Chapter, Chi Omega.

8. *FF*, 1 December 1923, 14 February 1920.

9. Ibid., 26 March 1921.

10. Frances Shelly Bennett (FSCW 1920), questionnaire response; Woody, *Women's Education,* 202–3.

11. College Government Association Handbook 1928, 26.

12. Faculty Senate Minutes, vol. 2, 140; FF, 20 September 1929, 17 January 1930.

13. *FF*, 1 March 1919.

14. 20 February 1921, 26 February 1921; *DD*, 21 February 1921; *FF,* 23 February 1924, 28 February 1925, 21 February 1930.

15. *FF*, 16 October 1920.

16. Ibid., 8 November 1924, 18 October 1929; *DD*, 21 October 1929.

17. *FF*, 15 October 1921.

18. *DD*, 12 October 1925.

19. Mary Logan McCullough (FSCW 1928) to author, 22 November 1993.

20. Ibid.; Annie MacKay (FSCW 1927) to author, 26 November 1993.

21. *FF*, 2 October 1923.

22. Ibid., 30 April 1921, 17 May 1919, 24 April 1920.
23. Ibid., 6 May 1922.
24. BOC, vol. 5, 15. A letter from Conradi to Cawthon contained the unexplained phrase: "It was necessary for you to get on your way at the sanitarium without being reminded too much of your connections here at the college." EC Papers.
25. *FF,* 3 October 1925.
26. Ibid.; Dodd, "Formative Years," 108.
27. *FF,* 17 October 1925.
28. Tampa *Morning Tribune,* 2 February 1926.
29. FSCW Catalogue, 1924–25, 177; J. G. Kellum to Anna M. Tracy, 4 February 1926, EC Papers.
30. *DD,* 20 November 1925; *FF,* 7 March 1930.
31. The Wisteria Tea Room became the Sweet Shop; BOC, vol. 5, 227.
32. *FF,* 22 May 1926; Mary Logan McCollough (FSCW 1928) to author, 22 November 1993; *FF,* 15 January 1927.
33. Ibid., 2 October 1926, 26 September 1930.
34. *DD,* 11 November 1925; *FF,* 17 November 1925, 15 December 1926.
35. BOC, vol. 5, 378; *FF,* 28 September 1927.
36. *FF,* 21 November 1925, 13 February 1926; "To the Faculty," 17 September 1924, EC Papers.
37. *FF,* 24 January 1925.
38. *DD,* 14 November 1925.
39. *FF,* 17 November 1925, 21 November 1925.
40. Ibid., 30 November 1925.
41. FSCW Catalogue, 1921–22, 27, 1924–25, 30.
42. Ibid., 1925–26, 33.
43. *FF,* 22 November 1927.
44. Ibid., 5 March 1927, 22 November 1927.
45. Ibid., 12 October 1928, 26 April 1929.
46. Ibid., 11 February 1928; College Government Association Handbook 1928, 26; *FF,* 10 December 1927, 11 February 1928.
47. *FF,* 16 April 1921
48. *DD,* 19 March 1926; FSCW Catalogue, 1925–26, 34; India Steed Wells (FSCW 1927); *FF,* 5 March 1927, 2 April 1927.
49. *DD,* 1 October 1928. Methodist, 488; Baptist, 365; Presbyterian, 261; Episcopalian, 208; Catholic, 52; Christian Scientist, 27; Jewish, 20. The remainder were affiliated with miscellaneous denominations. FSCW Catalogue, 1927–28, 37.
50. *FF,* 28 January 1922.
51. *DD,* 22 May 1922.

52. Ibid., 31 May 1922, 8 July 1922, 11 July 1922, 12 July 1922, 12 September 1922.
53. *FF,* 21 May 1923, 29 March 1924. Her throw was 100' 8.5". *DD,* 19 March 1926; *FF,* 19 March 1927, 27 March 1920, 15 May 1920, 4 February 1928.
54. *FF,* 5 March 1927.
55. Colman Letters, 2 December 1917; *FF,* 30 November 1918.
56. *FF,* 13 November 1926, 27 November 1926, 30 November 1928.
57. Ibid., 20 September 1929; Dr. Grace Fox (FSCW 1928), interview by author, 17 April 1991.
58. *FF,* 8 February 1929; Dr. Grace Fox (FSCW 1928), interview by author, 17 April 1991; Ella Scoble Opperman, "The Story," 22–23. Typewritten manuscript.
59. Opperman, "The Story," 22–23; *FF,* 13 December 1929.
60. Dr. Grace Fox (FSCW 1928), interview by author, 17 April 1991.
61. Faculty Senate Minutes, vol. 1, 81.
62. Ibid.
63. *FF,* 28 October 1916.
64. Edward Conradi to A. A. Murphree, 15 October 1917, AAM Corres.; *DD,* 9 October 1917. At the time, Kappa Delta, Chi Omega, Alpha Delta Pi, Delta Delta Delta, and two local organizations had chapters at FSCW; Kappa Alpha, Alpha Tau Omega, Sigma Alpha Epsilon, and Pi Kappa Alpha had chapters at the University of Florida. The Board considered the argument that the fraternal organizations were undemocratic and subjected those not asked to join to undue embarrassment.
65. *FF,* 15 October 1921, 30 September 1922.
66. Ibid., 17 January 1925; *Smith's Weekly* (Tallahassee), 10 October 1924; *DD,* 5 October 1928, 4 February 1929.
67. *FF,* 24 November 1923, 19 February 1927; *DD,* 5 October 1928.
68. Mona Alderman Canova (FSCW 1925), questionnaire response; Susan Miller Cowles (FSCW 1952, 1968, 1971). The chapter bought the Windom House.
69. *DD,* 24 August 1923, 27 April 1929.
70. FSCW Catalogue, 1926–27, 23.
71. *FF,* 4 February 1928.
72. Ibid., 15 October 1921; Opperman, "The Story," 21.
73. Opperman, "The Story," 110–115.

Notes to Chapter VIII (pages 199–218)

1. *FF,* 24 October 1930.
2. BOC, vol. 7, 66. The land had been part of Governor William D.

Bloxham's (1881–1885, 1897–1901) plantation. The college paid $10,000 for the property, now the site of Alumni Village.

3. *FF,* 24 October 1930.

4. Ibid.; President's Report, 12 October 1932, 13–14, 19 October 1934, 12–13.

5. *FF,* 30 July 1931, 9 March 1934; President's Report, 19 October 1934, 13.

6. President's Report, 15 October 1936, 10; BOC, vol. 7, 514; Leon County Deed Book #29, 34. Purchase price was $3,000. *FF,* 27 September 1935; *DD,* 1 September 1936, 8.

7. BOC, vol. 7, 15–16. Purchase price was $1,000. *FF,* 16 January 1931. Dorman Hall occupies this site now.

8. BOC, vol. 7, 186; *FF,* 3 February 1933, 22 November 1935.

9. President's Report, 19 October 1934, 12.

10. *FF,* 2 October 1931, 22 September 1933, 25 September 1931; President's Report, 19 October 1934, 12. The caretaker was also the head carpenter for the college.

11. *FF,* 22 September 1933.

12. Ibid., 10 October 1930, 26 November 1937; Sanborn Map, Florida State University East Campus, 1947. The Bellamy Building now sits on the site of the basketball courts, Thagard Health Center on the volleyball courts, and the Aquatic Center where the soccer and hockey field lay. The site of Deviney Hall was the archery range. *FF,* 27 March 1931; President's Report, 12 October 1932, 12–13.

13. *FF,* 11 March 1932; *DD,* 5 October 1934; *FF,* 10 November 1939.

14. BOC, vol. 6, 368, 473; *FF,* 24 October 1930, 18 April 1940.

15. The J. M. Raymond Construction Company built the plant.

16. *FF,* 6 March 1931, 24 October 1930; *DD,* 12 January 1931, 16 September 1934.

17. *FF,* 10 October 1930; President's Report, 12 October 1932, 10; *FF,* 24 October 1930.

18. Dorothy Bryant McGahagin (FSCW 1944), "Class of 1944," 19. Alumni Association, Florida State University.

19. President's Report, 12 October 1932, 10.

20. *FF,* 26 June 1931, 9 October 1931; Survey #3004; President's Report, 12 October 1932. The contractor, J. M. Raymond, had also built the original section in 1927–28. Cost for the addition was approximately $100,000.

21. BOC, vol. 7, 200.

22. Louisa Conradi Ekermeyer (FSCW 1928), interview by author, 18 November 1992. Elizabeth Conradi Boone graduated in 1921.

23. BOC, vol. 7, 163.
24. *FF,* 1 December 1933.
25. BOC, vol. 7, 553.
26. *FF,* 11 December 1931, 1 December 1933
27. BOC, vol. 7, 204.
28. *FF,* 8 April 1932; BOC, vol. 7, 222; *FF,* 16 January 1931, 8 April 1932, 3 November 1933.
29. President's Report, 12 October 1932, 12–13.
30. *FF,* 27 March 1931, 16 February 1934.
31. Ibid., 12 May 1933; Survey #3004. The ornamental steelwork came from the Farquar Machinery Company of Jacksonville, Florida.
32. *FF,* 30 June 1933; President's Report, 19 October 1934, 11; Sanborn Map, Florida State University East Campus, 1947; *FF,* 11 October 1935.
33. *FF,* 1 December 1933, 15 December 1933; BOC, vol. 7, 381; Faculty Senate Minutes, 1934–36, 128. The estimated cost of repairs was $64,000.
34. BOC, vol. 7, 553.
35. Ibid., 172.
36. The doors now stand on either side of the entrance to the Ruby Diamond Auditorium. *FF,* 6 January 1933.
37. President's Report, 19 October 1934, 9.
38. BOC, vol. 7, 482, 487, 521, 560.
39. *DD,* 1 September 1936, 9.
40. *FF,* 4 October 1935, 20 March 1936. Robert and Company, Inc., of Atlanta supervised the work along with Mendenhall. H. S. Baird Construction Company of Jacksonville did the actual work. The contents of the cornerstone are now part of Special Collections.
41. President's Report, 15 October 1936, 8; 20 July 1940, 6. Mendenhall estimated reconstruction would cost $200,000.
42. BOC, vol. 7, 532.
43. John J. Tigert to L. M. Bristol, cited in Bristol, *Focal Points,* 64.
44. BOC, vol. 7, 532. Eighteen years later Tigert insisted that he had discussed the matter with Conradi on several occasions, and that while Conradi "preferred to have the date remain as it was, he offered no serious objection." John J. Tigert to L. M. Bristol, cited in Bristol, *Focal Points,* 64.
45. Cary D. Landis to John J. Tigert, 22 April 1935, cited in Bristol, *Focal Points,* 65.
46. BOC, vol. 7, 540.
47. Governor Albert W. Gilchrist (1909–1913) had bequeathed $10,000 to each of the state's institutions of higher learning.

48. *Lewis et al v. Gaillard et al,* Florida Reports, vol. 61, January Term, 1911, cited in Bristol, *Focal Points,* 46–67.

49. Report of the Business Manager, 10 December 1936, 96; BOC, vol. 7, 540; Faculty Senate Minutes, 1937–40, 18; *FF,* 11 December 1936.

50. President's Report, 10 November 1930, 87.

51. *FF,* 16 January 1931. The newspaper cited a contemporary study by Raymond Walters, Dean of Swarthmore College.

52. Carolyn Krentzman (FSCW 1937–39) and Bonnie Krentzman Mannheimer (FSCW early 1940s), FSU OHC.

53. *FF,* 12 February 1932. Other southern state-supported women's schools considered in the survey were Georgia State, South Carolina State, Texas State, and Virginia State; northern schools were Vassar, Wellesley, and Mount Holyoke.

54. President's Report, 15 October 1936, 50, 28 September 1938, 27; *FF,* 7 January 1938.

55. President's Report, 28 September 1938, 5.

56. Mary Lou Norwood (FSCW 1947), FSU OHC.

57. Dr. Anne Pates (FSCW 1936), FSU OHC.

58. *FF,* 28 June 1935, 20 September 1935.

59. Ibid., 2 October 1936, 9 October 1936.

60. President's Report, 15 October 1936, 9.

61. *FF,* 12 February 1937; BOC, vol. 8, 316.

62. *FF,* 1 July 1938.

63. Survey #3004; *DD,* 18 September 1938, 17 September 1939. The main section was 200' x 41'; each wing was 112' x 41'.

64. *FF,* 29 September 1939; *DD,* 17 September 1939; *FF,* 21 April 1939.

65. *FF,* 28 July 1939.

66. Edward Conradi to Dixie Hollins, 15 August 1939, EC Corres.

67. FSCW Catalogue, 1939–1940, 40–41. The totals included a $12 registration fee, $14 infirmary fee, $18 student activity and buildings fee, $16 laundry fee, $1.25 post office box rent, and $164 for board in the Dining Hall.

68. *FF,* 1 July 1938; FSCW Catalogue, 1939–1940, 23; *DD,* 18 September 1938; *FF,* 25 November 1938.

69. *FF,* 17 March 1939, 13 October 1939, 7 November 1941. Downstairs dining rooms were 53' by 100', upstairs were 53' by 80'.

70. "Lassie," 11 September 1940.

71. Ibid., 17 March 1939.

72. FSCW Catalogue, 1939–1940, 24; BOC, vol. 9, 220; *FF,* 26 July 1940. This skeleton is now displayed at the Museum of Florida History, Tallahassee.

73. President's Report, 28 September 1938, 7; *FF*, 17 March 1939. This is now called Dogwood Way.
74. President's Report, 19 October 1934, 8; *FF*, 30 October 1936; President's Report, 15 October 1936, 40.
75. *FF*, 8 April 1938, 6 May 1938.
76. Ibid., 22 July 1938, 2 December 1938. Longmire died on 18 July 1938.
77. President's Report, 28 September 1938, 22.

NOTES TO CHAPTER IX (PAGES 219–239)

1. *FF*, 19 October 1928; "Facts about Florida State College for Women," EC Papers.
2. FSCW Catalogues, 1930–1940. Of approximately 88 faculty members hired between 1930 and 1940, 70 had only master's or bachelor's degrees. Some of those instructors hired between 1915 and 1940 with only bachelor's or master's degrees who later earned doctorates were Katherine Montgomery, Grace Fox, Venila Shores, Sarah Herndon, Mary Noka Hood, Edna McIntosh, Nita Pyburn, Ruth Schornherst, and Anna May Tracy.
3. *Laws of Florida*, 1933, vol. I, 515–16; *FF*, 22 September 1933.
4. Florence Steinberg Weil (FSCW 1933) to author, 9 December 1993; Sue Chaires Boynton, Tedy Parker King, Cornelia Watson Gause, Mary Lou King, Floread B. Lee, Tam T. Milton, Charlotte Cooper, Jean Wood Crow, FSU OHC; Wallace W. Reichelt (Associate Professor, History, 1948–1978), FSU OHC.
5. *FF*, 16 October 1931.
6. President's Report, 19 October 1934, 14, 28 September 1938, 6; *FF*, 17 March 1933; Dodd, "Formative Years," 112. The downward trend in enrollment reversed itself almost immediately, but the legislature did not restore salaries until after 1947.
7. She received her bachelor of arts degree from Barnard College and her master of arts degree from Bryn Mawr.
8. *FF*, 25 September 1931, 28 July 1933, 24 September 1937, 22 September 1939.
9. Faculty Senate Minutes, vol. 2, 149; Dr. Daisy Parker Flory, interview by James P. Jones, 15 December 1976.
10. BOC, vol. 7, 513, vol. 8, 38, 75, 171; Dodd, "Formative Years," 116–118; This arrangement enabled any teacher 65 years or older and employed for at least ten years to elect a special assignment under direct supervision of a dean or the school's president instead of teaching. The Board calculated special status salary at 20% of the instructor's average salary for the past 5 years plus 1% for every year at the

institution. *FF*, 30 July 1937; BOC, vol. 2, 86; *DD*, 12 December 1937; *FF*, 4 February 1938; BOC, vol. 8, 207.

11. *DD*, 9 May 1939.

12. Sara Krentzman Srygley (FSCW 1936), interview by James P. Jones, 1 June 1977; Rhea Bond Miller (FSCW 1944), FSU OHC; Marian Conn Bashinski (FSCW 1938), FSU OHC; Mary Settle (FSCW 1931) to Robin Sellers, 5 May 1993.

13. Dr. Daisy Parker Flory (FSCW 1937), interview by James P. Jones, 15 December 1976.

14. President's Report, 19 October 1934, 15–16; *FF*, 10 July 1936.

15. President's Report, 15 October 1936, 11–13; *FF*, 10 July 1936; FSCW Catalogue, 1938–39, 47.

16. President's Report, 15 October 1936, 12.

17. William G. Dodd to Edward Conradi, 24 January 1938, EC Papers.

18. The most visible and active of the new company included Paul Finner (1922, Psychology), Herman Kurz (1922, Botany), William Hudson Rogers (1922, English), Olivia Dorman (1924, Classics), Harold Richards (1925, Physics), Kathryn Abbey (1926, History), Ralph Eyman (1928, Education), Guy Diffenbaugh (1928, English), Coyle Moore (1928, Sociology), and Owen Sellers (1931, Music).

19. *FF*, 24 November 1933.

20. BOC, vol. 7, 8, passim.

21. Speech delivered by Alban Stewart to Faculty Senate, September 1932, EC Papers. Stewart noted the enrollments as: Smith, 2,060; Simmonds [sic], 1,558; Wellesley, 1,550; Mount Holyoke, 982, Radcliff, 1,038; Goucher, 806. FSCW had 1,776 registered in February 1932.

22. Ibid.

23. Faculty Senate Minutes, 30 May 1931.

24. Ibid.

25. Edward Conradi to Charlotte Beckham, 9 May 1932, EC Papers.

26. BOC, vol. 7, 417; *FF*, 28 September 1934, 17 May 1935.

27. *FF*, 23 February 1934; Student Handbook 1935-1936, 12; *FF*, 5 October 1934.

28. Miriam Peterson Andrews (FSCW 1938), interview by author, 6 December 1993.

29. *FF*, 5 October 1934; Student Handbook 1935-1936, 21. According to the handbook, the business section was the area between Duval and Calhoun streets, and St. Augustine and Tennessee streets.

30. Student Handbook, 1935–1936, 16.

31. Mary Reed Bridges (FSCW 1939) to author, 25 January 1994.

32. *FF*, 10 February 1933; Athletic Association Minutes, 2 October 1935.

33. *FF,* 9 April 1937, 23 April 1937.
34. Ibid., 4 February 1938, 1 December 1939.
35. "Lassie," 28 September 1940, 28 October 1940, 31 October 1940.
36. Ibid., 2 October 1936, 13 November 1936, 4 December 1936.
37. Minutes of Cut Committee and Cases Considered, Book 1, 11, 67. Registrar's Office, Florida State University.
38. *FF,* 4 December 1936.
39. Ibid., 6 January 1939.
40. Ibid., 17 January 1936.
41. Ibid., 10 October 1930, 6 November 1931, 20 October 1933, 26 October 1934, 18 October 1935, 2 October 1936, 12 October 1937, 7 October 1938, 20 October 1939.
42. Ibid., 2 October 1936.
43. Ibid., 17 October 1930.
44. Ibid., 29 September 1933, 16 October 1936, 24 September 1937, 20 October 1939.
45. Ibid., 20 October 1939.
46. Ibid., 31 October 1930, 7 November 1930, 6 November 1931, 27 September 1935, 1 November 1935, 6 November 1936.
47. Ibid., 21 October 1938, 4 November 1938, 27 October 1939.
48. Ibid., 26 April 1940.
49. *Smith's Weekly* (Tallahassee), 31 October 1924; *Flastacowo* 1933, np.; *FF,* 16 January 1931; *Flastacowo* 1933, np.; Student Handbook 1935-36, 98.
50. Athletic Association Minutes, 25 September 1933; *FF,* 12 January 1934.
51. *FF,* 20 March 1936, 14 May 1937.
52. Ibid., 3 May 1935.
53. Myrtle E. Dolbee, Report on the history of the Alpha of Florida Chapter of Phi Beta Kappa, nd.; A. A. Murphree to Edward Conradi, 25 October 1926; Notes from the Records, 2, Phi Beta Kappa Scrapbooks, cited hereafter as PBK Scrapbooks.
54. A. A. Murphree died in 1927.
55. James Miller Leake to Arthur R. Seymour, 18 February 1929, PBK Scrapbooks.
56. Joseph Roemer to Arthur Seymour, 28 March 1929; Myrtle E. Dolbee to Professor Joseph Roemer, 6 April 1929; Joseph Roemer to Myrtle Dolbee, 10 April 1929, PBK Scrapbooks.
57. Dr. Daisy Parker Flory, conversation with author, 16 September 1994.
58. *Alumnae News,* vol. 6, no. 3: 3; *FF,* 1 March 1935.
59. Report made by Mrytle E. Dolbee, nd., 19–20. PBK Scrapbooks. The Beta Chapter of Florida of Phi Beta Kappa was installed at the University of Florida in 1938.

60. *FF,* 2 October 1936, 12 November 1937, 17 March 1939; *Jacksonville Journal,* 12 May 1939.
61. Minutes of Cut Committee and Cases Considered, Book 1, 23 January 1939, np. Registrar's Office, Florida State University.
62. *FF,* 7 May 1937.
63. President's Report, 12 October 1932, 80–81
64. BOC, vol. 7, 457; *DD,* 16 September 1934; *DD,* 16 September 1934; *FF,* 30 October 1936; President's Report, 15 October 1936, 80.
65. Dr. Loretta Ellias (FSCW 1940), FSU OHC.
66. Marian Conn Bashinski (FSCW 1938), FSU OHC; *FF,* 12 March 1937.
67. President's Report, 15 October 1936, 94-105.
68. *FF,* 12 February 1932, 30 October 1936; Carolyn Krentzman (FSCW 1937–1939) and Bonnie Krentzman Mannheimer (FSCW early 1940s), FSU OHC.
69. *FF,* 23 October 1936, 25 November 1932.
70. *DD,* 16 September 1934; *FF,* 5 November 1937.
71. Katherine Blood Hoffman (FSCW 1936), interview by author, 23 October 1993.
72. Dr. Loretta Ellias (FSCW 1940), FSU OHC.
73. Ibid.
74. CGA Book, vol. 2, 1 August 1932, 13 October 1933.
75. *FF,* 22 March 1935, 21 February 1936
76. *DD,* 18 September 1936, 20 September 1936, 4 March 1937.

NOTES TO CHAPTER X (PAGES 240–261)

1. Edward Conradi to the Board of Control, 3 August 1940, EC Corres.
2. *Florida Times Union,* 8 July 1940, 35.
3. BOC, vol. 8, 376.
4. Hamilton Holt to Edward Conradi, 19 July 1940. Rollins College Archives, Deland, Florida.
5. BOC, vol. 8, 376–80.
6. *Florida Alligator* editor to Edward Conradi, EC Corres.
7. BOC, vol. 8, 378–80.
8. "Lassie," 21 February 1941.
9. Doak S. Campbell, *Problems in the Education of College Women: A Study of Women Graduates of Southern Colleges,* Field Study No. 6 (Nashville, Tennessee: George Peabody College for Teachers, 1933); *FF,* 5 April 1935, 3 October 1941.
10. "Lassie," 8 October 1941.
11. Mart Pierson Hill (FSCW 1942), FSU OHC.
12. *DD,* 16 October 1941.

13. Doak Campbell to Edward Conradi, 8 July 1943, EC Papers; President's Report, 20 August 1942, 5; *DD*, 1 December 1944, 1.
14. E. R. Smith to Doak Campbell, 8 December 1941, DC Corres.
15. *FF*, 12 May 1944, 29 September 1944, 3 November 1944, 12 October 1945.
16. Ibid., 12 May 1944, 29 September 1944, 9 March 1945; *DD*, 9 March 1945, 1, 22 March 1945, 4.
17. President's Report, 20 August 1942, 6.
18. Students who held nursing scholarships lived in the Infirmary; Edward Conradi to Chairman, 21 November 1940, EC Corres.
19. Olivia Dorman to Edward Conradi, 13 September 1941, EC Corres.
20. Wilbur W. Whitehurst to J. G. Kellum, 12 September 1941, DC Corres.
21. Olivia Dorman to Edward Conradi, 13 September 1941, EC Corres; Doak Campbell to Henry P. Adair, 3 February 1942, DC Corres; *DD*, 11 January 1943, 1; BOC, vol. 10, 460.
22. "Lassie," 8 October 1941.
23. FSCW Catalogue, 1941, 43; Olivia Dorman to Doak Campbell, 12 August 1942, DC Corres.
24. "Lassie," 10 May 1941.
25. Ibid., 15 December 1941, 10 January 1942; Edith McCollum to Olivia Dorman, 26 November 1941, DC Corres.
26. *FF*, 27 November 1943, 29 September 1944.
27. President's Report, 24 November 1944, 7.
28. *DD*, 17 September 1944, 6; *FF*, 6 October 1944, 13 October 1944; *DD*, 26 September 1944.
29. Doak S. Campbell, *A University in Transition,* (Tallahassee: Florida State University, 1964), 22, cited hereafter as Campbell, *Transition*; *DD*, 10 January 1945, 7; The Shores Building, housing the School of Library and Information Studies, occupies the site presently.
30. *FF*, 4 May 1945.
31. Campbell, *Transition,* 22.
32. *FF*, 11 May 1945; Campbell, *Transition,* 23; *FF*, 29 September 1944.
33. *FF*, 10 November 1944.
34. *Alumnae News*, vol. 37, no. 4, 3; *DD*, 10 January 1945, 7.
35. President's Report, 24 November 1944, 7, 1 November 1946, 8; *DD*, 14 January 1945; President's Report, 1 November 1946, 8.
36. BOC, vol. 12, 84, 163, 262, 453; *FF*, 12 October 1945.
37. *FF*, 18 February 1940.
38. Ibid., 26 July 1940, 4 October 1940.
39. "Lassie," 11 October 1940.
40. Burke-Wadsworth Act, adopted 16 September 1940, required all men

aged 21 to 35 to register for one year's military service within the United States.

41. *FF,* 20 September 1940.
42. "Lassie," 15 October 1940, 1 January 1941; Carolyn Krentzman (FSCW 1937–1939) and Bonnie Krentzman Mannheimer (FSCW early 1940s), FSU OHC.
43. Olivia Dorman to Edward Conradi, 29 October 1940, EC Corres.
44. *FF,* 14 February 1941, 21 February 1941; the base commander was Colonel Jacob Wuest; *FF,* 21 February 1941.
45. At the 50th Reunion of the Class of 1943 (Tallahassee, Florida, 2–3 April 1993), one of the memories most vividly recalled was of the rule of four to leave campus.
46. *FF,* 14 March 1941, 18 April 1941; *DD,* 21 April 1941, 1.
47. "Lassie," 8 December 1941; Maryanne Cannon Hartwell (FSCW 1945), FSU OHC.
48. Dr. Loretta Ellias (FSCW 1940), FSU OHC.
49. "Lassie," 10 December 1941.
50. J. T. Diamond to Doak Campbell, 17 February 1942, 2, DC Corres.
51. *FF,* 20 February 1942.
52. Ibid., 6 February 1942. Richards and others were wrong about the bombs, but Nazi submarines sank several tankers along the Atlantic Coast of Florida between February and May 1942. Mart Pierson to Lucy Lester, 6 February 1942, Campus Defense Council; *FF,* 13 February 1942; "Lassie," 17 February 1942.
53. *FF,* 20 February 1942, 9 October 1942
54. Marjorie Morrison Moylan, "Magnolias and Mavericks," 143, unpublished memoirs. By permission of Marjorie M. Moylan.
55. *FF,* 16 October 1942.
56. "Lassie," 17 February 1941.
57. Marion Hay, Mary Settle, Nellie-Bond Dickinson, Owen Sellers, H. D. Mendenhall, Royal Mattice, and many others; *FF,* 23 February 1945; *DD,* 26 February 1945; BOC, vol. 12, 371.
58. Dr. Katherine Montgomery, Alumni Files, Florida State University.
59. *FF,* 9 January 1942, 25 September 1942; *Flastacowo* 1943, 197; *FF,* 5 February 1943, 14 January 1944; Norma Pennoyer Kerkow (FSCW 1943), Alumni Files, Florida State University.
60. *FF,* 12 February 1943.
61. "Lassie," 27 September 1941.
62. *FF,* 9 January 1942.
63. "Lassie," 11 January 1943.
64. Ibid., 19 February 1943; Louise Pittman Minton, (FSCW 1944), "50th

Anniversary," 50, Alumni Association, Florida State University; "Lassie," 11 May 1942; *DD*, 7 May 1942, 5; *FF*, 15 January 1943; Gloria Shuman Gaines (FSCW 1945), "Confessions of the Even Spirits of '44," 52, Alumni Association, Florida State University; Mary Lou Norwood (FSCW 1947) to author, 22 November 1994.

65. *DD*, 1 January 1943, 1; *FF*, 25 September 1942.
66. "Lassie," 2 October 1942.
67. *FF*, 12 March 1943, 2 April 1943, 7 May 1943, *Flastacowo* 1943, 203.
68. Martha Fain Brooks, Betty Lewis Harrison, Class of 1945 meeting, 16 November 1994.
69. Campbell, *Transition,* 67; *DD*, 24 March 1944; *FF*, 24 March 1944; *FF*, 31 March 1944.
70. *DD*, 30 March 1944; *FF*, 31 March 1944, 7 April 1944, 21 April 1944, 12 May 1944.
71. *FF*, 28 March 1941, 17 November 1944. The chimes were a gift to the college from the classes of 1934 and 1936, originally installed in the library tower but moved to Westcott in 1937; *DD*, 16 February 1945, 9 May 1945; *FF*, 11 May 1945.
72. Dorothy Nelson Binger (FSCW 1946), FSU OHC.
73. Louise Peeples Jackson (FSCW 1947) to author, 28 January 1993.
74. *DD*, 8 October 1945, 10; *FF*, *19* October 1945, 30 November 1945, 18 January 1946, 8 February 1946.
75. *FF*, 4 November 1938.
76. Richard Mayo (Director of Marching Chiefs, 1971–1976), interview by author, 19 April 1993, FSU OHC; *FF*, 10 March 1939.
77. Sue Chaires Boynton, Tedy Parker King, Cornelia Watson Gause, Mary Lou King, Floread B. Lee, Tam T. Milton, Charlotte Cooper, Jean Wood Crow, FSU OHC; *FF*, 6 December 1940.
78. *FF*, 7 November 1941, 12 December 1941; Owen Sellers to J. G. Kellum, 30 October 1941, DC Corres.; Charlotte Cooper (FSCW 1943), Alumni Files, Florida State University; President's Report, 20 August 1942, 17; *FF*, 2 April 1943.
79. Richard Mayo (Director of Marching Chiefs 1971–1976), interview by author, 19 April 1993, FSU OHC.
80. Marjorie Morrison Moylan (FSCW 1944) to author, 21 June 1994; *DD*, 11 November 1943, 1; *FF*, 24 November 1944.
81. *FF*, 14 November 1941, 13 February 1942, 27 November 1943.
82. Ibid., 18 October 1940, 28 November 1941; *DD*, 25 November 1941.
83. *FF*, 27 November 1942, 23 April 1943, 7 May 1943, 27 November 1943.
84. *Sunday News-Democrat* (Tallahassee), 3 December 1944.

85. *FF*, 24 November 1945.

NOTES TO CHAPTER XI (PAGES 262–275)

1. *Laws of Florida*, 1947, Chapter 23669, Sect. 1. The legislative act was actually a committee substitute for House Bills Number 1 and 42. Cited in Bristol, *Focal Points*, 38.
2. Rhodes, "Legal Development," 205.
3. Ibid., 231; *Laws of Florida*, 1925, Chapter 10288, Sec. 1, 524–25.
4. Bristol, *Focal Points*, 53; Edward Conradi, "Survey," EC Papers; Report of the Educational Survey Commission of 1929, 429, 740.
5. *FF*, 5 March 1937.
6. Bristol, *Focal Points*, 37-55 passim.
7. *FF*, 11 April 1939, 25 April 1941.
8. Enrollment dropped from 3,438 in 1940–41 to 681 in 1943–44; *FF*, 30 April 1943.
9. Board of Control to Lacy G. Thomas, 14 May 1943, DC Corres.
10. *DD*, 7 September 1944.
11. Ibid., 17 September 1944, 6, 26 September 1944, 1.
12. Ibid.; Bristol, *Focal Points*, 43; *DD*, 5 April 1945, 1.
13. *FF*, 30 March 1945, 4; Bristol, *Focal Points*, 43.
14. Memorandum, December 1944, DC Corres.
15. *FF*, 13 April 1945.
16. *DD*, 11 April 1945, 1; *FF*, 13 April 1945. Representative Bourke Floyd of Apalachicola proposed the study. *FF*, 2 February 1945; *DD*, 8 April 1945, 1, 17 April 1945, 1. Henry S. Baynard of St. Petersburg introduced the bill.
17. *DD*, 24 April 1945, 4
18. *FF*, 18 January 1946. Typically, the legislature had appropriated only $450,000 for the dormitory. *DD*, 10 May 1946, 7.
19. *FF*, 22 November 1946; Survey #3004.
20. BOC, vol. 12, 522; Doak Campbell to the Faculty, 15 July 1946; R. K. Shaw to Doak Campbell, 25 July 1946, DC Corres. Shaw figured the cost of the bus would be approximately $1,008 per month.
21. Bristol, *Focal Points*, 44; *DD*, 20 August 1946, 1.
22. Milton W. Carothers to Doak Campbell, 18 August 1946, DC Corres.
23. *DD*, 22 August 1946, 1, 27 August 1946, 1
24. BOC, vol. 13, 7–10; Bristol, *Focal Points*, 44; *DD*, 4 September 1946, 1, 6 September 1946, 1, 8 September 1946, 1.
25. *DD*, 6 December 1946, 11; Olivia Dorman to Doak Campbell, 20 September 1946, DC Corres; *FF*, 6 December 1946.
26. *FF*, 5 October 1946, 7 February 1947.

27. Ibid., 31 January 1947, 4 April 1947; *DD*, 3 November 1946, 6; *FF*, 1 November 1946.
28. *FF*, 15 November 1946; Report of Thanksgiving Committee on Results of Thanksgiving Votes, 8 November 1946, DC Corres; *FF*, 22 November 1946; Athletic Association Minutes, 8 January 1947.
29. *FF*, 8 November 1946.
30. Louise Gehan (FSCW 1938) to Doak Campbell, 7 November 1945, DC Corres.
31. BOC, vol. 12, 522; *DD*, 6 January 1947, 4.
32. Bristol, *Focal Points*, 5960; *Sunday News-Democrat*, 26 January 1947, 1; *FF*, 31 January 1947.
33. *FF*, 11 April 1947.
34. Florida Citizens Committee on Education, "Education and the Future of Florida," 1947, 290.
35. *FF*, 7 February 1947, 4 April 1947.
36. *DD*, 20 February 1947, 1.
37. *FF*, 1 November 1946.
38. BOC, vol. 13, 334; "Thanks for the Memories," Class of 1947 Reunion, np.
39. *DD*, 15 April 1947, 4, 20 April 1947, 6, 7 May 1947, 1.
40. *Laws of Florida*, 1947, Section 1, Chapter 23669, cited in Bristol, *Focal Points*, 38.
41. BOC, vol. 13, 338.
42. Mart Pierson Hill (FSCW 1942), FSU OHC.
43. *DD*, 9 June 1947, 1. McAllister was also president of the Association of Governing Boards of State Universities and Allied Institutions.

Sources

Manuscript Collections

A. A. Murphree Correspondence. P. K. Yonge Library of Florida History, University of Florida, Gainesville, Florida.

A. A. Murphree Letterbooks. Special Collections, Strozier Library, Florida State University.

Doak Campbell Correspondence. Florida State Archives, Tallahassee, Florida.

Edward Conradi Correspondence. Florida State Archives, Tallahassee, Florida.

Edward Conradi Papers. Special Collections, Strozier Library, Florida State University.

Miscellaneous

Acts of the Legislature. Chapter 6540, Acts of 1913.

Adams, Asa Allen. "Before and After in Florida Institutions." *Florida Grower*, 41, no. 2 (February 1933): 5–24.

Adams, Alfred Hugh. "A History of Public Education in Florida." Ph.D. diss., Florida State University, 1962.

Allen, Frederick Lewis. *Only Yesterday.* New York Perennial Library, Harper & Row, 1964.

Armstrong, Orland Kay. *The Life and Work of Dr. A. A. Murphree.* Gainesville: Orland Kay Armstrong, 1928.

Athletic Association. Minutes of the Meetings. Special Collections.

Avant, Fenton Davis. *The Davis-Wood Family of Gadsden County and Their Forebears.* Easley, South Carolina: Southern Historical Press, 1979.

———. *My Tallahassee.* Tallahassee, Florida: L'Avant Studios, 1983.

Baker, Liva. *I'm Radcliffe! Fly Me!* New York: Macmillan Publishing Co. Inc., 1976.

Bellamy, Raymond. "History of the Department of Sociology at FSU." Typewritten manuscript. Special Collections.

Board of Control. Minutes of the Meetings of the Board of Control, State of Florida, 1905–1947.

Brevard, Caroline Mays. *A History of Florida.* New York: American Book Company, 1904.

Bristol, L. M. "The Buckman Act: Before and After; A Study in Historical Sociology." Unpublished manuscript, 1946. Florida State Library, Tallahassee, Florida.

———. *Three Focal Points in the Development of Florida's State System of Higher Education.* Lectures given at the College of Education, University of Florida. Gainesville: University of Florida Press, 1952.

Bush, George Gary. *History of Education in Florida.* Bureau of Education Circular of Information No. 7, 1888. Washington, D.C.: Government Printing Office, 1889.

Campbell, Doak S. *Problems in the Education of College Women: A Study of Women Graduates of Southern Colleges.* Field Study No. 6. Nashville, Tennessee: George Peabody College for Teachers, 1933.

———. *A University in Transition.* Tallahassee: Florida State University, 1964.

Class of 1947, Florida State College for Women. "Thanks for the Memories." Alumni Files.

College Government Association. Secretary's Book. Special Collections.

Conradi, Edward. "Calendar of Campus Improvements." Typewritten manuscript. Conradi Papers.

———. "Facts about Florida State College for Women." Typewritten report. Conradi Papers.

———. *Memoirs of Edward Conradi, President of FSCW 1909–1941.* Tallahassee, Florida: Florida State College for Women, 1945.

Crook, Mary Ruth Weaver, (FSCW 1944). "Tallahassee Lassie 1940–1944," Letters from Mary Ruth Weaver to her family in Kissimmee, Florida. Typewritten manuscript. By permission of Mary Ruth Weaver Crook.

Deed Book, FSCW/FSU. Mendenhall Building, Florida State University.

Diamond, Rowena. "History of Florida State College for Women." Typewritten manuscript. Special Collections.

Dodd, William G. "Early Education in Tallahassee and the West Florida Seminary, Now Florida State University," Part I. *Florida Historical Quarterly,* 28 (July, 1948): 1–27.

———. "Florida State College for Women: Notes on the Formative Years." Typewritten manuscript: 1958–59. Special Collections.

———. *History of the West Florida Seminary.* Tallahassee: The Florida

State University, 1952.

Dunn, Hampton. *Yesterday's Tallahassee*. Miami, Florida: E. A. Seemann, 1974.

Flastacowo. 1910–1915; 1921–1947.

Florida Citizens Committee on Education. "Education and the Future of Florida." Tallahassee, 1947.

Florida Education Association Journal.

Florida Female College Catalogue, 1905–06, 1908–09.

Florida Female College. Bulletin of the State College for Women, 1908.

———. Minutes of the Meetings of the Faculty Senate. 1905–1909. Special Collections.

Florida House Journal, 1850–51; 1866.

Florida Senate Journal, 1846–47; 1850–51; 1881; 1889.

Florida State College. *Argo*. 1901–1903.

Florida State College for Women Catalogue, 1910?–1948.

Florida State College for Women. *Alumni Bulletin*.

———. College Bulletins, 1916–1947.

———. *College Government Association Handbook*, 1928. Special Collections.

———. Customs and Regulations Book, 1918. Special Collections.

———. Minutes of Cut Committee and Cases Considered, Books 1–2. Registrar's Office, Florida State University, Tallahassee.

———. Minutes of the Meetings of the Faculty Senate. Vol. I, 1905–1920; Vol. II, 1920–1940. Special Collections.

———. *Student Handbook*, 1935–1936. Special Collections.

———. *The Talisman*, 1906–1914.

———. *YWCA Student Handbook*, 1911–1912. By permission of Hallijeanne Chalker.

Florida State University. "Alumni News."

———. Blueprints. Mendenhall Building, Florida State University.

France, Mary Duncan. "The Evolution Controversy in Florida, 1921–1928." M.A. thesis, Florida State University, 1973.

Gaines, Gloria Shuman, (FSCW 1945). "Confessions of the Even Spirits of '44." Alumni Files.

Groene, Bertram H. *Ante-Bellum Tallahassee*. Tallahassee: Florida Heritage Foundation, 1971.

"History of the Library," Typewritten manuscript, no author cited. Special Collections.

Kendall, Elaine. *"Peculiar Institutions": An Informal History of the Seven Sister Colleges*. New York: Putnam, 1976.

Kuehl, Warren. *Hamilton Holt: Internationalist, Journalist, Educator*.

Gainesville: University of Florida Press, 1960.

Laws of Florida, 1850–51, 1852–53, 1856, 1868, 1870, 1895, 1905, 1925, 1927, 1947.

McGahagin, Dorothy Bryant. "FSCW Class of 1944." By permission of Dorothy Bryant McGahagin.

Minton, Louise Pittman (FSCW 1944). "50th Anniversary." Alumni Files.

Moylan, Marjorie Morrison. "Magnolias and Mavericks." Typewritten memoirs. By permission of Marjorie Moylan.

Opperman, Ella Scoble. "Annals of the School of Music, 1905 to 1947." Typewritten manuscript. Special Collections.

———. "The Story." Typewritten manuscript. Special Collections.

Orr, Milton Lee. *The State-supported Colleges for Women*. Nashville, Tennessee: George Peabody College for Teachers, 1930.

Pipkin, Beulah, ed. *The Class of 1919: Florida State College for Women*. Handwritten letter collection, 1969.

Pitchford, Rachel. "A Leading Woman's College," *Florida Highways* (November 1941): 10–11, 38–42.

Proctor, Samuel. "The University of Florida: Its Early Years, 1853–1906." Ph.D. diss., University of Florida, 1958.

Rhodes, Francis A. "The Legal Development of State Supported Higher Education in Florida." Ph.D. diss., University of Florida, 1948.

Sanborn Maps, 1903, 1016, 1926, 1936, 1947.

Saverio, Emil. Loyalty Oath. RG402, S249. Florida State Archives.

Shores, Venila. "Some Historical Notes Concerning Florida State College for Women." *Third Yearbook of the Tallahassee Historical Society.*

State Department of Public Instruction. *Annual Reports of the Superintendent of Public Instruction of the State of Florida*, 1905–1947.

———. *Biennial Reports of the Superintendent of Public Instruction of the State of Florida*, 1905–1947.

———. *Biennial Report of the Superintendent of Public Instruction of the State of Florida*, 1894.

———. *Biennial Report of the Board of Control of the State Educational Institutions of Florida*, 1906–1948.

State of Florida. Florida Master Site File, Survey #3004. Department of State, Bureau of Historic Preservation, Tallahassee.

Steinfuhrer, Julius. Loyalty Oath. RG402, S249. Florida State Archives.

Tebeau, Charlton W. *A History of Florida*. Miami: University of Miami Press, 1971.

University of Florida Catalogue, 1904-05.

U.S. Statutes at Large, Vol. III.

Vicinus, Martha. "Distance and Desire: English Boarding-School Friendships," *Signs: Journal of Women in Culture and Society,* 9 (Winter 1984): 601–622.

Walker, Sandra Hull and William W. Rogers. "In Defense of Professor Arthur W. Calhoun: A Florida State College For Women Co-ed Speaks Her Mind." Unpublished paper. By permission of William W. Rogers.

Woody, Thomas. *A History of Women's Education in the United States.* New York: The Science Press, Vol. II, 1929.

Newspapers

Chapel Hill Weekly.
Evening Sun (Clearwater).
Daily Democrat (Tallahassee).
Democrat and Weekly Record (Tallahassee).
Florida Flambeau (Florida State College for Women).
Florida State News (Tallahassee).
Florida Times-Union (Jacksonville).
Jacksonville Journal.
Miami Metropolis.
Morning Sun (Tallahassee).
Semi-Weekly True Democrat (Tallahassee).
Smith's Weekly (Tallahassee).
Sunday News-Democrat (Tallahassee).
Tampa Morning Tribune.
Weekly True Democrat (Tallahassee).

Scrapbooks

Davis, Alberta Lee. Special Collections.
Kellum, J. G. Special Collections.
Monroe, Kathlyn. Memory Book. James P. Jones Collection.
Moor, Beth Walton. Special Collections.
Opperman, Ella Scoble. Special Collections.
Phi Beta Kappa. Special Collections.
Robinton, Elizabeth. Alumni Association, FSU.
Schwalmeyer, Maude. Special Collections.
Stone, Jeanne Compton. By permission of Mode Lee Stone, Jr.

Interviews

Andrews, Miriam Peterson (FSCW 1938). Interview by author, 6 December 1993.

Ashbrook, Angeline Yent (FSCW 1910–1912). Interview by James P. Jones, 28 December 1976.

Boots, Nancy Stewart (FSCW 1938). Interview by author, 11 June 1994.

Cowles, Susan Miller (FSU 1952). Interview by author, 12 July 1994.

Duparc, Rovanna (FSCW 1944; Assistant Professor, Food and Nutrition 1945–47, 1961–77). Interview by the author, 11 May 1993.

Ekermeyer, Louisa Conradi (FSCW 1928). Interview by author, 17 November 1992.

Flory, Daisy Parker (FSCW 1937; Dean of the Faculties and Professor, Political Science 1942–1984). Interview by James P. Jones, 15 December 1976; Interview by author, 16 September 1994.

Fox, Grace (FSCW 1928; Professor, Physical Education 1933–1971). Interview by author, 17 April 1991.

Hoffman, Katherine Blood (FSCW 1936; Professor, Chemistry 1940–1984). Interview by author, 23 October 1993

Lang, Lucy (FSCW 1926). Interview by author, 5 April 1993.

McCord, Betty Mack (FSCW 1937) and Guyte, Jr. Interview by author, 10 January 1994.

Meginniss, Pat Thomas (FSCW 1947). Interview by author, 17 April 1993.

Slemons, Ella Taylor Bisbee (FSCW 1919) and Theresa Yaeger Palmer (FSCW 1919). Interview by James P. Jones, 24 March 1977.

Srygley, Sara Krentzman (FSCW 1936; Professor, Library Science 1941–1976). Interview by James P. Jones, 1 June 1977.

Stewart, Alban, Jr. Interview by author, 27 April 1993.

Tracy, Anna May (FSCW Dietitian, 1922–1956). Interview by James P. Jones, 29 December 1976.

Weil, Florence Steinberg (FSCW 1933). Interview by author, 9 December 1993.

FSU Oral History Collection

Barber, Lylah Scarborough (FSCW 1929).

Bashinski, Marian Conn (FSCW 1938).

Binger, Dorothy Nelson (FSCW 1946).

Boynton, Sue Chaires (FSCW 1943), Tedy Parker King (FSCW 1945), Cornelia Watson Gause (FSCW 1941), Mary Lou King (FSCW 1943), Floread B. Lee (FSCW 1941), Tam T. Milton (FSCW 1942), Charlotte Cooper (FSCW 1943), Jean Wood Crow (FSCW 1942).

Bulloch, Mary Dorothy (FSCW 1927).

Dickinson, Nellie-Bond (Professor of Modern Dance, 1935–1963).

Ellias, Loretta (FSCW 1943; Professor, Biological Science, 1945–1987).

Hartwell, Maryanne Cannon (FSCW 1945).

Higgs, Lucille (Assistant Director, University Library, 1949–1985).

Krentzman, Carolyn (FSCW 1937–1939) and Bonnie Krentzman

Mannheimer (FSCW early 1940s).

Liske, Sue Love (FSCW 1942).

Mayo, Richard (Director of Marching Chiefs, 1971–1976)

Norwood, Mary Lou (FSCW 1947).

Pates, Anne (FSCW 1936; Professor, Biological Science, 1949–1980).

Reichelt, Wallace W. (Associate Professor, History, 1948–1978).

Stone, Jeanne Compton (FSCW 1928).

Additional Contributors

Allen, Eleanor Claire Beeson, FSCW 1929

Auxier, Lucy Pope, FSCW 1933

Barkley, Ruth Richardson, FSCW 1934

Bennett, Frances Shelly, FSCW 1920

Black, Gladys Martin, FSCW 1918

Black, Mary Elizabeth Lowe, FSCW 1930

Blackburn, Emilie, FSCW 1929

Blain, Marguerite Lumpkin, FSCW 1922

Blanchard, Chris Morrison, FSCW 1947

Bow, Amelia Black, FSCW 1941

Bowden, Beryl Lovvorn, FSCW 1924

Bowen, Wilhelmina Whitted, FSCW 1920

Bridges, Mary Reed, FSCW 1939

Brooks, Martha Fain, FSCW 1945

Browning, Juanita Lawrence, FSCW 1930

Burnett, Marion Phillips, FSCW 1933

Cameron, Dorothy H., FSCW 1942

Canova, Mona Alderman, FSCW 1925

Carter, Elsie Jones, FSCW 1924

Carter, Linda, FSU 1970

Carter, Betty, FSCW 1948–1952

Chalker, Hallijeanne

Chapman, Florence, FSCW 1936

Chapman, Janine, FSU 1965

Chitty, Betty Nickinson, FSCW 1941

Christian, Mary Rimbey, FSCW 1920

Coleman, Bernice Conklin, FSCW 1929

Cone, Jennie Rae Nall, FSCW 1935

Cox, Beverly, FSU 1954–1955

Cox, Verta Wilson, FSCW 1928

Crago, Harriet Kirk, FSCW 1947

Crawford, Caroll, FSU 1956

Creary, Dempsey, FSCW 1928

Crichton, Ethel Webb

Dennis, Lois Dossey, FSCW 1946

Englert, Alice Summitt, FSCW 1947

Farrell, Dorothy Parker, FSCW 1940

Fleckenstein, Louis

Fraser, Margaret Van Cleve, FSCW 1928

Gallant, Mary, FSCW 1931

Goddard, Alice Winter, FSCW 1926

Goldman, Sue Searcy, FSCW 1945

Gonzales, Annette

Graham, Martha King, FSU 1956

Greiff, Frances Traxler, FSCW 1946

Grove, Lucille Reece, FSCW 1925

Harmon, Gwendolyn S., FSCW 1942

Harrison, Betty Lewis, FSCW 1945

Hart, Marjorie Mackey, FSCW 1933

Hemenway, Oakley St. John, FSCW 1917

Henderson, Mary Leslie Keen, FSU 1953

Hodgdon, Carleen Vinal, FSCW 1934

Howell, Loraine Chamberlin

Howie, Jean Lewis, FSCW 1945

Hull, Catherine Welch, FSCW 1941–1942

Jackson, Louise Peeples, FSCW 1947

Jennings, Dora Foster, FSCW 1918

Jones, Pearl Walsh, FSCW 1923

Keel, Susan, FSCW 1947

Kershaw, Virginia Dean, FSCW 1928

King, Marguerite L., FSCW 1942

Dunkman, Cornelia Engle, FSCW 1923

Kurz, Rose, FSCW 1943

Lang, Lucy, FSCW 1926

Martin, Ethel Blanchard, FSCW 1943

Marxsen, Sarah Lewis, FSCW 1947

Matheny, Jeanne Felkel, FSCW 1942

Mattice, Margaret Teague, FSCW 1933

May, James

McClellan, Martha, FSCW 1934

McConnell, Frances

McCullough, Mary Logan, FSCW 1928

McEwen, Winnie Warren, FSCW 1915

McKay, Annie, FSCW 1927

Miller, Rhea Bond, FSCW 1944

Moore, Maude Clyatt, FSCW 1921

Mores, Katherine

Mozo, Grace Bail, FSCW 1942

Mulvaney, Evelyn Cobb

Mulvaney, Glenn

Newell, Hazel, FSCW 1928

O'Driscoll, June Hadsell, FSCW 1945

Ogilvie, Ethel Henry, FSCW 1924

Page, Ruby Ebert, FSCW 1945

Phillips, Herbert E., FSCW 1942

Pierce-Ruhland, Harriet T., FSCW 1944

Powell, Edna Haynie, FSU 1949

Renfro, Margaret S., FSCW 1938

Riley, Ruth Jones, FSCW 1947

Rolland, Madeline, FSCW 1936

Rutland, Martha Jane Brown, FSCW 1946

Sale, Louise Yonge Buck, FSCW 1926

Settle, Mary, FSCW 1931

Skipper, Bobbie Rice

Smith, Pearl C., FSCW 1922

Smith, Patty Hill, FSCW 1946

Stalling, Bess A.

Strickland, E. G.

Thompson, Ina S., FSCW 1924

Tomyn, Anne Norris, FSCW 1937

Triplett, B. J. Singleton, FSCW 1947

Turner, Jere, FSCW 1944

Turner, Harriet B., FSCW 1942

Turner, Sue Ellen, FSU 1972

Ward, Olive Duggan, FSCW 1933

Wells, India Steed, FSCW 1927

Whitfield, Nancy

Willis, Frances E. Battle, FSCW 1941

Yancey, L. Elizabeth, FSCW 1942

Ziegler, Terry Bannerman, FSCW 1929

Index

FEMINA PERFECTA

Text design and graphics by Gayle Norris
in Garamond with display lines
in Caslon Open Face and Belwe
Fleurons ornaments and Letraset Decorative Initials
Cover design by Ed Augustyniak and Gayle Norris
Computer photo enhancements by David Poindexter
Printed by Boyd Brothers, Inc.
Panama City, Florida
on Repap Matte Text
bound in Repap Matte Cover
with Ultra II end papers